THE PRESIDENT AND FOREIGN AFFAIRS

Evaluation, Performance, and Power

Ryan J. Barilleaux

PRAEGER SPECIAL STUDIES • PRAEGER SCIENTIFIC

New York • Philadelphia • Eastbourne, UK
Toronto • Hong Kong • Tokyo • Sydney

Library of Congress Cataloging in Publication Data

Barilleaux, Ryan J.
  The president and foreign affairs.

  Bibliography: p.
  Includes index.
  1. Presidents—United States. 2. United States—
Foreign relations—1945—   .I. Title.
JK570.B285 1985   353.03′23   84-26282
ISBN 0-03-002883-3 (alk. paper)

Published in 1985 by Praeger Publishers
CBS Educational and Professional Publishing
a Division of CBS Inc.
521 Fifth Avenue, New York, NY 10175 USA
©1985 by Praeger Publishers

All rights reserved

56789 052 987654321

Printed in the United States of America
on acid-free paper

For Marilyn

ACKNOWLEDGMENTS

Like any author, I am indebted to those who have helped me along the way. I have been particularly fortunate in receiving assistance from many great and good people.

This book has had two godfathers. The first, Bruce Buchanan, inspired my interest in the topic of presidential evaluation and directed my dissertation on that subject. He has consistently given me sound guidance and I have borrowed more than a few ideas from him. I have learned much from working with this scholarly gentleman and he never flags in his determination to help me do the best work I can do. The other godfather is Herbert Levine, who taught me by word and by example what it means to be a professional scholar. It is by his example that I work.

I want to thank as well a number of people who have given me much help and advice in order to make this book possible and to make it a better work. Jack Levy helped me to sharpen my analysis. Charles Cnudde, Steven Baker, George Edwards, Steven Shull, Bert Rockman, Thomas Cronin, Gordon Hoxie, and Robert Clinton all made comments on this research and helped me to avoid many serious problems. Michael Greenberg and John Phillip Rogers gave me not only useful advice, but also helped me to cross-check my research in several places. James Pinedo first taught me about word-processing equipment and my colleague Robert Webking taught me to use an IBM Personal Computer. Rosalind Federman typed most of the manuscript and suffered my idiosyncracies with grace. All of my colleagues in the Department of Political Science at the University of Texas at El Paso encouraged me and gave me the benefit of their experience, particularly Z. Anthony Kruszewski. A countless number of librarians and archivists helped me to locate the materials I needed. I want also to thank Dottie Breitbart, Lisa MacLeman, and the staff at Praeger for their help and advice.

Finally, there are those whose contributions are reflected in this book, but whose help is much greater. My mother has always supported my efforts, and my late father always believed in his son's abilities. My wife, to whom this work is dedicated, has always believed in me and helped me along. She also asked me some hard questions about this book along the way that made me clarify my thinking.

It is traditional at this point to thank those who provided the money to make a research project possible. Financial support for this book came from me and my family. No federal grant money was used to support this research, nor any support other than from employment. I do, however, want to thank the University of Texas System for providing me with word-processing resources.

Everyone mentioned here deserves some share in the credit for whatever I have accomplished. Of course, I accept full responsibility for whatever errors and misjudgments remain.

El Paso, Texas
August 1984

CONTENTS

	Page
ACKNOWLEDGMENTS	vii
INTRODUCTION: THE PRESIDENTIAL ORDEAL	1

Chapter

1 THE CONVENTIONAL WISDOM — 4

    Identifying the Conventional Wisdom — 6
    Examining the Conventional Wisdom — 23
    Notes — 27

2 CRISES — 31

    The Taiwan Strait Crisis, 1954-55 — 32
    The Bay of Pigs Crisis, 1961 — 48
    Notes — 65

3 NON-CRISIS SECURITY ISSUES — 72

    SALT I — 73
    SALT II — 94
    Notes — 111

4 NON-CRISIS NON-SECURITY ISSUES — 119

    The Trade Expansion Act of 1962 — 120
    The Trade Act of 1970 — 137
    Notes — 150

5 TOWARD A NEW WISDOM — 158

    Results of the Case Studies — 159
    Toward More Effective Evaluation — 163
    Implications of This Study for the Presidency — 169
    Manifesto for a General Theory of
        Presidential Evaluation — 171
    Notes — 177

	Page
APPENDIX	179
BIBLIOGRAPHY	202
INDEX	210
ABOUT THE AUTHOR	216

INTRODUCTION:
THE PRESIDENTIAL ORDEAL

The president of the United States is always on trial. As the chief of foreign affairs, he bears the burden for U.S. policy. Consequently, his performance under that burden is continually judged by Congress, the public, the press, and international observers. Moreover, this constant scrutiny is akin to the ancient trial by ordeal, for the president's performance is assessed by how well he holds up under his burden. Just as trials during the Dark Ages judged guilt or innocence by a subject's reaction to ordeals of fire, water, or combat, so the chief executive is evaluated. Yet, what are the standards of this presidential ordeal? Concomitantly, how good are they for evaluating effectively his performance?

These questions are the chief concerns of this book. Its aim is to identify the current standards for evaluating presidential performance, to examine them in the light of historical experience, and to suggest a better way to evaluate presidents. Currently, there is no clear idea of the criteria used to evaluate presidents--whether it be evaluation by citizens or scholars--little is known about the value of these standards.

The area of foreign affairs is a good example of this problem. Many authorities can describe the president's power and roles in foreign affairs, including that of commander in chief, chief diplomat, or merely chief manager of the foreign policy process, yet such discussions rarely offer specific ideas of just what those duties involve. Moreover, it is unclear how such duties are translated into criteria for evaluating performance.

Yet evaluations are made, as they must be, by professional president-watchers and amateur observers. Everyone, from expert analysts to the general public, engages in these evaluations, and all have their opinions of how he's doing. The public is continually questioned in opinion polls about their views on the president's handling of his job, and scholars and editorialists regularly produce midterm assessments and end-of-term judgments on the chief executive. In a democratic republic such as the United States, this sort of activity is to be expected and perhaps encouraged, for it enhances the idea of official accountability. It is, however, undertaken according to standards neither explicitly stated nor clearly understood.

Evaluation is important to everyone, from presidents to citizens, particularly in the vital area of foreign affairs. U.S. democracy places primary responsibility for foreign policy in the hands of the president. In the period since World War II, foreign policy has been predominantly a presidential burden and he is held responsible for it by the electorate. It is therefore important that evaluative standards in this area be thoughtful and realistic, in order to render effective judgments of presidential performance. Indeed, the democratic evaluation of performance in the White House demands such standards, for evaluative criteria indicate expectations, and expectations in turn influence policy making. As this book shall reveal, there is a strong tendency among the general public, commentators, and even scholars to think in terms of foreign policy "wins" and "losses."[1] Such expectations color presidential behavior, as chief executives seek to deliver on expectations and avoid politically dangerous "losses."[2]

At the same time, the quality of standards for evaluating presidential performance affects how past presidential actions and policy managements are judged, and can thus influence future presidential policy making. Presidents, their advisors, and the community of commentators and scholars seeking to influence foreign policy all rely upon history for guidance in constructing policy processes and making decisions, so they need accurate evaluative standards if they are to make good use of historical precedents. Without these standards, their views of what other presidents have done, and how previous officeholders have handled the foreign affairs presidency, will be seriously flawed. Better policy and better policy mechanisms can be developed only if our understanding of the past is accurate. As this book shall reveal, the current understanding of presidential reality is flawed, in that it overestimates the president's ability to influence events. Consequently, attempts to draw lessons from the history of the foreign affairs presidency are impaired by the misjudgments of the conventional views.

In short, thoughtful and realistic standards for evaluation are imperative, however the conventional wisdom on how to judge presidents is wrong. It leads to faulty assessments of presidential foreign policy performance, and a continuation of such faulty evaluations could be dangerous to the nation.

John Kennedy once remarked that "Domestic politics . . . can only defeat us: foreign policy can kill us." Since it is the president who is charged with the greatest responsibility for this vital policy area, it is imperative that he be evaluated by realistic standards. While the criteria for presidential assessment will always represent some ideal of what the president ought to do or achieve, they must also fundamentally reflect the realities of the foreign affairs presidency.

Conventional wisdom fails this test, resulting in a misperception of what presidents can accomplish, what they can be held responsible for, and what factors influence their achievements. This book can help to explain why presidents can or cannot live up to the expectations of the conventional wisdom, and what can be done to remedy this situation. The gap between expectations and reality requires adjustments to the foreign policy process and to the criteria for evaluation.

The purpose of this book is to examine the presidential ordeal and suggest ways to sharpen its instruments. Chapter 1 is a description of the conventional wisdom. Chapters 2, 3, and 4 analyze that wisdom through six case studies of presidential foreign policy making. Finally, in Chapter 5 the process of closing the gap between expectations and reality is begun.

NOTES

1. One need only observe the commentary and reporting on the Reagan administration's intervention in Lebanon for evidence of this view.
2. See Bruce Buchanan, "Assessing Presidential Performances: Can We Do Better?" (Paper presented at the American Political Science Association, New York, N.Y., September 2, 1981).

1

THE CONVENTIONAL WISDOM

The evaluation of presidential performance is a subject with which few president-watchers deal explicitly. Scholars, editorialists, and the general public all judge presidents, but they seldom identify the criteria by which they choose to evaluate incumbents. Indeed, for the most part, discovering a guide to presidential evaluation involves gleaning evaluative criteria from various observers' more general comments on the presidency or on foreign policy. Accordingly, this study begins by identifying the standards expressed by three groups: scholars, commentators, and the general public.

The criteria of these groups can be synthesized into what may be considered the "conventional wisdom" on presidential foreign policy performance. This "wisdom," which has never before been explicitly stated, represents the current state of the presidential ordeal.

The most mysterious aspects of this consensus are the general public's standards for presidential evaluation. While opinion polls generally sample approval of the job the president is doing, they do so without reference to how such decisions were reached. In the Gallup Poll, which regularly samples opinion in this matter, the relevant question takes the form of "Do you approve of the way _____ is handling his job as president?"[1] Although opinion is also sampled on more specific aspects of performance, such as the president's "handling" of foreign policy or of the Vietnam War, the approach is essentially the same: evaluations are given, but without the respondents' antecedent calculations of how to evaluate performance.[2] The components of "handling" are not defined.

The response to this situation has been a great deal of research aimed at identifying the factors affecting public evaluations, and the results of such research indicate patterns in public assessments of presidents.[3] These patterns reveal that the public tends to form its evaluation of presidential performance from events and outcomes.[4] As one scholar, Samuel Kernell, has put it, "contrary to existing reports events and conditions which intuitively seem to be important determinants of a president's popularity are in fact the primary explanatory variables."[5] Conditions such as war, international crises, and economic conditions account for fluctuations in public evaluations of presidential performance. In other words, the general public is concerned with results; its judgment of how well a president is handling foreign policy depends on the outcomes he appears to achieve.

Only slightly less mysterious are the standards of editorialists. Commentators regularly render judgments on presidents and their conduct of foreign policy, but the standards which underlie those judgments must usually be inferred by their readers. Of course, editorialists are supposed to render such judgments, but they should state their reasons for doing so. In practice, however, most do not articulate their criteria for presidential evaluation, even those who focus much of their attention on the presidency. A review of eight commentators on the presidency and foreign affairs (David Broder, Hedley Donovan, Joseph Kraft, Flora Lewis, James Reston, Hugh Sidey, George Will, and Theodore White) for the years 1980-84 demonstrates the pattern of judgment by standards that are not often clearly stated.[6]

When analyzed, however, their remarks do reveal performance criteria. These editorialists share the public's concern for achievements and outcomes, but registered interest in other factors as well. Most discussed the importance of the processes of foreign policy making, and some emphasized presidential character and political skills as well. As would be expected, several judged presidents according to the particular policies they pursued: Flora Lewis and Joseph Kraft on pursuit of arms control; George Will on maintenance of national strength; and David Broder on human rights. At the same time, these writers expressed a greater awareness of the limitations on presidential power than appear in public expectations, although they continued to consider outcomes an important criterion for evaluation.

Implication of evaluative standards is also the norm in the scholarly literature on the presidency and foreign policy, for few scholars deal directly with the question of evaluating or appraising presidents. Of the 28 scholars reviewed in this study (see Appendix), only a handful explicitly addressed the question of how presidents should be evaluated.

Among the handful who made their standards explicit, the authors were concerned with a diversity of topics. Some considered the issue of assessing presidential "greatness," while others concentrated on presidential effectiveness in managing the foreign policy decision process. Their criteria ranged from Richard Neustadt's questioning of a president's "feel" for the nature of his power,[7] to Alexander George's five rules for effective decision making,[8] to Clinton Rossiter's list of qualities necessary for presidential effectiveness (bounce, cunning, affability, political skill, a sense of history, the "newspaper habit," and a sense of humor).[9] These authors laid out lists of evaluative criteria as simple as Neustadt's four questions for presidential assessment[10] and as complex as Thomas Bailey's forty-three "yardsticks"[11] for measuring presidential greatness.[12]

The norm, however, is for scholars only to imply standards for presidential evaluation. Consequently, it is necessary to extract evaluative criteria from authors' comments on the presidency and foreign policy. Once analyzed, however, the remarks of these scholars exhibit no lack of evaluative criteria. Their standards can be brought together with those of commentators and the general public to produce the "conventional wisdom" on presidential evaluation. While generally implicit, this wisdom defines current expectations of presidential foreign policy performance.

IDENTIFYING THE CONVENTIONAL WISDOM

Although the various authors and observers surveyed certainly do not share a set of clear, consistent, and well-defined standards of presidential appraisal, it is possible to extract from their analyses something of a consensus regarding the proper criteria for judging presidential performance. As noted above, similarities in the concepts and relationships addressed by the various observers allow a synthesis of the conventional wisdom to be made.

That synthesis has been derived through a three-step process. First, the standards of each observer were identified and clarified. For scholars, these standards are drawn from representative works of each author. The range of scholars reviewed herein represent both contemporary opinion (e.g., Alexander George and Thomas Cronin) and classic works that are still influential (e.g., Harold Laski, whose 1940 book was reissued in 1980 with a new introduction by James MacGregor Burns). The views of commentators were drawn from a survey of each editorialist's columns for the years 1980-84.[13] Finally, for public standards, the relevant criteria were discerned from the literature on interpreting public opinion.

The writings of these observers were surveyed with an eye toward their comments implying responsibilities of the president in foreign affairs, his role in that policy area, and discussions of the role of the president in the U.S. political system. While a few observers explicitly stated criteria for evaluating presidents, in most cases the criteria were inferred from comments implying assessments of performance. Each observer's criteria are stated in terms as close to the author's as possible, but also as explicit standards for assessing performance. (The Appendix provides a listing of president-watchers and their standards.)

The process of definition is continued in the second step, wherein the criteria of each author are expressed as general concepts (see Appendix, Step 2: Observers' Criteria as General Concepts). A survey of the criteria identified in the first step was undertaken to produce a list of 28 general concepts/criteria reflected in the various observers' evaluative standards (e.g., the criterion of Executive management by the president, which is reflected in the lists of nearly all authors surveyed here). This step facilitates comparability among the standards of the various president-watchers, thus making it easier to extract the conventional wisdom.

Drawing together the common threads from the several observers occurs in the third step, which presents the conventional wisdom as a synthesis of the generalized criteria (see Appendix). In this synthesis, as in the discussion of the standards of the conventional wisdom to follow, related concepts among the 28 identified are collapsed into a few categories.[14]

8 / THE PRESIDENT AND FOREIGN AFFAIRS

There are three reasons for this collapsing of categories. First, for the reason of parsimony: it is much easier to develop a sophisticated and manageable analysis of presidential evaluation with fewer categories than with 28. Second, for the reason of coherence: it is important to link together related concepts (e.g., Goal-setting, Policy coherence, and Policy initiation in the category of Policy direction and design) which reflect similar features of the foreign affairs presidency. Studying a general category such as Policy direction and design or Management and oversight is more useful than attempting to tease out some two dozen criteria and their implications for the presidency. Moreover, reducing the number of categories of criteria provides a better reflection of the reality of the presidential ordeal. This is the third reason for the collapsed categories: most observers deal with a handful of criteria, rather than two dozen or so standards. Only one of the 36 president-watchers surveyed in this study offered a long, overlapping list of standards.[15] The rest discussed a brief set of core issues. In the same way, the synthesis of the conventional wisdom focuses on core issues which provide a coherent and parsimonious guide to evaluation.

The result is what may be considered the conventional wisdom on presidential evaluation in foreign affairs. Its components are: Policy direction and design; Organization and staffing; Management and oversight; Consensus-building; and Achievements/outcomes. The first four of these pertain to the policy process, while the last is seen as their result.

> Policy direction and design: The president's performance in foreign affairs is to be judged according to his ability to provide policy direction and design. This criterion includes the development of foreign policy goals for the nation, unified through a comprehensive design which guides policy formation and action by providing a sense of priorities, policy coordination and coherence, perspective for individual issues and cases, and the capacity for future planning.

This criterion is either implied or clearly stated in most discussions of the foreign affairs presidency. Because the president is the central foreign policy actor of the United States, he is expected to give direction and coherence to that policy. Among the observers surveyed in this study, this requirement ranged from a minimal specification that the president set the goals for U.S. foreign policy, to a demand that he provide a comprehensive or "grand design" for it.

First, the president must provide the nation with foreign policy goals: he is to set the course. At minimum, this means that he must have a clear notion of what policies he wants to pursue--whether they be human rights detente with the Soviet Union, or strengthening ties with allies. Furthermore,

> there is the need for a president to come to office not only with a sense of the general direction in which he wishes to move, but a sense, also, of the direction in which the times require him to move.[16]

According to the observers who offer this criterion, it is the president's responsibility to point a direction in which policy ought to go. "He must resolve the policy questions that will not yield to quantitative, empirical analysis. . . ,"[17] such as attempting to reconcile the support for Israel with the necessity for Arab oil,[18] and offer goals and priorities for U.S. foreign policy. He is expected to choose from among the competing policy alternatives available to the United States by indicating what he seeks to accomplish in foreign affairs. Without this indication, the observers agree, the nation has no policy and will drift into danger.

Beyond merely stating goals and priorities, the president is further expected to produce a comprehensive design which will shape and guide foreign policy. This call for a grand design is a central issue in the criteria of several observers and consistent with the views of most others. Foremost among those observers arguing the need for a comprehensive policy design is Henry Kissinger who considers this requirement crucial to presidential success in foreign affairs.

Indeed, Kissinger prefaces his memoirs with a discussion of his thoughts on the president and foreign policy, and addresses this criterion at length. He states that

> I believed that no nation could face or even define its choices without a moral compass that could set a course through the ambiguities of reality and thus make sacrifices meaningful.[19]

A grand design is necessary to make policy coherent, and to contribute to the effectiveness of policy:

> A new administration has the right to ask for compassion and understanding from the American people. But it must found its claim not on pat technical answers to difficult issues; it must above all ask the right questions. It must recognize that, in the field of foreign policy, we will never be able to contribute to building a stable and creative world order unless we first form some conception of it.[20]

In the same vein, Robert Hunter also calls for a comprehensive policy design which he summarizes in the term "world view." According to Hunter, the president must see to it that policy is unified through

> a world view for American foreign policy that can provide a basic framework for judging alternative policies toward diverse parts of the world. . . . If an incoming president is wise, he will take care before scrapping the policies of his predecessor, until he at least understands them and is able to establish his own world view--one that has some chance of advancing the U.S. national interest, can be sustained over a period of time, and will outlast his own tenure of office.[21]

Flora Lewis, foreign affairs columnist for the New York *Times*, echoes this view as well. She sees a comprehensive design as important to the president and to the nation as a whole. In a broad sense, for Lewis, this design is essential to national survival:

> The American President next year, new or
> familiar, will need to start over with a
> fresh look at the changing world and a
> conscious effort to develop and explain a
> global policy. . . . The effort at redefi-
> nition, to put bits and pieces of reaction
> back into a coherent American attitudinal
> plane, can be more decisive for the future
> than the name of the winner.[22]

Moreover, this task of assembling a grand design for policy is essentially a presidential one: "The great Presidential task that nobody else can perform is giving voice to America's purposes in a way that educates and assures, that provokes awareness of a complex reality and gives steady guidance in dealing with it."[23] It is his responsibility to give direction to U.S. foreign policy, and to do so in a comprehensive and unified way.

Not only is he required to provide direction, design, and policy formation in an initial sense, but to provide coherent perspectives on individual issues, policies, programs, and decisions. In other words, the observers agree, the president must not only have a fundamental idea of what he wants to accomplish, but he must also be able to relate to his subordinates (and to the nation, and sometimes the world) how individual problems and issues are relevant to the overall design. What this means is that, in the press of the daily conduct of foreign policy, the president must be able to articulate how the matter at hand (e.g., a crisis in Central America or a new international trade bill) relates to his grand design and thus how it is to be handled.

This can be termed the issue of perspective. Observers such as I. M. Destler and columnist Joseph Kraft maintain that the various "pieces" of foreign policy--issues, programs, decisions--must be given perspective for how they fit together into the overall U.S. approach to the world, and it is the president who is responsible for providing this perspective.[24] Perspective on a daily basis, and, according to president-watchers, an important part of the design itself.

The next two criteria concern organization, staffing, management, and oversight. All four of these factors are certainly related, but it is possible to make distinctions between, on the one hand, Organization and staffing, and on the other, Management and oversight. The primary distinction is that, in practice, Organization and staffing temporally precede Management and oversight. This distinction will become more apparent shortly.

> Organization and staffing: The president's performance in foreign affairs is to be judged according to his ability to effectively organize and staff the foreign affairs government. This judgment is based on the quality and effectiveness of the organizational scheme the president establishes for handling foreign affairs, his ability to work within that scheme, and the individuals he chooses to make it work.

Most observers agree that two important presidential responsibilities are to make high-quality appointments and to structure the decision process for effective decision making. Structure is important because the president does not stand alone, but depends on his foreign affairs government for information, analysis, and advice. At the same time, organizational structure must be given life by the personnel of the foreign affairs government, so staffing is likewise important.

A president's organizational scheme affects decisions and policy by shaping the decision process. As Theodore Sorensen, former aide to President Kennedy, noted in a moment of understatement, "Procedures do, of course, affect decisions."[25] Indeed, many president-watchers are keenly interested in the effects of organization on presidential policy making.

One scholar, Alexander George, sees the criterion of effective organization as crucial to the effectiveness of the president's entire policy process. Moreover, it is important for the president to understand his own role in the organizational scheme he establishes:

> The first and foremost task that a new president faces is to learn to define his own role in the policymaking system; only then can he structure and manage the roles and relationships within the policymaking system of his secretary of state, the special

assistant for national security affairs, the secretary of defense, and other cabinet and agency heads with responsibility for the formulation and implementation of foreign policy.[26]

The scheme that the president establishes to operate foreign policy influences what information reaches him, how options and choices are handled, and what sort of advice he receives. As commentator David Broder has observed, "What counts in the long run is how well he [the President] manages the processes of politics."[27] Broder, like George and other president-watchers, sees the structure of the president's foreign affairs government as important, because all policy flows through it.

In the same way, these observers emphasize staffing as an important evaluative standard. Staffing provides a means for making the president's organizational scheme work, by animating it with the individuals who will help him achieve his goals. Thomas Cronin observes in this vein:

> An effective president shrewdly uses his recruitment resource not only as a means of rewarding campaign supporters and enhancing his ties to Congress but also as a vital form of communicating the priorities and policy directions of his administration.[28]

For Cronin, then, appointments serve as an important means for implementing the president's policy design. Other observers reflect this view, emphasizing as does Clinton Rossiter that presidents are helpless without effective aides:

> If the modern Presidency, as I have insisted, is irrevocably institutionalized, the modern President must do better than Washington and Lincoln on this score, for he can no longer expect to accomplish anything unless he surrounds himself with able technicians as well as wise statesmen and shrewd politicians.[29]

Even when they are not as poetic as Rossiter, the president-watchers of the conventional wisdom give great attention to the criterion of staffing. Louis Koenig, who insists on a high "quality of counsel" from a president's subordinates, argues that staffing is crucial to presidential power:

> Power for the President reflects, among other things, the quality and usefulness of his staff. Upon them he depends for the funneling of information and problems to himself and the communication and interpretation of his directives to those sectors of the huge, sprawling executive branch that administers the diplomatic, economic, military, scientific, intelligence, and psychological phases of foreign policy.[30]

Reflecting this view, Gordon Hoxie goes so far as to lay down four useful rules for presidential staffing: the president choose a principal aide whose career involves experience in the service of more than one politician; that presidential assistants must avoid publicity; that the president avoid emotional dependence on his chief aide; and that a central staff figure emerge.[31]

Taken together, these various observations, combined with the remarks of other president-watchers, illustrate the organizational and staffing criterion of the conventional wisdom. The view of the conventional wisdom is that the president must master both aspects of this standard: the president must develop an effective organization, and understand his own role in whatever scheme he establishes; and, he must animate that structure with effective and useful subordinates.

> Management and oversight: The president's performance in foreign affairs is to be judged according to his management and oversight of the information and decision processes of foreign policy, his subordinates, and policy implementation. The president must insure that policy is consistent with his comprehensive design, that all necessary work is properly carried out, and that the mechanisms and personnel of his administration are coordinated in their operations. He must also make provisions for crisis management.

Interestingly, this criterion receives the greatest attention from the observers of the conventional wisdom. It is among the evaluative standards of nearly all of the president-watchers surveyed in this study, and some authors even state explicit conditions or standards by which this criterion is to be used to evaluate incumbents.

The various authors' discussions of Management and oversight range widely in their emphasis, from E. S. Corwin's specification that the conduct of the day-to-day business of foreign affairs is a presidential responsibility,[32] to Clinton Rossiter's equation of effective presidential management with presidential success:

> What sort of technician was he? How efficiently did he organize his energies, direct his Lieutenants, and thus exercise his powers? Lincoln could be an indifferent administrator and yet a great President, but the rise of the modern state has made it impossible for an inefficient President to discharge even a fraction of his duties with much hope of success.[33]

Regardless of these varieties of emphasis, however, the great majority of observers focus on the importance of Management and oversight in some aspect. Consequently, in the conventional wisdom this criterion is complex, and requires of a president sophisticated administration.

First, a president must manage the mechanisms, personnel, and processes of the foreign policy government. Richard Pious, a scholar who has devoted much attention to presidential management of foreign relations, focuses on this requirement in his assessment of the presidency:

> The major problem for presidents has not been the absence of authority or institutional conflict with Congress: it has been the weakness of the president as a <u>manager</u> of foreign relations. There is no unity of purpose within the executive branch. Often the national security "communities"--diplomatic, military, and intelligence--are rivals, working at cross-purposes or against the White House.[34]

16 / THE PRESIDENT AND FOREIGN AFFAIRS

The president must understand how to deal with these problems of management, i.e., how to cope with the large and diverse governing machinery over which he presides. Concurrent with his responsibilities for establishing an effective organizational scheme for foreign policy, he must make the mechanisms work. Hedley Donovan, a commentator with experience as senior counselor to President Carter, demonstrates how these matters are connected:

> A crucial executive ability, above all for the Chief Executive of the U.S., is perceptiveness about people. This will bear on the quality of the President's appointments and his ability to mold his people into an effective Administration.[35]

The president must manage more than people. The fearfully complex systems and institutions in his care need executive oversight and control. It is not enough to say the president "can hire managers"; as he delegates, he must know how to keep track of the delegated work; he must understand what his managers are managing. Robert Hunter also contributes to this argument, listing as the third of his twelve "general propositions" for presidential performance the criterion of effective management:

> Setting policies and priorities in foreign policy is critical, but so too are the mechanisms and the process that the president establishes to help him create and carry out a foreign policy. A president who neglects that engine--in either its design or its operation--is sure to have mammoth difficulties, probably in times of quiet, and surely in times of crisis.[36]

But these president-watchers go beyond merely stating a need for good management. Indeed, they insist that the president be "master in his own house"; i.e., he must clearly be in charge, and not attempt to avoid or delegate his responsibilities. Just as Donovan argued that the president must manage his managers, so do other observers emphasize this requirement for decisive presidential control. For Roger Hilsman, one of the president's three chief roles in foreign affairs is as the "ultimate decider" of foreign policy: while he cannot decide on all the thousands of matters in this policy area, he is obligated to make decisions of great fatefulness (e.g., whether to commit U.S. troops to a conflict) or resolve disputes which cannot be settled in the lower levels of decision making (e.g., deciding which agency will have primary charge over a particular program or issue).[37] Likewise, Flora Lewis reflects the judgments of many observers about decisions in her comment on an unresolved conflict within the Reagan administration: "Normally, a presidential decision should have settled the matter."[38] The implication is clear--the president must not only manage, he must also take charge and take responsibility for making his foreign affairs government work. Finally, Hunter summarizes this focus on presidential control and decisiveness in management with the question "Who governs?" He explains:

> The success or failure of U.S. foreign policy is the responsibility of the president of the United States--to the degree that the United States itself can be instrumental in determining its own fate. . . . The president must make the choices when foreign and domestic policies conflict; no president, now or in the future, can abdicate this role. Senior officials under his command may succeed or fail at their respective tasks, but they are there by presidential choice. The responsibility is truly his.[39]

The dual requirement of effective presidential management and decisive presidential control of his administration is reflected in the several observers who affirm the importance of this criterion. Moreover, they add to these standards specific responsibilities within the managerial realm--beyond overall management, they specify decision process management, crisis management, and effective oversight.

The foremost analyst of the requirements of decision process management is Alexander George. He suggests evaluating the president according to how well he fosters effectiveness in the decision process, and lays out five rules for effective decision making: ensure that sufficient information on the situation at hand is obtained and adequately analyzed, in order to provide a valid diagnosis of the problem; facilitate consideration of the major values and interests affected; assure a search for a wide range of options and a reasonably thorough evaluation of the expected consequences of each; provide for careful consideration of problems involved in implementing the various options; and, maintain receptivity to indications that current policies are not working out well, and cultivate an ability to learn from experience.[40]

George gives strongest statement to decision-process standards to which other observers also allude. They expect the president to insure that a problem or issue is well understood, that alternatives presented to him are realistic and leave room for presidential discretion, and that no significant bit of information or analysis is left out of the considerations.

As Rossiter noted, the modern state is highly institutionalized. In terms of the foreign affairs presidency, this means that the president must work through an elaborate bureaucracy in making decisions. That is why attention is given to the organizational scheme the president establishes for his decision making, and that is why these observers are also concerned about managing the decision process. Just as George is concerned about the necessities for effectiveness in that process, so are Destler, Kissinger, Hunter, and others concerned about how the president can make it work to his advantage. These latter three each offer their own advice regarding the decision process, with Kissinger providing some general guidelines to which the others would likely agree:

> To be helpful to the President the machinery for making decisions must therefore meet several criteria. It must be compatible with his personality and style. It must lead to action; desultory talk without operational content produces paralysis. Above all, it must be sensitive to the psychological relationship between the President and his close advisors: it must enable the President's associates to strengthen his self-confidence and yet give him real choices, to supply perspective and yet not turn every issue into a test of wills. It must give scope to genuine presidential discretion without promoting megalomania

that often develops in positions where one
encounters few equals. At the same time,
if every single decision is funneled into
the President's office, he will lose the
benefit of technical competence and accumu-
lated experience of the permanent officials.[41]

In the same way, the president-watchers expect him to develop facilities for crisis management. Just as Hunter noted the strain on routine policy processes in times of crisis, so do the various observers pronounce a presidential responsibility for managing crises. Indeed, Thomas Cronin lists this criterion as one of the seven components of his presidential "job description."[42] He notes that, for better or worse, crises are presidential responsibilities in which "a president is often little more than the victim of the interplay of events and institutions. . . ."[43] The president is obligated to do something about whatever crisis is at hand, and president-watchers thus expect him to develop means for coping with such occurrences. They are not very specific on just what it is presidents must do to manage crises, only that the chief executive must do so.

The final specific requirement under this criterion is that the president exercise effective oversight. This responsibility was alluded to in Donovan's remark about knowing "what his managers are managing," but president-watchers do see it as distinct. Two scholars who focus on oversight are Peter Cowhey and David Laitin, who describe presidential oversight as a fundamental responsibility for seeing to it that all necessary work is done and done properly.[44] As Cowhey and Laitin explain it, oversight is a feature of management, but not the same as decisive control or the handling of crises and decision making. Rather, oversight is what Roger Hilsman summarizes in his second of three presidential foreign policy roles--the president as "ultimate coordinator." Hilsman describes this function as follows:

> Once a policy is set, the departments and
> agencies involved in implementing the pol-
> icy can be counted on to accomplish the
> vast bulk of the necessary coordination
> with one another. But as with disagreement
> over issues, there can be simple failures
> and gaps. Ultimately, it is the President

> who must prod and push to make sure
> that everyone is doing what he should.45

This task may be performed by the president himself or by one of his subordinates under presidential direction, but Hilsman, Cowhey and Laitin, and others agree that it is a presidential responsibility.

The president is thus required to effectively manage, coordinate, and oversee his foreign affairs government. As the observers of the conventional wisdom see it, management is such that it can affect a president's ability to achieve his aims. As James Reston commented in this vein on President Reagan's unwillingness to firmly control his senior advisors:

> [I]s harmful to the President because there is a continuing doubt about whether he's really in command of a steady, continuing policy.
>   Accordingly, his proposals are increasingly rejected by the Congress and the allies. And the confusion of his staff is at least partly to blame.46

> Consensus-building: The president's performance in foreign affairs is to be judged according to his ability to build and maintain a consensus in support of his policies and decisions. A president should possess the requisite political skills to seek out, establish, and maintain the limits of his consensus.

Just as the president is charged with guiding and initiating policy and making decisions, so do president-watchers expect him to build a consensus in support of both. This criterion, as expressed by the various observers, varies from Richard Neustadt's observation that presidents must work by consensus, because "Presidential _power_ is the power to persuade,"47 to commentator Hugh Sidey's expectation of an effective president being able to command consent: "He [Reagan, with the congressional vote supporting the sale of AWACs to Saudi Arabia] won another vote of confidence. That is the way government is supposed to work."48

The observers of the conventional wisdom adhere to this criterion for several reasons. At base, this standard grows out of the understanding that, without consensus of some sort, the president is limited in his ability to implement his policies and decisions. This understanding is captured in Neustadt's remark about "the power to persuade." At a higher level, some observers see consensus as important because foreign policy is the policy of a nation, and without consensus national policy is limited. Consequently, analysts such as James Reston seek a foreign policy which receives bipartisan support.[49]

Beyond these two levels, some observers extend to consensus an importance that is gained from an idea of democratic legitimacy. These authors see consensus as an end in itself, because the president is the chief foreign policy actor of a democracy, and thus needs consensus because it is democratic. (While no observers in this study suggested that the president ought not to be democratic, only a few stressed this feature of consensus.) An example of these analysts is George Reedy, who observes that the president "must persuade enough of his countrymen of the rightness of his decisions so that he can carry them out without destroying the fabric of society."[50] The usual example given in this regard is the Vietnam War, for which President Johnson was unable to maintain support. Without a supporting consensus, they maintain, the war lacked democratic legitimacy. Also in this group is Richard Pious, who argues that presidents have relied too heavily on prerogative power to conduct foreign affairs. He thus infers a standard of presidential performance which involves a president's seeking consensus rather than pressing prerogative claims.[51]

Most observers of this study focused on consensus as a necessary tool of the presidential conduct of foreign affairs. They view it as a concomitant of the checks and balances of the U.S. political system, so the president must master its techniques. To do so involves a variety of political skills, ranging from what Emmett Hughes calls a "sense of timing,"[52] to what others describe as skills in anticipating and overcoming opposition,[53] coalition-building,[54] and mastering the arts of both public and private persuasion.[55]

Yet, beyond their remarks calling for consensus and their hints about the skills necessary to achieve it, these observers fail to define exactly what they mean by consensus. They are not clear on what it is, how it is measured, or how to tell if a president is working to develop it. In the conventional wisdom, then, a rather ambiguous notion of consensus is outlined as an important criterion.

In short, this criterion is a simply stated, and yet ambiguous one: the president must build and maintain a consensus behind his policies, for whatever reason. In this requirement, president-watchers find easy agreement. But to do so requires certain political skills of persuasion and judgment. Again, the authors can agree in their recommendations; however, they do not go beyond these expectations. None of the observers offers any more explicit guidelines for how a president is to build a consensus, or how he is to develop the necessary skills to do so. The conventional wisdom thus holds a simple, but important, expectation regarding a requirement which is both vague and demanding at the same time.

> Achievements/outcomes: The president's performance in foreign affairs is to be judged on the outcomes and results he is able to achieve.

This final criterion is significant for two reasons: first, because it forms the standard by which the public evaluates presidents; and, second, because of its relationship to other criteria in the writings of other president-watchers. The public forms its judgments of presidents based on this criterion, and most of the commentators in this study also regard it as important. Moreover, many scholars included this standard. Consequently, the criterion of Achievements and outcomes is relevant to all of the three groups surveyed here, and is therefore relevant to this study as well.

It is particularly relevant in the sense of its relation to the other criteria. To be specific, the thrust of the observations of the president-watchers surveyed here, whether scholars, commentators, or the general public, is such that these observers implicitly posit a relationship between the first four criteria and this final one. References to what will contribute to presidential success or effectiveness, whether they be Clinton Rossiter's demand for administrative mastery or Henry Kissinger's prescription of a grand design, betray a subtle but powerful relationship between criteria in the views of these observers. So does the public's assessment of a president's "handling" of foreign policy according to the outcomes he is able to achieve. In short, that relationship predicts that fulfillment of the several evaluative criteria will lead to (or strongly aid) success in foreign policy outcomes.

Fulfillment of criteria ⟶ Success

The nature of this relationship, as posited by the conventional wisdom, is such that outcomes constitute an evaluative criterion which is dependent on the first four criteria. It is thus the dependent variable in the conventional wisdom's "calculus" of presidential performance: according to this view, if the president fulfills the necessary criteria, he should achieve success in foreign policy.

This relationship is important to note because it illuminates the essence of the conventional wisdom: the consensus of president-watchers is that presidential success or effectiveness is heavily dependent upon the president's ability to fulfill the several criteria of direction, organization, management, and consensus. In other words, the conventional wisdom implies that good process will yield good outcomes.

It is this view which becomes the focus of attention in addressing the second central issue of this study, i.e., "How useful are these standards for assessing presidential performance?" This issue is difficult to address, but it is important to do so, for the presidential ordeal is only as good as its instruments. The rest of this study will be directed toward addressing this second issue, evaluating the evaluative criteria, and sharpening the instruments of the presidential ordeal.

EXAMINING THE CONVENTIONAL WISDOM

Since the conventional wisdom posits a relationship between policy process and policy outcomes, an examination of this view requires a comparative study of presidential policy making in circumstances of both success and failure. In this way, it will be possible to isolate the role of the four "process" criteria in determining outcomes. While such a study of "test" should not be seen as definitive, it will provide a means for the historical record to cast doubt on or provide supporting evidence for the process-outcomes relationship.

This requires a series of cases undertaken in the "disciplined-configurative" mode of analysis. In this mode, several cases are examined in terms of the same general and theory-related variables.[56] To employ this mode of analysis requires a guiding theory to organize analysis (i.e., the conventional wisdom), a "class" of cases relevant to that theory, and a selective, focused treatment of cases. In this last matter, as long as the researcher is sensitive to the circumstances of each case, he is less interested in its idiosyncracies than in how the case illuminates the theory under scrutiny.

As for the cases to be studied, a definition of the relevant class is in order. This study will examine cases in foreign policy which can be identified as successes or failures for the president. In the interest of contemporary relevance, cases will be drawn from the post-World War II era.

While the ultimate goal of presidential evaluation is a general evaluation of a president's performance, a focus on particular cases has two distinct advantages. First, because cases are coherent and somewhat discrete phenomena (even if inevitably linked to other events and circumstances), they allow a focused analysis of events in order to isolate the role of presidential performance in determining outcomes. Second, a focus on cases is consistent with presidential evaluation as it actually occurs under the conventional wisdom: president-watchers focus much of their attention on such cases as the Bay of Pigs crisis, the decision of whether to deploy the MX missile, the negotiation and ratification of the SALT treaty, the Reagan administration's intervention in Lebanon, or attempts to pass a new international trade bill. A focus on cases does no violence to current evaluations, but also enables a constructive examination of the conventional wisdom.

The cases were selected from incidences of presidential success or failure in foreign policy, but the researcher must also ensure comparability and variety among cases by developing a typology for foreign policy cases.[57] This typology will identify the various issue-areas of presidential involvement in foreign affairs, i.e., types of foreign policy problems. This typology will make it possible to match similar cases (comparability) and cover the range of cases (variety) arising in foreign policy. It thus provides the framework for analysis illustrated in Table 1.1 and contains three issue-areas.

TABLE 1.1

Framework for Analysis

	Crises	Non-Crisis Security Issues	Non-Crisis Non-Security Issues
Success:	*Taiwan Strait Cuban Missiles Lebanon, 1958 Mayaguez	*SALT I North Atlantic Treaty Test Ban Treaty	*Trade Expansion Act, 1962 GATT Camp David Accords Foreign Assistance Act, 1967
Failure:	*Bay of Pigs Berlin, 1961	*SALT II Skybolt Open Skies	*Trade Act of 1970 Jackson-Vanik Amendment

*These cases are examined in this study.

1. Crises: Crises are defined in this study as those situations of high threat to national security, in which the president and other decision makers perceive themselves to be so threatened and under great time pressure to deal effectively with the threat. Perception is important as a determinant of foreign policy crises, because how the president perceives the nature, gravity, and urgency of a case will greatly influence how he will behave in responding to that situation. The second factor in this definition is time urgency, because threat and urgency combine to yield situations which demand, or which the president believes demand, a quick and effective response to the threat.

In the Taiwan Strait crisis (1954-55), President Eisenhower was successful in his attempt to defend U.S. interests in the Far East, project U.S. power abroad, and maintain the security and morale of Taiwan while avoiding war with China. In the Bay of Pigs crisis (1961), President Kennedy met defeat in his attempt to defend U.S.

interests and project national power. This case is a clear failure of policy making in a crisis.

2. Non-crisis security issues: This category contains those cases which are not crises, but which directly involve defense and security issues: arms control, weapons systems, security alliances, and military readiness. Security issues are readily distinguishable, but this category includes those cases not of the same threat and urgency as crises.

This study will examine the cases of the two SALT treaties. In the case of SALT I, President Nixon was able to achieve his goal of concluding and ratifying an arms agreement with the Soviet Union. In SALT II, President Carter achieved a second arms treaty with the Soviet Union, but was unable to obtain its approval by the U.S. Senate.

3. Non-crisis non-security issues: This category includes those cases which involve neither crises nor are directly related to defense and national security. In one sense this is a "remainder" category, but in another sense the issues included here are related: issues which are often given less attention than crises and questions of security, but which nevertheless fall in the realm of foreign affairs. Issues such as those of international trade policy, diplomacy, and foreign aid tend to be seen as qualitatively different from security issues.

This study shall examine two cases of international trade policy. In the Trade Expansion Act (1962), President Kennedy obtained passage of a major initiative in trade policy: one which increased presidential authority to negotiate tariff reductions and ushered in the Kennedy Round in international trade talks. In the failure of the Trade Act of 1970, President Nixon was unable to renew lapsed provisions of the 1962 act, as well as to move toward more free trade.

In Chapters 2, 3, and 4, these six cases will be examined through the "disciplined-configurative" mode of analysis. Chapter 5 will look at the results of the case studies, consider their implications for the conventional wisdom, and suggest a better way for evaluating presidential performance in foreign affairs.

NOTES

1. See Thomas E. Cronin, The State of the Presidency, 2nd ed. (Boston: Little, Brown, 1980), pp. 328-29; and George Edwards, The Public Presidency (New York: St. Martin's Press, 1983), pp. 253-57.

2. Edwards, The Public Presidency, p. 253.

3. See for example, ibid. and the sources cited therein, as well as Samuel Kernell, "Explaining Presidential Popularity," American Political Science Review 72 (June 1978):506-22; Donald R. Kinder, "Presidents, Prosperity, and Public Opinion," Public Opinion Quarterly 45 (Spring 1981):1-21; Lee Sigelman, "Dynamics of Presidential Support: An Overview of Research Finding," Presidential Studies Quarterly 9 (Winter 1979):206-16; Stephen J. Wayne, "Great Expectations: What People Want from Presidents," in Rethinking the Presidency, ed. Thomas E. Cronin (Boston: Little, Brown, 1982), pp. 185-99; John E. Mueller, War, Presidents, and Public Opinion (New York: John Wiley and Sons, 1973); and "Poll Cites Qualities of Ideal President," New York Times, October 9, 1983, p. 32.

4. Kernell, "Explaining Presidential Popularity"; Mueller, War, Presidents; Wayne, "Great Expectations." While the Kernell study is widely regarded as definitive, Edwards, The Public Presidency, disputes these findings, arguing that outcomes are not the major factors affecting public evaluations. Rather, he contends that "Citizens seem to focus on the president's efforts and his stands on issues rather than on his personality or how his policies affect them or even whether his policies are successful in the short run" (p. 253). Yet, as Edwards admits, "policy efforts" are "nebulous" (ibid.), thus begging the question of what they are. It seems reasonable to assume that outcomes and results, which Kernell and others identified as important and which seem intuitively significant, are fundamental to assessing "policy efforts." Moreover, Edwards focuses on the term "handling" in many opinion polls, as if the word has precise meaning, but ignores the rampant ambiguity of such a question. In sum, it is quite unlikely that he has cast any doubt on these findings.

5. Kernell, "Explaining Presidential Popularity," p. 515. The original was in italics.

6. David Broder, columns in Washington Post, January 1980-January 1984; Hedley Donovan, "Fluctuations on

the Presidential Exchange," *Time*, November 9, 1981, pp. 121-22; Hedley Donovan, "Job Specs for the Oval Office," *Time*, December 13, 1982, pp. 20-29; Joseph Kraft, "The Post-Imperial Presidency," New York *Times Magazine*, November 2, 1980, pp. 31-95; Joseph Kraft, columns in Washington *Post*, January 1980-84; Flora Lewis, columns in New York *Times*, January 1980-84; James Reston, columns in New York *Times*, January 1980-84; Hugh Sidey, "Assessing a Presidency," *Time*, August 18, 1980, pp. 10-15; Hugh Sidey, "The Presidency," a regular column in *Time*, January 1980-February 1984; George Will, columns in *Newsweek*, January 1980-March 1984; George Will, columns in Washington *Post*, January 1980-January 1984; and Theodore H. White, *America in Search of Itself: The Making of the President, 1956-1980* (New York: Harper and Row, 1982).

7. Richard E. Neustadt, *Presidential Power*, rev. ed. (New York: John Wiley and Sons, 1980), p. 147.

8. Alexander L. George, *Presidential Decisionmaking in Foreign Policy: The Effective Use of Information and Advice* (Boulder, Colo.: Westview Press, 1980), p. 10.

9. Clinton Rossiter, *The American Presidency*, 2nd ed., Time Reading Program Special Edition (New York: Time, 1963), p. 154.

10. Neustadt, *Presidential Power*, p. 147.

11. Ibid., pp. 147-61. See also the Appendix to this book.

12. Thomas A. Bailey, *Presidential Greatness*, reissued with a new preface (New York: Irvington, 1978), pp. 262-66. The Appendix to this book condenses Bailey's test by grouping similar points together.

13. Except in the cases of Hedley Donovan and T. H. White: White's book, *America in Search of Itself*, cited above, served as an excellent summary of his views, while Donovan's two essays for *Time* ("Fluctuations" and "Job Specs"), also cited above, summarize his views.

14. The author's development of general concepts and the synthesis thereof were cross-checked by two colleagues who reviewed all the material. The author wishes to express special thanks to John Phillip Rogers and Michael Greenberg for their assistance and advice. Inter-rater reliability was high in the cross-checks, and the results given here reflect a consensus of the raters.

15. Bailey, *Presidential Greatness*, pp. 262-66.

16. Harold J. Laski, *The American Presidency, An Interpretation* (New York: Universal Library, 1940), p. 29.

17. George Reedy, The Twilight of the Presidency (New York: World, 1970), pp. 28-29.
18. This example is borrowed from Cronin, The State of the Presidency, p. 155.
19. Henry Kissinger, White House Years (Boston: Little, Brown, 1979), p. 55.
20. Ibid., p. 66.
21. Robert Hunter, Presidential Control of Foreign Policy, Washington Papers, vol. 10, no. 91 (New York: Praeger, 1982), p. 92.
22. Flora Lewis, "Now Back to the World," New York Times, November 4, 1980, p. A19.
23. Flora Lewis, "Sleeping with Elephants," New York Times, January 16, 1981, p. A23.
24. See I. M. Destler, Presidents, Bureaucrats, and Foreign Policy (Princeton: Princeton University Press, 1974), pp. 4-7 and 89-94.
25. Theodore Sorensen, Decision-Making in the White House (New York: Columbia University Press, 1963), p. 3.
26. George, Presidential Decisionmaking, p. 146.
27. David Broder, "It's Up to Reagan Now," Washington Post, January 21, 1981, p. A9. In that column, Broder stressed organization of the processes of government. Emphasis added.
28. Cronin, State of the Presidency, p. 167.
29. Rossiter, American Presidency, p. 155.
30. Louis Koenig, The Chief Executive, rev. ed. (New York: Harcourt, Brace, and World, 1968), p. 235.
31. R. Gordon Hoxie, "The Not So Imperial Presidency: A Modest Proposal," Presidential Studies Quarterly 10 (Spring 1980):204.
32. Edward S. Corwin, The President: Office and Powers, 4th ed. (New York: New York University Press, 1957), p. 226.
33. Rossiter, American Presidency, p. 155.
34. Richard Pious, The American Presidency (New York: Basic Books, 1979), p. 332.
35. Donovan, "Job Specs," p. 22.
36. Hunter, Presidential Control, p. 91.
37. Roger Hilsman, The Politics of Policy Making in Defense and Foreign Affairs (New York: Harper and Row, 1971), pp. 18-20.
38. Flora Lewis, "A Policy or $1,000?" New York Times, December 4, 1981, p. A31.

39. Hunter, Presidential Control, p. 90.
40. George, Presidential Decisionmaking, p. 10.
41. Kissinger, White House Years, p. 40.
42. Cronin, State of the Presidency, pp. 156–58.
43. Ibid., p. 157.
44. Peter Cowhey and David D. Laitin, "Bearing the Burden: A Model of Presidential Responsibility in Foreign Policy," International Studies Quarterly 22 (June 1978): 281.
45. Hilsman, Politics of Policy Making, p. 20.
46. James Reston, "Who Advises Reagan?" New York Times, April 27, 1983, p. A27.
47. Neustadt, Presidential Power, p. 10.
48. Hugh Sidey, "The Art of Enticement," Time, November 9, 1981, p. 31.
49. James Reston, "The State of the Union," New York Times, January 20, 1980, p. E19.
50. Reedy, Twilight of Presidency, p. 29.
51. Pious, American Presidency, p. 419.
52. Emmett John Hughes, The Living Presidency (New York: Coward, McCann, and Geoghegan, 1972), p. 111.
53. Lawrence E. Lynn and David F. Whitman, The President as Policymaker (Philadelphia: Temple University Press, 1982), p. 280.
54. Cronin, State of the Presidency, p. 168.
55. Hilsman, Politics of Policy Making, p. 21.
56. For a detailed discussion of this mode of case-study analysis, see Harry Eckstein, "Case Study and Theory in Political Science," in The Handbook of Political Science, vol. 7, ed. Fred I. Greenstein and Nelson W. Polsby (Reading, Mass.: Addison-Wesley, 1975); Alexander George, "Case Studies and Theory Development: The Method of Structured, Focused Comparison," in Diplomacy: New Approaches in History, Theory, and Policy, ed. Paul G. Lauren (New York: Free Press, 1979); and Norman Thomas, "Case Studies," in Studying the Presidency, ed. George Edwards and Stephen Wayne (Knoxville: University of Tennessee Press, 1983).
57. Presidential success or failure was assessed by two tests: whether the case is generally regarded as a success or failure; and, whether or not the president achieved his goals in the case. Both criteria had to agree in order for a case to be selected. While the bulk of cases in foreign policy fit into a third, indeterminate category, use of success and failure better illuminates the role of the "process" criteria in affecting outcomes.

2

CRISES

Crises are often seen as important tests of U.S. foreign policy and policy makers, so they naturally come to be seen as tests of the chief foreign policy actor. They present situations that demand special presidential attention and action, and are thus extremely relevant to the issue of presidential evaluation. An important role of the president is to be crisis manager for the United States, and foreign policy in the modern era has been marked by a series of crises: the invasion of South Korea, the Taiwan Strait crisis, the Suez crisis, crises in Berlin, the Congo, Indochina, and the Middle East, the Bay of Pigs crisis, the Cuban missile crisis, the Iranian hostage crisis, and several others.

These situations constitute a special category in foreign affairs. They usually suspend normal procedures of decision making and policy formation, demand extraordinary amounts of time and energy from the president and his advisors--all compressed into a brief period, and threaten important values of the president and the nation.

It is thus imperative that presidential crisis management be properly understood. Two cases from recent history can help to develop that understanding: the Taiwan Strait crisis of 1954-55 and the Bay of Pigs crisis of 1961. In the first case, President Eisenhower was confronted with a threat against U.S. interests in the Far East, and he managed to achieve his goals in protecting those interests. In the Bay of Pigs crisis, President Kennedy failed in his attempt to project U.S. power in response to a crisis situation he perceived in Cuba, thus engendering long-term problems for the United States in the Caribbean region. While these cases do not precisely mirror one another, they

32 / THE PRESIDENT AND FOREIGN AFFAIRS

do provide a useful contrast of presidential policy making in a crisis. In each case, the president attempted to defend U.S. interests as he saw them through a projection of national power, albeit with different results. The following case studies will examine the factors affecting the outcomes of these cases.

THE TAIWAN STRAIT CRISIS, 1954-55

The Taiwan Strait crisis of 1954-55, during which Communist China threatened several offshore islands held by the Nationalist Chinese on Taiwan, stands as an important case for studying presidential success in coping with a crisis.[1] For in this case President Eisenhower was able to achieve his several objectives, which included maintaining the security and morale of the Nationalists, and avoiding war with China. This study will examine the reasons behind his success.

Summary of Case

On September 3, 1954, Chinese Communist artillery began shelling the island of Quemoy, which is located opposite the eastern Chinese city of Amoy. In the United States and on Taiwan, this attack was regarded as a prelude to a full-scale Chinese invasion of Taiwan, which never materialized. For the months between September 1954 and May 1955, however, an atmosphere of crisis pervaded, as the United States and China drew close to war. By May, the tension had subsided, and China made overtures toward negotiations.[2]

The U.S. response to this crisis was a complex combination of diplomacy, threat, and maneuver, for the affair drew out over a nine-month period, but it revolved around a few key decisions and actions of President Eisenhower and his advisors. It began to take shape soon after the president received word of the shelling on the evening of September 3, when he began consulting several of his advisors regarding the U.S. response.[3]

From the beginning, this affair was seen by the administration as a crisis directly involving the United States.[4] Because it was the effective guarantor of Taiwan's security, the United States was a direct participant in this conflict. Moreover, because President Truman had interposed ships of the U.S. Navy between China and Taiwan to underscore the U.S. commitment, military actions against Taiwan would, as in Eisenhower's words, "have to run over the Seventh Fleet."[5] The president thus faced what he and his administration regarded as a crisis for the United States. He believed that an immediate response was necessary, and throughout the several months of the affair there existed a pervading sense of urgency.[6] Indeed, his comments to the National Security Council, during its first meeting after the beginning of the crisis, illustrates the gravity with which he viewed the situation: "We're not talking about a limited, brush-fire war. We're talking about going to the threshold of World War III."[7]

Because of the nature of this crisis, the president, who was at his summer White House in Denver during September, convened the National Security Council at nearby Lowry Air Force Base on September 12.[8] At this meeting, attended by Vice-President Nixon, Secretary of State John Foster Dulles, his undersecretary, Gen. Walter Bedell Smith, Defense Secretary Charles Wilson, and the Joint Chiefs of Staff,[9] the question of the U.S. response to the Chinese action was discussed. With Gen. Matthew Ridgway dissenting, the Chiefs presented a plan for Nationalist bombing of the Chinese mainland and the active U.S. military defense of the offshore islands. They argued that loss of the islands would be disastrous to Nationalist morale, so the United States had to defend them.[10] In his dissent, Army Chief Ridgway responded that military leaders should give military and not psychological advice.[11] He and the other Chiefs agreed, however, that Taiwan could be defended successfully without the islands.[12] The president did not react favorably to the Chiefs' plan, because he regarded it as too provocative of a general war.[13] He cautioned the whole group of the dangers that the crisis involved.

Secretary of State Dulles then presented his analysis, arguing that the United States resist Communist pressure while not committing itself to defense of Quemoy and Matsu. He thus proposed that the problem be presented to the United Nations Security Council, in order to obtain a resolution calling for a cease-fire in the area. Dulles concluded his remarks with the observation, "Whether Russia vetoes or accepts such a plan, the United States will gain."[14] The president accepted this suggestion.

In the time following the meeting, the administration worked on the Dulles plan. Dulles worked to bring Nationalist leader Chiang Kai-shek and British Foreign Secretary Anthony Eden in line with the idea of a Security Council resolution, which was to be introduced by New Zealand.[15] At the same time, President Eisenhower sought to reassure Chiang of the U.S. commitment to defend Taiwan by concluding a mutual security treaty with the Nationalist government.[16]

On January 18, 1955, the tension heightened when Communist forces captured the island of Ichiang, which had been held by a small contingent of Nationalist troops. This island lay near the Tachens archipelago, where a Nationalist infantry division was stationed.[17] This move inaugurated a second phase of the crisis, which followed the artillery attacks against Quemoy, Matsu, and Ichiang in the autumn of 1954. This second phase complicated the crisis in its increased pressure on Taiwan and the United States, which was accompanied by pressure from conservative Republicans on the Eisenhower administration to respond to the Chinese with force.[18]

This second phase initiated another round of meetings and decisions for the president and his advisors. On January 20, Eisenhower met with Secretary Dulles and other officials to consider a new Nationalist request: that the United States guarantee the security of Quemoy and Matsu. This request precipitated the need for a decision from the president.[19]

At this meeting, Secretary Dulles argued for a shift in policy. He told the president that, while the Communists ought not to be allowed to capture all of the offshore islands, the Nationalists might not be able to hold any of the islands without U.S. help. He thus recommended that the United States assist in the evacuation of the Tachens, while renewing a promise to assist in the defense of Quemoy and Matsu.[20] The president, who had reviewed both the military and political aspects of the offshore islands dispute, accepted this suggestion. At the same time, he authorized a request to Congress for presidential authority to use force to protect Taiwan, the nearby Pescadores islands, and "related positions."[21]

On the following day, another meeting took place in the president's office. At this meeting, attended by Secretary Dulles, Secretary Wilson, Deputy Defense Secretary Anderson, the Joint Chiefs, and State Department Policy

Planning Chief Robert Bowie,[22] the Chiefs argued against the president's decision to evacuate the Tachens. They contended that defending or reinforcing the islands would be easier than evacuating them, but that argument was opposed by the president himself.[23] The president rejected the Chiefs' arguments on both political and military grounds: he disagreed with their judgment that defense of the Tachens would be easier than evacuation, and he estimated that the political consequences of evacuating the islands would be negligible. The decision to evacuate was then reiterated.

One week later, on January 28, the Formosa Resolution passed Congress, recognizing the president's authority to act with force in defense of Taiwan. Before the end of February, the evacuation of the Tachens was complete.

Armed with a congressional resolution, Eisenhower now faced the third, and tensest, phase of the crisis. When Secretary Dulles returned from a trip to Asia in early March, he reported that the Taiwan Strait situation was far more serious than he had imagined.[24] He was convinced that the Communists were determined to take Taiwan even if the Nationalists abandoned Quemoy and Matsu.[25] In response to this danger, Dulles publicly threatened U.S. resistance and nuclear retaliation against China.[26] The president, adopting a strategy designed to "keep the Communists guessing,"[27] intimated that nuclear weapons might be involved in an American response to Chinese aggression. Speaking to the press on March 16, he told reporters that "I see no reason why they [nuclear weapons] shouldn't be used just exactly as you would use a bullet or anything else."[28] One week later, he compounded the ambiguity of his possible action in another press conference. When asked about the possible use of nuclear weapons to defend Quemoy and Matsu, the president responded that "The only thing I know about war is two things: the most unpredictable factor in war was human nature, but the only unchanging factor in war was human nature. And the next thing is that every war is going to astonish you in the way it occurred, and the way it is carried out."[29]

One month later Eisenhower's ambiguity paid off. On April 23, at a meeting of Third World nations, Chinese Foreign Minister Chou En-lai expressed a willingness to negotiate with the United States over Taiwan and the Far East.[30] By May 22, an informal cease-fire was underway in the Taiwan Strait.

In the conduct of this crisis, Eisenhower managed to achieve his objectives. At base, he wanted to maintain the security of Taiwan, but he also wanted to avoid war over the offshore islands.[31] Second, he wanted to restrain Nationalist adventurism, but without destroying their morale. Finally, he wanted to avoid the military confrontation he suspected would lead to World War III, but he would not do so if it meant appearing to surrender on the security of Taiwan.[32] To reach these goals, he pursued a diplomatic solution, reassurance of the Nationalists, ambiguity for the Communists, veiled threats, and avoidance of confrontation. The president was thus successful in dealing with this crisis.

Policy Direction and Design

The first criterion of the conventional wisdom of particular relevance to this case is that of Policy direction and design. President Eisenhower met all the requirements of this criterion, providing direction and perspective to his aides and others over the course of the nine-month affair.

Eisenhower had inherited from his predecessor a delicate situation. President Truman had stationed the Seventh Fleet in the Taiwan Strait to demonstrate the U.S. commitment to defend Taiwan, but no clear policy existed in the matter of the offshore islands. Once the crisis in the strait arose, however, the president was pressed for a policy regarding this unsettled subject.

To provide direction, the president had to develop a clear sense of his own objectives in this area, and then to convey his course to the necessary parties. His objectives, discussed above, revolved around a dual emphasis on the security of Taiwan and a firm desire to avoid war. Moreover, because he regarded Nationalist resolve essential to the defense of Taiwan, the president sought to insure that the morale of Chiang Kai-shek's forces was not destroyed. With these goals in mind, he set about designing his policy for responding to the crisis.

The first group to receive instruction in this area was the National Security Council. On September 12, 1954, at the council's first meeting after Quemoy was shelled, the president offered the group his analysis of the significance of the crisis and the sort of course he wanted to

Crises / 37

take. In response to the Joint Chiefs' plan of bombing mainland China, Eisenhower immediately informed the group of the gravity of the crisis: he remarked on the imminence of World War III. This warning was soon coupled with a policy decision by the president designed to state an overall policy: the president endorsed Secretary Dulles' suggestion of a United Nations Security Council resolution requesting a cease-fire. With these two acts, Eisenhower informed his administration that he wished to avoid aggression in resolving this grave crisis.

At the January 1955 meetings, after the capture of Ichiang, the president again made it clear to this senior group that he wanted to avoid aggression and unnecessary conflict. Consequently, he decided on the evacuation of the Tachen islands. Once again, he rejected a plan by the Chiefs, this time to defend the Tachens, in favor of a less conflictive policy.

Beyond the National Security Council, the president conveyed his design and perspective to two other groups, his nation and external parties. With regard to external parties, Eisenhower was concerned about three: the Nationalist Chinese, the Communists, and the British. Since maintenance of Nationalist morale was one of his objectives, the president took several steps to deliver his message. Soon after the decision to pursue a U.N. resolution was made in September, Assistant Secretary of State Walter Robertson was dispatched to Taiwan to convince the Nationalist leaders of the wisdom of that course. Later, in December, when the Nationalists were still concerned about U.S. assistance, the president consented to a mutual security treaty between the United States and Taiwan. Even when, in April, he sought to minimize the Nationalist commitment of troops to the offshore islands, the president insisted that any withdrawal of troops be directed by Chiang himself.[33] In sum, Eisenhower wanted Chiang to be clear on the U.S. intent to aid Taiwan and to continue treating him as an ally.

He was also concerned about the Communist Chinese. Not only were the U.N. resolution, the Formosa Resolution in Congress, and the mutual security treaty all designed to demonstrate U.S. resolve, but the president sent further signals of his intent in other messages. His two press conference statements in March 1955, intended to "keep the Communists guessing," were another way of informing Peking of the president's course: by delivering a vague threat, he intended to inform the Communists of how far he might be willing to go to defend Taiwan (i.e., with nuclear weapons).[34]

The president was also concerned with making his course clear to the British. He strongly desired Western allied unity in this affair, as in all affairs regarding confrontation with the Communists, so he sought to gain the support of the British leaders. This task was accomplished through meetings between Secretary Dulles and British Foreign Secretary Eden,[35] and through private letters to Prime Minister Churchill.[36]

Eisenhower thus felt compelled to convey his course to three external parties. The policy he outlined was not intended to be the same as that he had given the National Security Council, but the reasons for this discrepancy are obvious. He informed his own advisors of his genuine intentions, but as a bargaining tactic he had to paint a different picture for his Chinese adversaries. Moreover, since he was concerned about Nationalist morale, his messages to that group stressed commitment, and left out his reservations about being tied to a guarantee of U.S. defense of the offshore islands.[37] This strategy of several versions of a president's course will be discussed again below, but it is clear that policy direction and design may involve presenting more than one design to different parties.

This observation can also be applied to the course Eisenhower outlined at home. He secured from Congress the Formosa Resolution, demonstrating his willingness to defend Taiwan, as well as ratification of the mutual security treaty. Moreover, his press conference statements on nuclear weapons in March led to a brief war scare in the nation.[38] The policy design presented to Congress and the public was different from that expressed in the privacy of the National Security Council, in large part because Eisenhower could not state publicly anything he did not want the Communist Chinese to hear.

What comes from these actions is an affirmation of the fact that presidents send different messages to different groups. In the National Security Council, Eisenhower emphasized restraint. To the Nationalists, he emphasized commitment. To the British, he emphasized resolve tempered with caution. Finally, to the Communists and to the nation, he outlined a policy of "brinkmanship."

To assess the president's performance in fulfilling this criterion, then, it is necessary to disaggregate the concept of Policy direction and design, for the policy that Eisenhower outlined and his perspective on the crisis were manifested in more than one portrayal of his intentions. In dealing with the public and with his adversary, the president portrayed his course in terms of resolve. In dealing with his operative foreign affairs government, he portrayed his course in a more complex form. In his own mind, as final policy arbiter and crisis manager, he maintained a clear notion of what he wanted. That he achieved his objectives implies that the president understood the necessity of conveying his course in different forms to different groups.

Policy design, then, is more than a simple act of clarifying and stating a president's overall policy direction. It is a complex process for clarifying ends and means, and may itself become part of the means for achieving presidential goals. Indeed, in this case, Eisenhower's skill in presenting different policy designs to different audiences aided him in his efforts to influence Communist behavior. Because policy direction is complex, the president must have a clear perspective on how the various components of his foreign policy fit together. The evidence suggests that Eisenhower was successful in this case in part because he fulfilled the requirements of this criterion in its complex form.

Management and Oversight

The second criterion of importance to this case is that of Management and oversight. An important requirement of this criterion is that the president insure that his policy design is being followed. As the preceding section indicates, Eisenhower had a clear idea of his course and worked to see that it was followed. He laid out his policy to his advisors on several occasions, and made sure that they understood his views in this crisis. Second, he sent messages to external parties and to the nation regarding his policies.

In pursuit of this policy, the president took actions beyond those described above. He directed Secretary Dulles in diplomatic contacts with Britain and Taiwan,[39] and advised the secretary on his statements to the press regarding several aspects of the crisis.[40] Moreover, the president dispatched Admiral Arthur Radford and Assistant Secretary of State Walter Robertson to Taiwan when he wanted Chiang to fall in line with his idea of withdrawing most of the Nationalists' troops from the offshore islands.[41] He thus combined several strands of activity to see that his policy design was implemented: public statements, admonitions to subordinates, direction of Secretary Dulles, private letters, messages to Congress, personal emissaries, and oversight of his subordinates.

Indeed, oversight was important to the president's handling of the crisis, as he insured that his subordinates effectively carried out his plans. Oversight is another requirement of this criterion. The president carefully oversaw Secretary Dulles's actions during this period, even advising him on several specific matters: what to say to the press on the importance of the Tachen islands,[42] how to deal with Foreign Secretary Eden,[43] and on negotiating with Chiang Kai-shek.[44] Besides Dulles, the president used Radford and Robertson as his personal emissaries to Chiang, in order to oversee discussions of his plan to reduce troop levels on the offshore islands.[45] Moreover, he reviewed the orders and deployment of the Seventh Fleet during the crisis,[46] and probed the reasoning behind military advice he received from the Joint Chiefs of Staff.[47] In sum, the president was closely involved in oversight of all U.S. actions in this crisis. Not only did he skillfully use his subordinates to carry out his plans, but he also instructed them in their work and reviewed its quality. As in his probing of the Chiefs' assessment of the military aspects of the Tachens situation, Eisenhower insured that his administration served him well.

This area also involved maintenance of an effective decision process for formulating U.S. policy. First, the president moved to obtain adequate information and analysis on the crisis, and from a variety of sources. As soon as he was informed of the shelling of Quemoy on September 3, 1954, Eisenhower sought analysis from senior officers in the Defense and State departments.[48] Several days later, at the special meeting of the National Security Council on September 12, he received more analysis, from Secretary of State Dulles and from the Joint Chiefs of Staff. As would be the pattern throughout the crisis, the president heard conflicting arguments: the Chiefs advocated military action, and the secretary of state pressed for a diplomatic solution.[49] This pattern was repeated in the January 1955 meetings regarding the Tachen islands. The president also had other sources of information and analysis. He received reports from Ambassador Karl Rankin in Taiwan,[50] intelligence from the CIA,[51] and strategic advice from Prime Minister Churchill.[52] In March, when Dulles reported that the overall situation was worse than expected, the president dispatched Col. Andrew Goodpaster, the White House staff secretary, to confer with the commander-in-chief of the Pacific Fleet.[53] Goodpaster's report provided further analysis. Finally, throughout the crisis, Eisenhower supplemented all of these sources with his own study of the situation. As a military commander and a politically sensitive statesman, he was able to draw on his own analysis of the various aspects of the crisis for help. Indeed, in a private letter he wrote in February 1955 to his friend and onetime colleague Gen. Alfred Gruenther, the president analyzed with precision the political and military problems wrapped up in the crisis: considerations of military strategy, geopolitics, Western unity and morale, and the possibility of general war.[54] He was thus able to obtain information from a variety of sources.

This variety of sources, combined with the differing views offered by the Joint Chiefs, secretary of state, and others, made it possible for the president to proceed from a rather thorough study of events and circumstances. He also acted to facilitate consideration of the major values and interests involved in this case, which consideration occurred over the nine months of the crisis.

Indeed, the president and his advisors had no choice but to examine the various values and interests involved in the crisis: arguments over these values were coming to the administration from all sides. Churchill offered Eisenhower a Western strategic view of the interests at stake, while at home he was assailed by those he called "the truculent and the timid, the jingoists and the pacifists."[55] One group counseled military action, while the other advocated surrender of the offshore islands to China. The Joint Chiefs offered one view of the interests at stake, and the secretary of state another. The president also had his own views, but listened to the various analyses.

From the beginning, the crisis was seen as revolving around certain key issues: Nationalist morale, U.S. prestige, the security of Taiwan, and the price of peace. There were debates and conflicting reports among the president's advisors on each of these points. The Chiefs maintained that any loss of territory would destroy Nationalist morale,[56] and that the Nationalists alone could not defend the offshore islands.[57] Churchill maintained that the supreme goal was the security of the United States' ally Taiwan, so the islands must be discarded as a secondary entanglement.[58] Secretary Dulles held Nationalist morale as an important issue, for which he first rejected the idea of evacuating the Tachens and then came to accept it.[59] Democrats, led by Adlai Stevenson, argued that nuclear war was being foolishly risked over "these little islands."[60] Finally, the president saw all of these issues as interrelated, arguing in his private letter to Gruenther that a balance of interests had to be struck. For this reason, he retained personal control over the U.S. response.[61]

Just as the process of information-gathering, analysis, and value-consideration proceeded throughout the crisis, so did consideration of the various options available to the United States. The options changed somewhat over the different phases of the crisis as circumstances changed. Yet the broad categories of options remained the same over the course of the nine-month affair, with continual reassessment of each.

The first category of options was military. The choices here ranged from various levels of defense, as in aid to defenders on Quemoy, the Tachens, or Taiwan, to the Chiefs' plan of retaliation against the Chinese mainland. Eisenhower, fearing the consequences of an overt U.S. commitment to defend the offshore islands, and working hard to avoid what he believed would become World War III, maintained a policy of defense of the islands only in the event of a full-scale invasion of Taiwan.[62] War was not seen as an option in the aggressive sense, but defense against attack was certainly considered.

The second category of options was diplomatic. The policy adopted at the September 12 meeting, that of seeking a United Nations resolution, was the only real manifestation of these sorts of options, although Eisenhower used diplomacy to reassure Chiang Kai-shek of the U.S. commitment to defend Taiwan. After the capture of Ichiang, diplomatic options were no longer actively considered.

The third category of options contained those actions designed to demonstrate U.S. resolve. In this category were the Formosa Resolution, which was to show U.S. determination to employ force in defense of Taiwan, just as the mutual security treaty was to cement the U.S. commitment. Also in this category was the move to evacuate the Tachen islands, which was intended not only as a way to avoid confrontation but also as a means for resolving the crisis through a conciliatory move.[63] Most significantly, however, this category includes the "brinkmanship" of Eisenhower and Dulles, which the President saw as a way to demonstrate resolve.[64] By resorting to ambiguity in his public statements on the question of nuclear weapons being involved in the Taiwan conflict, Eisenhower sought a strategic solution to his problem.

These options were all considered in one form or another as the crisis progressed, and their consequences were studied as well. Eisenhower saw any military option as a last resort, which he wanted to reserve for a response to a Chinese attack, but he feared that the Communists might soon acquire it, so he sought a solution through means other than military in nature.[65] After he and his advisors were convinced that the diplomatic option had failed, in the capture of Ichiang, Eisenhower felt that the only choice left to him was to clearly demonstrate American resolve in the face of Chinese aggression.[66]

The idea of this solution revolved around Eisenhower's conviction that a demonstration of resolve could offset a possible war by forcing the Communists to back down from a confrontation with the United States.[67] Accordingly, he and Dulles reasoned that a conciliatory withdrawal from the Tachens, following closely as it did the Formosa Resolution, might encourage China to end the crisis.[68] When that policy failed, the president looked to a plan to minimize trouble.[69] But this move was soon followed by the ambiguous announcement of the policy regarding nuclear weapons, which Eisenhower felt would demonstrate resolve and deter aggression.[70] In his memoirs, the president comments both on his belief at the time that a Chinese attack on Taiwan was unlikely, and on his conviction that resolve in the face of an aggressor can deter him.[71]

In following all these steps toward an effective decision process, Eisenhower sought to think through a solution to the crisis. An overall feature of his analysis and decision process was the sort of discussion exemplified in the meetings of the National Security Council. In the meeting on September 12, and the March meetings on the subject of the Tachen islands, Eisenhower encouraged discussion and debate of the various choices facing him. In each of these meetings, the secretary of state and the Joint Chiefs of Staff disagreed on the proper policy. Such a practice as this was a conscious tactic of the president, which he employed to seek out the best choice in any decision.[72] The range of policy choices represented in these discussions was not as wide as, say, the public debate which included the Democrats and the China lobby, but there was significant disagreement among the president's advisors.

Because of the nature of the affair, with shifting circumstances over time, the president and his advisors moved through these steps continuously in a constant assessment and reassessment of circumstances, behavior, options, and policies in force. All the available evidence indicates a continuous process of analysis and review.[73] In March, Eisenhower planned Nationalist troop withdrawals from the offshore islands to minimize trouble. Although he had given up on diplomatic solutions in January, he accepted the Chinese offer to negotiate when circumstances changed in April.[74]

In the general matter of management and oversight, then, the president's conduct met the requirements of this criterion. He worked to insure that his policy design, in its complex form, was understood and that it was effectively implemented. Moreover, he engaged in a close oversight of his subordinates throughout the crisis, while managing the decision and policy process toward a resolution of the affair. Indeed, his own contributions to analysis and strategic bargaining highlight Eisenhower's overall fulfillment of the requirements of this criterion.

Consensus-building

The final criterion of particular relevance to this case is that of Consensus-building, but not for reasons predicted by the conventional wisdom. For in this case the president's record as regards consensus was at best mixed, and this crisis illuminates some problems with the conventional view of consensus.

Eisenhower certainly sought to develop support for his policies, both at home and among the United States' allies. On the domestic side, the president sought congressional approval of his policies in the form of the

Formosa Resolution and the mutual security treaty with Taiwan, hoping that these actions would demonstrate a domestic consensus.[75] Abroad, he was concerned about support from Western allies, particularly Britain, and the Nationalist government on Taiwan as well. After the diplomatic option failed, and the United States moved to other policies in 1955, the president was unable to draw Britain into support for his policies. He exchanged several letters with Churchill,[76] and Dulles met with Eden on more than one occasion,[77] but Britain would not endorse the U.S. policy. Canada also wrote itself out of the scene in March 1955, which angered the president.[78] This disagreement between the United States and her allies was so great that Eisenhower later commented that its effect was to "threaten a split between the United States and nearly all its allies."[79]

As for the Nationalists, an important part of the president's response to this crisis was Nationalist cooperation with U.S. policy. He sought to bring Chiang Kai-shek into support for his moderate policy in the Taiwan Strait, and was able to convince Chiang both to evacuate the Tachen islands and to reduce troop levels on other islands. He accomplished this cooperation by continual assurances to Chiang of the U.S. commitment, as in the security treaty and the Formosa Resolution, and in treating Chiang as a valued ally: the troop withdrawal plan put Chiang in control of troop movements, not the United States.[80]

Yet, for all these efforts, the results were mixed. The president won the congressional actions he wanted, and achieved Nationalist cooperation as well. But he encountered significant opposition from U.S. allies, while at home there was no sense of clear support for his policies. The Democrats, led by Stevenson, complained angrily that the president was risking war over the offshore islands; after the first press conference of March "brinkmanship" brought a war scare and further criticism of Eisenhower's handling of the crisis.[81]

Eisenhower thus achieved mixed results from his consensus-building efforts. The war scare decreased in late March, when the president and his press secretary suggested that war was unlikely, but criticism and uneasiness about his handling of the crisis did not dissolve completely.[82] The president, nevertheless, defined domestic consensus in terms of congressional votes, so he felt that he had a consensus.[83]

Here is where this case illuminates some interesting aspects of consensus. Because the conventional wisdom is unclear regarding the nature and measurement of consensus, it is difficult to state whether or not Eisenhower fulfilled the requirements of this criterion. At best, his record was mixed--that has been established. Yet he achieved support in the ways he considered most crucial: in congressional votes and from the Nationalists. He was willing and able to act without a broad public consensus or the support of Western allies.

These facts point to the ambiguity of consensus in the conventional wisdom. Is it to be conceived narrowly or broadly? Does it include external parties, or is consensus only a domestic issue? Is it necessary, or only desirable? If consensus means the minimum support necessary to act, regardless of controversy or whatever, then Eisenhower did meet this criterion. If, however, consensus means something broader, which can certainly be inferred from the discussion of consensus in the conventional wisdom, then the president did not meet this standard. In an era of supposedly bipartisan foreign policy, he was harshly criticized by the Democrats, and by members of his own party.[84] In an era of supposed Western unity against Communism, he could not gain the support of Churchill.

Because of this ambiguity, the results are mixed and Eisenhower's record muddled. But this fact did not prevent him from acting in this crisis, which raises the question of the relevance of consensus to presidential performance.

This question of relevance also grows out of the ambiguity of the conventional wisdom. Given the broad power of the president in foreign affairs, particularly in times of crisis, the lack of a broad consensus in no way impeded Eisenhower's crisis management. In this sense, consensus was irrelevant to the president's ability to act. The Formosa Resolution recognized the president's power to act, but it did not create that power. On the other hand, if consensus means something broader, particularly if it involves the legitimacy of presidential action, then consensus is more relevant to this case, yet still ambiguously so.

For Eisenhower achieved congressional approval for the Formosa Resolution and the mutual security treaty, but not a broader consensus. Consequently, without a clear definition of consensus from the conventional wisdom, the question of legitimacy remains unanswerable.

Other Criteria, Other Factors

A fourth criterion of the conventional wisdom has not been addressed above because it is less important than the other three to this case. At the same time, an understanding of the case would be incomplete without consideration of another factor which lies outside that consensus.

In the matter of conventional wisdom, Organization and staffing did not play a decisive role. As would be expected in a crisis, the president was closely involved with all aspects of the affair, and did not engage in the "overstaffing" of issues for which he is often unjustly criticized. The preceding analysis has demonstrated how the president supervised the decision and policy implementation processes, not depending on his subordinates to make policy. The foreign policy machinery that Eisenhower had established functioned adequately, so it did not affect policy making either in malfunctioning or in saving the day. Perhaps this criterion can only be significant when Organization and staffing have some extraordinary effect, whether bad or good, but in the matter of the Taiwan Strait this criterion does not provide any particular insights.

Outside of the conventional wisdom, there lies an important fact that certainly helps to explain the president's success in this case. That is the fact that the preponderance of power lay with the United States. Although the president was justifiably concerned that Chinese motivations might be so strong that American power would not deter aggression, and that the Soviet Union might aid China if conflict erupted, the United States still held the upper hand against China.[85] Eisenhower was attempting to avoid the war that would bring U.S. power to bear against China, but the fact of that power aided his cause. As Alexander George and Richard Smoke have noted, before the crisis began, the U.S. commitment to Taiwan was unclear, but as events progressed China came to see how far the United States would go to defend the Nationalists.[86] The factor of U.S. power certainly played a part in the eventual outcome of the crisis.

48 / THE PRESIDENT AND FOREIGN AFFAIRS

A factor such as this one is not included in the conventional wisdom, which gives little attention to the circumstances and conditions in which presidential performance occurs. Occasional references are made to such conditions, as in Robert Hunter's remark that "The success or failure of U.S. foreign policy is the responsibility of the president of the United States--to the degree that the United States itself can be instrumental in determining its own fate . . .," but the overall consensus focuses on presidential behavior without reference to circumstances.[87] This case has demonstrated how such a view is obviously flawed.

Conclusion

Explaining the president's success is possible only by reference to the important factor of the international power circumstances in this case. For Eisenhower's performance in this case cannot alone explain the outcome of the affair: not only did he fail to fulfill completely the requirements of Consensus-building, but his performance vis-à-vis Policy direction and Management do not account for his ultimate success. Skillful management and a clear direction were certainly important, but these actions exploited rather than created a favorable power situation.

The president's performance, then, was effective in that he took advantage of the conditions at hand, rather than achieving success strictly because of fulfillment of the conventional wisdom's criteria.

This case has demonstrated not only the incompleteness of these standards, in excluding the conditions in which performance occurs, but it has also illuminated the ambiguity of the conventional wisdom to be both vague and inaccurate for guiding presidential performance.

THE BAY OF PIGS CRISIS, 1961

The 1961 Bay of Pigs crisis provides an excellent case for studying a presidential failure in foreign affairs, for in this case President Kennedy clearly failed in his attempt to manage an assault by Cuban exiles on Castroist Cuba in defense of U.S. interests, and to project U.S. power. In this case, not only did he and his administration act under the belief that they were in a crisis, but the fate of the invasion force at the Bay of Pigs was a major defeat for the president and a serious embarrassment for the U.S. government. Consequently, this affair, once called "the most screwed-up operation there has ever been," has come to represent a low point in U.S. policy, and understanding its roots in presidential decision making can aid in examining the nature of presidential foreign policy making.[88]

First, it is clear that this affair was seen as a crisis by Kennedy and his advisors. Not only is it generally recalled as such by Kennedy aides such as Theodore Sorensen, the president's chief assistant, but it is apparent that the president himself perceived the situation as one of high threat and great time urgency.[89] Upon entering office, Kennedy was concerned about the threat and urgency of the general international situation. As he emphasized in his first State of the Union message:

> Each day the crises multiply. Each day their solution grows more difficult. Each day we draw nearer the hour of maximum danger. . . . I feel I must inform the Congress that . . . in each of the principal areas of crisis, the tide of events has been running out and time has not been our friend.[90]

This general perception of crisis was particularly applicable in the case of Cuba. During his election campaign, Kennedy called Cuban President Fidel Castro a "dangerous and malignant . . . enemy on our very doorstep only eight minutes by jet from Florida," and advocated his overthrow.[91] Later, shortly before the invasion was launched, the new president told a television interviewer that "if we don't move now, Mr. Castro may become a greater danger than he is to us today."[92]

Summary of Case

Clearly, Kennedy perceived the Cuban situation to be both threatening and urgent, but was unaware of a CIA plan to invade Cuba until shortly after taking office. At that time, he inherited the plan for an exiles' invasion of

50   /   THE PRESIDENT AND FOREIGN AFFAIRS

Cuba, with secret U.S. support, from the Eisenhower administration. On the suggestion of Vice-President Richard Nixon, President Eisenhower had authorized the CIA to organize an anti-Castro political movement among Cuban exiles in the United States, and to secretly train a military force from those exiles willing to undertake guerrilla warfare against Castro in Cuba. As the 1960 presidential election progressed, the CIA developed plans and began preparation for such an operation.

Kennedy learned of the plan soon after his inauguration in January 1961. He had previously endorsed U.S. support for anti-Castro "freedom fighters"[93] and advocated the overthrow of Castro.[94] Upon learning of the plan, he was amazed by the magnitude of the large-scale amphibious invasion that the CIA was preparing to mount. He dismissed such a plan as "too spectacular" and insisted that the only plan acceptable to him would be a "quiet" landing of Cuban exiles in Cuba, with no U.S. military intervention.[95] In subsequent deliberations on the operation, Kennedy reiterated that insistence. An assault plan corresponded with his perception of a crisis, although he drew the line at overt U.S. assistance.

Nevertheless, the president understood the situation as one demanding immediate action. As Sorensen noted,

> the President had been told, this plan was now or never, for three reasons: first, because the brigade was fully trained, restive to fight and difficult to hold off; second, because Guatemala [where the exile brigade was training] was under pressure to close the increasingly publicized and politically controversial training camps, and his only chance was to send them back to Cuba, where they wished to go, or to bring them back to this country, where they would broadcast their resentment; and third, because Russian arms would soon build up Castro's army, Cuban airmen trained behind the Iron Curtain as MIG pilots would soon return to Cuba, large numbers of crated MIGs had already arrived on the island, and the spring of 1961--before Castro had a large jet air force and before the exile army scattered in discontent--was the last time Cubans could alone liberate Cuba.[96]

With these points in mind, he began to consider the invasion proposal.

Over the next two-and-a-half months, Kennedy and a select group of his advisors deliberated on the plan. They discussed it informally, and also attended several meetings on the Cuban invasion with CIA Director Allen Dulles, Richard Bissell, the CIA's head of covert operations, and the Joint Chiefs of Staff. At one of these meetings, on April 4, 1961, all of the president's advisors gave their approval to the plan. All were convinced that the invasion would be small and "quiet," as Kennedy had insisted, and that the guerrillas would be able to hide in the supposedly nearby Escambray Mountains if they were unable to establish a beachhead at the Cuban Bay of Pigs. Kennedy shared in this belief, which was later proven erroneous, but reserved final judgment on the operation until later.

On April 17, Kennedy decided to give the CIA the go-ahead on the mission. A brigade of about 1,400 exiles, with secret U.S. aid, invaded the Bay of Pigs. It was immediately clear that the plan was a failure. Castro's air force stopped the brigade's supply ships and quickly surrounded the invaders. The vast majority of those not killed were captured.

The administration was not only astounded by the failure of the mission, but also shocked to learn that the invasion was different from what Kennedy thought he had approved. It was a larger invasion than he had expected, and the brigade was cut off from the Escambray Mountains by huge swamps. Soon, the myth of no U.S. involvement in the operation was debunked, and the United States was denounced by several of its Latin American allies. As a result, the Bay of Pigs was soon marked as a crisis for U.S. foreign policy, and a failure for President Kennedy. It was a failure as a military operation, as an attempt to engage in covert operations, and it was a failure in terms of all the Kennedy administration's objectives.

Organization and Staffing

Writing about general decision making in the Kennedy White House, Theodore Sorensen commented that "procedures do, of course, affect decisions."[97] That remark was a particularly telling one, for the Organization and staffing of the Kennedy administration was an important variable in the case of the Bay of Pigs, because the structure of Kennedy's foreign affairs government had an impact on the decision process.

Scholars of presidential decision making are fond of the Kennedy organizational system, which was marked by its informal channels of information and access. This approach has been labeled the Collegial Model of Policy Making, because it eschewed a hierarchical decision mechanism in favor of collegially related advisors revolving around the president.[98] In this model, the president is at the hub of a policy-making wheel, and his advisors and executive branch officials are the spokes of the wheel: information and advice flow to the president from several competing sources, rather than through one bureaucratic process. Alexander George has praised this approach for its flexibility, informality, and nonbureaucratic nature, and it had those characteristics.[99] But this system was dependent on proper coordination from the president, and his ability to use the loose structure to ensure adequate deliberation on policy questions. Since the system was highly informal in its approach to decision making, there were few routines for mandating such deliberations.

In the Bay of Pigs decision, this structure had an impact on the Kennedy administration's deliberative process. In the Eisenhower administration, the Cuban invasion plan had been the concern of the Special Group,[100] a secret high-level committee for examining and approving covert operations.[101] The general matter of Cuba was also discussed in the National Security Council. All this changed under Kennedy, who dismantled what he considered to be the overly bureaucratic Eisenhower national security apparatus. The National Security Council, which hardly met, was not in charge of the Cuban invasion. Neither was the Special Group, which continued to debate details of the operation but exercised no directive authority over it.[102] Rather, Kennedy relied on an informal, select group of his advisors to deliberate on the plan.

This informal group was not a committee in the sense of having clear responsibility over the plan or discussions about it, as the ExCom would be during the Cuban missile crisis, but was a loose assembly that constituted the Collegial Model in action. This group consisted of the secretaries of state, defense, and treasury, the attorney general, an assistant secretary of state, the president's assistant for national security, his Special Assistant Arthur Schlesinger, Jr., and those minor officials Schlesinger called "appropriate assistants and bottle-washers."[103] The president and this group met occasionally with CIA officials Dulles and Bissell and the Joint Chiefs of Staff, and senior members of it met with the president either at one or in small numbers. At one meeting in April 1961, Senate Foreign Relations Committee Chairman William Fulbright joined the discussion. Over the course of the 80-odd days during which the plan was considered, the group or sets of its members met with the president several times on this matter.

For all of the meetings of all of these officials, the administration's deliberations were marked by an absence of coordination from President Kennedy. There was no staff work to support plan evaluation by senior officials, nor were any of the members of the ad hoc advisory group assigned to provide independent assessments of the project.[104] Indeed, the Taylor Commission Report, which summarized the administration's official investigation of the Bay of Pigs affair, stated that "Top level direction was given through ad hoc meetings of senior officials without consideration of operational plans in writing and with no arrangement for recording conclusions reached."[105]

The absence of central direction in Kennedy's collegial system meant that coherence in policy making could not be achieved. Neither Kennedy nor any of his ad hoc group actually had a clear idea of what had been planned and approved, and what had not. All materials related to the plan, from briefing papers to maps, were kept by the CIA. Only one man, Richard Bissell, the CIA officer in charge of the invasion, knew the full extent of the plan.[106] Theodore Sorensen, Kennedy's senior advisor at the time, argues that the administration was too new to counterbalance the influence of the CIA, but the problem seems less one of newness than of a lack of coordination in the collegial system.[107] Such a system revolves around the president, and is thus dependent on him as the engine of the deliberative process. Kennedy's decision-making apparatus required coordination that it did not receive. Kennedy's newness may have been a broad condition which affected his performance in this case, but the organizational structure he employed had an impact on decision making: it produced a system that could only work effectively under close presidential supervision.

Another factor which falls in closely with organization is that of staffing, i.e., the people who inhabit the organization and their impact on it. Here is an important variable, for it helps to explain an influence on Kennedy which may account for some of his lack of coordination of the collegial decision apparatus.

The Bay of Pigs operation was planned and overseen by two men who received uncritical support from the members of the Kennedy administration. The CIA director, Allen Dulles, had been in intelligence work for decades and was regarded as a "legend." His deputy director for plans, i.e., chief of covert operations, Richard Bissell, known to many of the administration from his days on the faculty at Yale, was also highly regarded. Both are universally praised in memoirs of the affair, and faith in their abilities certainly helped to sway the decision process in their favor.[108]

Indeed, it is the generally uncritical support by the Kennedy administration for Dulles and Bissell which can provide some insight into how the organizational structure contributed to failure. Whereas the collegial system required competing sources of information and advice in order to be effective, as well as presidential orchestration of those sources, the members of the Kennedy administration found it difficult to challenge an ongoing plan advocated by such imposing figures as Dulles and Bissell.[109] Rather than a problem of newness alone, organization and staffing in the case of the Bay of Pigs were influential because the two combined to produce a situation which contributed to failure. The president did not properly coordinate his decision apparatus, and in part because of the reputation of Dulles and Bissell among his advisors, he did not feel pressed to mobilize that apparatus to critically study their plans.

This deference to Dulles and Bissell is one-half of the staffing issue. The other half is an issue raised by Schlesinger, Sorensen, and other memorialists of the Kennedy administration. It is the contention that the newness of the administration affected decision making in the case, and it is founded on the idea that "the new administration had not yet fully organized itself for crisis planning. . . ."[110] This argument may provide a partial explanation of what occurred, as was noted above, in that newness might be seen as a general condition characteristic of the administration. But too much must not be made of newness, because it was not a characteristic of several key actors. Secretaries Rusk and Dillon were not new to government, nor was Assistant Secretary of Defense Paul Nitze. Kennedy himself, while only recently inaugurated, was a sophisticated politician. Nor were the "best and the brightest" who served in the White House unaccustomed to argument and analysis. So, while the Kennedy administration was somewhat new as a body, it was not naive. Moreover, as General Taylor, who joined the White House staff after conducting the official investigation of the crisis, later commented, the lack of organization in the White House was a result of a negative attitude among Kennedy and his aides regarding organization and procedure rather than newness.[111]

Staffing did have some impact on this case, but that effect operated through the organizational system for decision making. Together, the two helped to produce the Bay of Pigs disaster. They also point to the relation of Organization and staffing to presidential performance in foreign affairs. For the organization a president establishes for his foreign affairs government mandates particular actions on his part, to ensure that the system works.

In Kennedy's case, the establishment of a collegial system of policy making, with the president as the hub of a wheel of advisors, meant that he had to exercise central coordination over the decision process. Concomitantly, his system required that he be highly skeptical of advice from any one source, and that he use his advisors as the agents of that skepticism.

Organization and staffing, which the conventional wisdom points to as important criteria for presidential performance, are more complex than just being matters of administrative preliminaries. These factors affect not only who occupies the positions of power and how they conduct business, but how the president must act to make his foreign affairs government work. Kennedy chose a particular administrative strategy, consciously scrapping the Eisenhower apparatus, but in the Bay of Pigs decision he did not properly perform his functions as chief. Of course, he did not work alone, but even the Taylor Commission noted that the absence of coordination in the Bay of Pigs affair originated at the top.[112]

Management and Oversight

If the factors of Organization and staffing were important to the Bay of Pigs decision, then so were the variables of Management and oversight. In the last section, the implications of Kennedy's decision structure and personnel were considered. In this section, that analysis will be complemented by a consideration of how Kennedy performed according to the Management and oversight criterion. The two factors, Organization and Management, are intimately related in this case, but they also have separate qualities.

Management is affected by structure, but there are issues of management that exist regardless of the organization and staffing a president employs. The first of these is the question of whether the president ensures that his policy design is being followed. In the case of the Bay of Pigs, Kennedy did not undertake to fulfill this responsibility. He and his advisors saw the use of a Cuban exile brigade as a way to topple Castro without actual aggression by the United States, and this was the main thrust of Kennedy's intentions in this affair.[113] On the one hand, Kennedy sorely wanted to "do something" about Castro, as his campaign speeches had made clear. He did not want to be charged as being "soft on Communism." At the same time, however, he insisted that there be no overt U.S. aggression. He was concerned about anti-U.S. reactions in Latin America and at the United Nations if the role of the United States was not well concealed.[114]

In accordance with this course, Kennedy allowed the CIA to continue planning the Cuban invasion, but explicitly prohibited U.S. military intervention.[115] Beyond this prohibition, however, he did little to ensure that his design was followed. Rather, the bulk of planning of the project was left to the CIA. He did ask the Joint Chiefs for a military evaluation of the operation, but made little use of his collegial system for oversight and analysis of the plan. Much faith was placed in the CIA to handle the affair. Moreover, Kennedy failed at crucial points to make his specific objectives clear: when pre-invasion bombing missions were to begin, he ordered the number of bombers reduced to a "minimal" level, leaving Richard Bissell to decide what that meant.[116] Bissell regarded this informal sort of decision making as "rather odd."[117] This episode was part of a larger pattern of imprecise and somewhat casual management.

As for directing the policy process, again, as noted above, Kennedy did not employ his collegial system of administration to check the work of the CIA. The Joint Chiefs were asked to assess the military aspects of the plan, but when they issued a vague and ambiguous report, Kennedy did not press for better analysis.[118] Besides this report, other experts who might have made useful contributions were not consulted. For example, Latin Americanists in the State Department were excluded from the decision process.[119] Kennedy consulted his advisors on the plan, and various aspects of it were debated in their meetings, but the project was essentially left to the CIA to handle. He did not effectively direct the policy process toward the implementation of his policy design.

Nor did Kennedy ensure that the decision process in the case of the Bay of Pigs was complete. First, nearly all of the information and analysis in this case came from the plan's advocates. The only other analysis that Kennedy sought was from the Joint Chiefs, and their report was rather ambiguous. Surprisingly, Kennedy, who exhibited political shrewdness so many other times, did not press for other evaluations of the plan when the Chiefs delivered their report. Not only did he not enlist other of his senior advisors to provide alternate sources of information and analysis, but he also failed to consult important expert sources of information about the plan. The State Department regional experts have already been mentioned, but there were also the intelligence branches of the CIA and the State Department.[120] None of these groups were either employed or consulted. Richard Bissell effectively controlled information and analysis of the proposed invasion.

Second, in consideration of values and interests relevant to the case, Kennedy and his advisors paid great attention to the possible political consequences of abandoning the invasion plan, particularly the charge of being "soft" on Castro.[121] This was tied to what Dulles called the "disposal problem," i.e., the matter of how to dispose of a force of highly motivated guerrillas without being charged as "soft." They did not, however, give much weight to the interests and consequences which would be involved if the plan was tried and failed (or even succeeded).[122] Alternative views of the values at stake were not ignored, but neither were they given extensive consideration.

It is at this point, in reference to consideration of alternative views, that Kennedy's actions and responses must be separated from those of his advisors. The president did try to remain open to arguments contrary to those of Dulles and Bissell, but his advisors did not help with this task, as illustrated in the case of Senator William Fulbright. When Fulbright voiced objections to the invasion plan at a meeting in April 1961, on the grounds that either success or failure of intervention would damage the reputation of the United States, he was coldly received by the advisory group. William Bundy, for example, felt the need to "rally" in support of the president against the senator's objections.[123] Likewise, none of Kennedy's other advisors displayed interest in Fulbright's arguments.

Kennedy's advisors did not help the president in that instance, because they did not give attention to dissenting views. So the president cannot be assigned complete blame for failure to consider such views. This failure cannot, however, eliminate the fact, discussed above, that Kennedy did not employ his collegial system to best advantage in considering interests and values. Rather than seeking alternative evaluations of interests and values, he relied on the judgments of Dulles and Bissell. Those who felt that the CIA's analysis of U.S. interests in the case were wrong, such as Fulbright, Schlesinger, and Undersecretary of State Chester Bowles, all had to take the initiative in demonstrating the existence of alternate views. Kennedy did not seek out such views, as his collegial system required.

In the same way, little was done regarding the other criteria of effective decision making: search for a wide range of options, and assess the consequences of various options. The search and evaluation of various options were in the hands of the CIA, specifically, those of Richard Bissell. As deliberations on the plan progressed, the range of options was defined by Bissell as proceeding with the invasion or calling it off. Kennedy had determined, on his own convictions, that U.S. military intervention would not be allowed. At the same time, he questioned Bissell about the possibility of infiltration of Cuba rather than invasion, but the CIA officer unilaterally judged that option unfeasible.[124] Because Kennedy relied on Bissell and his covert division of the CIA to do both planning and analysis, and did not seek out other evaluations, criticisms, analyses, or sources of information, he was left with little choice in the matter. As Arthur Schlesinger noted, Kennedy accepted Dulles's arguments regarding the "disposal problem" and Bissell's analysis of the invasion plan's feasibility.[125] Having placed his reliance in those experts, without establishing competing sources of information and analysis, Kennedy fell victim to their mistakes and misjudgments.

The president thus operated at the point in which his organization and staffing combined with his management to create problems for him. Although he was not alone in his administration, as no president is, he was the man at the center of the policy-making wheel in his collegial system. Not only does an effective decision process require certain steps which Kennedy did not ensure were taken, but he also failed to fulfill the role required of him by his organizational structure. When compounded with the problem of overreliance on Dulles and Bissell, these factors led to the Bay of Pigs disaster.

But Kennedy's advisors also had a hand in the decision, yet they did not press the president to doubt the efficacy of the CIA's plan. There are two reasons for that failure. The first is, as discussed above, Kennedy's own approach to the matter. The second is, surprisingly, Kennedy's skill in consensus-building.

Consensus-building

The criterion of Consensus-building is useful for explaining the outcome of the Bay of Pigs crisis, but in a way not predicted by the conventional wisdom. For Kennedy did not fail to meet the requirements of this standard; rather, he met them too readily. He won an easy consensus among his advisors, a fact that helped to precipitate the debacle at the Bay of Pigs.

The president had chosen a small group of advisors to help him in his deliberations on the invasion plan, and in part because of the small size and composition of this group he had little trouble developing a consensus. All members of the group were eager to help the president implement his policies and plans for the country, so none wanted to stand in the way of this bold operation.

This group was won over by Kennedy's skills as a welder of coalitions, skills that the conventional wisdom recommends as useful and good. The president's ability to draw together and maintain a consensus in the affair made it possible for him to proceed confidently with the plan, and to fail disastrously.

This case illustrates some interesting problems of the criterion of Consensus-building and the skills that it implies. First, as the limited advisory group shows, consensus involves the question of how to measure consent. Kennedy consulted only certain members of his administration, leaving out many relevant members of the State Department and CIA, and consulted the military only in a very limited way. He did not consult Congress, and certainly not the general public. Consensus was thus irrelevant outside of this highly limited group. Since the Cuban invasion was a covert operation, consensus-building did not extend beyond the range of the advisory group. While the political fallout from the failure of the operation was significant, public consensus was unimportant to whether or not the operation would occur. What was important was the decision makers' perceptions of public opinion, which may or may not have been accurate. Actual public consensus mattered much less than perceived public opinion. In that respect, Kennedy and his advisors were less interested in consensus-building than in following a consensus they believed already existed.

Crucial to this consensus-building was the president's political skill at inspiring his followers. The conventional wisdom implies that the president ought to possess those qualities which can aid him in welding an enthusiastic consensus in support of his decisions and policies, because such qualities will facilitate the achievement of the president's goals. Yet President Kennedy's inspirational qualities in this regard worked against him, for they helped to foster an easy consensus that ushered in disaster.

The evidence suggests that Kennedy's inspirational qualities stifled a healthy skepticism about the proposed invasion. What this means is that the "Kennedy charisma" created an atmosphere of assumed success. On Kennedy's part, this involved what his assistant Arthur Schlesinger described as Kennedy's ". . . enormous confidence in his own luck. Everything had broken right for him since 1956. He had won the nomination and the election against all the odds in the book. . . . Despite himself, even this dispassionate and skeptical man may have been affected by the soaring euphoria of the new day."[126] On the part of those around him, it was the sense that "Everyone around him thought he had the Midas touch and could not lose."[127] Even Admiral Arleigh Burke, chief of naval operations at the time and most active of the military leaders involved in the operation, confessed that he hesitated to speak up about his doubts regarding the plan in the presence of Kennedy, the "charmed young man."[128] In the same way, Adolph Berle of the State Department and Paul Nitze of Defense both swallowed their doubts because they wanted to rally behind the president.[129] Arthur Schlesinger, a special assistant to the president, opposed the plan but feared becoming a "nuisance."[130] Because Kennedy did not encourage dissent or doubt about the plan, he heard little.

Indeed, Kennedy's inspirational qualities contributed to the mistaken notion that the invasion as planned would be a success. They possessed him with a heady confidence in his own abilities, and they suppressed doubts among the president's advisors. Combined with the problems of organization and management, Kennedy's inspirational qualities helped to make disaster at the Bay of Pigs.[131]

The significance of what happened as regards consensus-building in this crisis is the light it sheds on problems with this criterion of the conventional wisdom. For the conventional wisdom suggests that effective consensus-building and inspirational skills are good, yet they did not help President Kennedy. Rather, by fulfilling the requirements of this standard, Kennedy fell victim to disaster. But there is a further problem, one which grows out of the ambiguity of this criterion. That is the failure of the conventional wisdom to define consensus: what it is, how it is measured. Was agreement among a select group of advisors really consensus, or is this criterion even relevant to a case such as this one?

The recommendations of the conventional wisdom are thus misleading and vague. For in this case consensus was achieved, and achieved easily, yet only a small and select group were allowed to consent. Moreover, the skills that the conventional wisdom suggests ought to improve a president's chances of acting effectively and achieving his goals only worked against President Kennedy, for they clouded his judgment and fostered docility among his advisors. Because Kennedy's organizational system depended on his direction to check and examine policy proposals, and had no autonomous procedures for doing so, the factors of Organization, Management, and Consensus-building combined to produce failure.

Other Criteria, Other Factors

Although four criteria were discussed as parts of the conventional wisdom on presidential performance, not all are relevant to an understanding of the Bay of Pigs, for not all of the criteria have a bearing on the failure of this case, so they did not provide any additional insights into what happened and why.

Policy direction and design does not offer much help in explaining the outcome of this case. Kennedy made it very clear to his administration, and, indeed, to the nation, what his general course was. During his presidential election campaign, he had offered to help anti-Castro forces, but refused direct U.S. aggression against Cuba.[132] When the CIA's invasion plan was presented to him, he firmly stressed his desire for a "quiet" landing of Cuban exiles on Cuba, with no U.S. military intervention.[133] So his general course was well known, even though his decisions on specific details of the operation (e.g., "minimal" air support) were somewhat cloudy. What is significant to note, however, is that Kennedy did not ensure adherence to his design once it had been established. A president must not only make his aims clear, but see to it that those goals are pursued. Kennedy outlined his intentions yet failed to follow through to see them carried out properly.

Beyond these criteria of the conventional wisdom, there are other factors which help to explain the Bay of Pigs and Kennedy's performance. Those other factors can be summarized in the fact that the president had limited control over events. Within the U.S. government the president's control was less than absolute. Even if Kennedy had been more skeptical of the CIA and had been more careful about supervising that agency, there still could have been mistakes, failures, and changes in plans beyond his reach. Because no president can implement all of his decisions unilaterally, he must depend on his subordinates to carry them out. Even with firmer control Kennedy probably would not have been able to prevent the CIA from bending his instructions into something different from what he expected. This phenomenon, also known as bureaucratic "slippage," created a gap between what the president thought he had authorized and what was implemented.

But even with those limitations on presidential power in mind, and even if by some chance the invasion had not been such a disaster, Kennedy's performance in the Bay of Pigs case did not live up to the requirements of the evaluative criteria. Neither did the president make effective use of his organizational system for governing, nor did he ensure that the necessary steps in an effective decision process were carried out. By failing to do so he failed to inform himself of the various options, their consequences, and the risks involved in the whole operation. Because of such failure he was unaware of the errors and misjudgments on which the plan was based. At the same time, he fulfilled the requirements of consensus-building but with adverse effects, for Kennedy's "leadership" qualities fostered docility in his advisors when they were supposed to make for more effective decision making. This docility may not have been strictly Kennedy's fault, but the unexpected and counterproductive effect of his inspiration calls into question the criteria of the conventional wisdom.

Much of the writing on presidential performance puts great stock in presidential "leadership," particularly the inspirational qualities that leadership implies and which are seen as important to consensus-building. Yet this case has demonstrated the possible adverse consequences of such qualities of which presidential observers, presidential advisors, and even presidents ought to be aware.

Perhaps the attention of many president-watchers has been misdirected, as they look to rapid or easy consensus-building. For, as this analysis has shown, the criterion of consensus-building is vague and somewhat misleading. It does not clearly mark the boundaries of consensus, nor demonstrate the relevance of this standard to varying cases. In those cases when the administration enjoys autonomy in action and is not required to act in concert with others, the relevance of consensus is unclear, because this criterion is unclear. In covert actions, for example, autonomy is high. On the other hand, when a president must work in concert with Congress, as with a treaty or when legislative approval is required for action, then consensus assumes the more straightforward form that presidential observers imply.

Conclusion

It is clear from the preceding analysis that President Kennedy failed to fulfill the requirements of two criteria of the conventional wisdom, and that his fulfillment of a third standard adversely affected the outcome of this case. Yet, does this mean, as the conventional wisdom suggests, that a bad policy process yielded a bad outcome?

In this case the answer to that question is yes. For the decision to go through with the Bay of Pigs invasion was predicated on a set of assumptions about circumstances and the likely course of events, and these judgments were wrong. The assumption about Castro's growing military capacity was seriously flawed: Castro already possessed sufficient strength to defeat invaders.[134] There was an assumption that, if the brigade encountered trouble at the beach, it could "fade" into the Escambray Mountains. In reality, the mountains were cut off from the landing site by a large swamp.[135] There was also an assumption that the exile invasion force would be joined by uprisings among the Cuban populace, but this assumption was never examined. As Robert Kennedy's notes from the Taylor Commission investigation reveal, "Evidently no probability of uprisings written up or put into memo form. No formal statement of opinion was given or asked for."[136] These and other dubious judgments regarding the likely fate of the invasion formed the tissue of suppositions on which the scheme was predicated, and which doomed the plan.

Since the scheme was based on misjudgments and erroneous information, an effective review process should have uncovered these flaws and mistakes. The U.S. government possessed the capacity to do so, but relevant expert personnel were either not consulted or not effectively employed. The Joint Chiefs' ambiguous and largely negative report on the military aspects of the operation was ignored, and the military was not asked for a more thorough analysis. Although the Chiefs sent the secretary of defense a memorandum which stated that none of the three landing sites under consideration for the brigade (of which the Bay of Pigs was one) was feasible for an invasion, none of the senior officials involved in the deliberations were aware of this judgment.[137] In the CIA, the branches of the agency not involved with the invasion planning were not consulted, although they contained expert analysts who knew of the lack of an indigenous anti-Castro resistance in Cuba,[138] and who possessed a more thorough understanding of Cuban topography than those training the exile brigade.[139] These resources possessed the sort of information that could have influenced the deliberations on the operation, but they were either excluded or improperly used.

Kennedy's deliberations did not make use of the resources at his command and it was his fault for not doing so. His collegial-decision system depended on his initiative to conduct an effective process of policy analysis and review, yet he provided none. Moreover, the president's failure was compounded by the docility fostered among his advisors who were reluctant to voice their doubts.

In this case, then, it was the president's failure vis-à-vis the criteria of the conventional wisdom that caused his ultimate defeat, plus the adverse effects of consensus. In this regard, the Bay of Pigs crisis is important for what it illuminates about these criteria: when they do matter, and where they are incomplete or vague. While not every presidential failure can be attributed to the president's failings, the fact that one can is important to note for students of the presidency.

NOTES

1. This crisis is known by several names: Quemoy-Matsu crisis (because of two major islands involved); Formosa Strait crisis (because Taiwan, a.k.a. Formosa, was more commonly called Formosa during the 1950s); and, the offshore islands crisis (because the islands in dispute lie directly off of the Chinese mainland). In this case study Taiwan will be used throughout.

2. See Dwight D. Eisenhower, Mandate for Change, 1953-1956 (Garden City, N.Y.: Doubleday, 1963), chap. 19, for a summary of the crisis.

3. Bennett Rushkoff, "Eisenhower, Dulles, and the Quemoy-Matsu Crisis of 1954-1955," Political Science Quarterly 96 (Fall 1981):466-67.

4. For confirmation of this assessment, see ibid., p. 467; Eisenhower, Mandate for Change, p. 464; and Alexander George and Richard Smoke, Deterrence in American Foreign Policy: Theory and Practice (New York: Columbia University Press, 1974), pp. 266-67.

5. Eisenhower, Mandate for Change, p. 463.

6. See ibid., chap. 19; and, Rushkoff, "Eisenhower, Dulles," pp. 466-67.

7. Rushkoff, "Eisenhower, Dulles," p. 464.

8. Robert A. Divine, Eisenhower and the Cold War (New York: Oxford University Press, 1981), p. 57; Eisenhower, Mandate for Change, p. 463; and Townsend Hoopes, The Devil and John Foster Dulles (Boston: Little, Brown, 1974), p. 266.
9. Hoopes, Devil and Dulles, pp. 265-66.
10. Eisenhower, Mandate for Change, p. 463; Rushkoff, "Eisenhower, Dulles," p. 468.
11. Rushkoff, "Eisenhower, Dulles," pp. 466-67.
12. Eisenhower, Mandate for Change, p. 463; Hoopes, Devil and Dulles, p. 265.
13. See Rushkoff, "Eisenhower, Dulles," p. 468; Eisenhower, Mandate for Change, p. 464; and Hoopes, Devil and Dulles, pp. 266-67.
14. Eisenhower, Mandate for Change, p. 464.
15. Ibid.
16. Ibid. See also Hoopes, Devil and Dulles, pp. 270-71.
17. Karl Lott Rankin, China Assignment (Seattle: University of Washington Press, 1964), pp. 218-19.
18. Hoopes, Devil and Dulles, p. 273; Eisenhower, Mandate for Change, p. 465.
19. Hoopes, Devil and Dulles, p. 273.
20. Eisenhower, Mandate for Change, p. 467.
21. Ibid.
22. Ibid.
23. "Meeting in the President's Office," January 21, 1955, Ann Whitman Diary Series, Dwight D. Eisenhower Library, Abilene, Kansas.
24. Eisenhower, Mandate for Change, p. 476.
25. Ibid.; and, "Memorandum for Files," March 11, 1955, Dwight D. Eisenhower Series, Eisenhower Library, Abilene, Kansas.
26. Divine, Eisenhower and the Cold War, p. 62; Rushkoff, "Eisenhower, Dulles," p. 476.
27. Divine, Eisenhower and the Cold War, p. 67.
28. Hoopes, Devil and Dulles, p. 278; Eisenhower, Mandate for Change, p. 477.
29. Eisenhower, Mandate for Change, p. 478.
30. Ibid., p. 482.
31. As George and Smoke note, it is reasonable to assume that China intended to wrest Quemoy and Matsu from Taiwan, whether by the pressure of shelling or the threat of invasion. This judgment is corroborated by the fact of a small-scale Chinese invasion of Quemoy in August 1954;

the Communist capture of Ichiang in January 1955; a build-up of Communist forces on the coast opposite Quemoy and Matsu; and, the revival of Communist pressure in the 1958 Quemoy crisis. See George and Smoke, Deterrence, pp. 266-67, 276-79, and 371-76.

32. See ibid., chap. 19; Rushkoff, "Eisenhower, Dulles," pp. 465-80; Hoopes, Devil and Dulles, chap. 17; and Divine, Eisenhower and the Cold War, pp. 55-66.

33. See Rushkoff, "Eisenhower, Dulles," p. 478.

34. See Eisenhower, Mandate for Change, pp. 477-78; Hoopes, Devil and Dulles, pp. 278-79; and, Divine, Eisenhower and the Cold War, pp. 62-64.

35. Eisenhower, Mandate for Change, p. 464.

36. See Rushkoff, "Eisenhower, Dulles," pp. 473-76, for a discussion of these letters, quotations from them, and their citations. See also Eisenhower, Mandate for Change, pp. 470-74 and Appendix O, for excerpts from some of this correspondence.

37. President Eisenhower to Gen. Alfred Gruenther, February 1, 1955, quoted in Fred I. Greenstein, The Hidden-Hand Presidency (New York: Basic Books, 1982), p. 23.

38. Divine, Eisenhower and the Cold War, pp. 62-63.

39. Rushkoff, "Eisenhower, Dulles," p. 469.

40. Ibid.

41. Eisenhower, Mandate for Change, p. 481.

42. "Call from the President," January 18, 1955, John Foster Dulles--Telephone Conversations Memoranda, Mudd Library, Princeton University.

43. "Thursday, October 7, 1954, Called Secy. Dulles," Eisenhower Diary Series, Dwight D. Eisenhower Library, Abilene, Kansas; and, "Call from President," October 7, 1954, John Foster Dulles--Telephone Conversations Memoranda, Mudd/Princeton.

44. Eisenhower, Mandate for Change, p. 611.

45. See Rushkoff, "Eisenhower, Dulles," pp. 478-79, n63; Robert Bowie (asst. secretary of state under Dulles), telephone interview with author, March 17, 1980.

46. "Telephone Calls, September 4, 1954," Eisenhower Diary Series, Eisenhower Library.

47. "Meeting in the President's Office," January 21, 1955, Ann Whitman Diary Series, Eisenhower Library.

48. See Rushkoff, "Eisenhower, Dulles," pp. 466-67.

49. See Eisenhower, Mandate for Change, chap. 19; Rushkoff, "Eisenhower, Dulles," pp. 466-67; and, Divine, Eisenhower and the Cold War, pp. 55-66.

68 / THE PRESIDENT AND FOREIGN AFFAIRS

50. Rankin, China Assignment, pp. 218-19.
51. "Meeting in the President's Office," January 21, 1955, Ann Whitman Diary Series, Eisenhower Library.
52. Eisenhower, Mandate for Change, pp. 471-72.
53. Ibid., p. 477.
54. See Greenstein, Hidden-Hand Presidency, pp. 20-24, for extensive quotations from the letter. Gruenther, who was supreme commander of NATO at the time, was Eisenhower's former chief of staff and an old friend.
55. Quoted in Greenstein, Hidden-Hand Presidency, p. 21.
56. Hoopes, Devil and Dulles, p. 265; Eisenhower, Mandate for Change, p. 463.
57. "Meeting in the President's Office," January 21, 1955, Ann Whitman Diary Series, Eisenhower Library.
58. Eisenhower, Mandate for Change, p. 472.
59. See Rushkoff, "Eisenhower, Dulles," pp. 473-78.
60. Quoted in Divine, Eisenhower and the Cold War, p. 63.
61. See Greenstein, Hidden-Hand Presidency, pp. 20-24.
62. Ibid., p. 23.
63. Eisenhower, Mandate for Change, pp. 472-73.
64. Ibid., pp. 477-78.
65. Greenstein, Hidden-Hand Presidency, pp. 23-24.
66. Ibid.
67. Eisenhower, Mandate for Change, p. 478.
68. Rushkoff, "Eisenhower, Dulles," pp. 473-74.
69. Ibid., p. 477.
70. Eisenhower, Mandate for Change, pp. 477-79.
71. Ibid., pp. 478-79.
72. See Greenstein, Hidden-Hand Presidency, pp. 246-47, for an excerpt from an interview with President Eisenhower in which he discusses this practice.
73. The burden of President Eisenhower's chapter on this crisis, the evidence from the files of the Eisenhower Library, Rushkoff's research, and the writings of Hoopes, Divine, and others is that Eisenhower kept searching for new information and approaches throughout the crisis. The letter to Gruenther, cited above, illustrates how the president reasoned through the various aspects of the affair; his goals were clear, and he remained flexible in his search for a means to achieve them and resolve the crisis.
74. See Eisenhower, Mandate for Change, pp. 480-83.

75. On the Formosa Resolution, the vote was 85-3 in the Senate and 410-3 in the House. On the mutual security treaty, the Senate approved that agreement by a vote of 64-6.
76. Eisenhower, Mandate for Change, pp. 470-76, Appendix O.
77. Rushkoff, "Eisenhower, Dulles," pp. 469, 474.
78. Eisenhower, Mandate for Change, p. 478.
79. Ibid., p. 459.
80. Rushkoff, "Eisenhower, Dulles," p. 478.
81. George and Smoke, Deterrence, p. 291.
82. Peter Lyon, Eisenhower: Portrait of the Hero (Boston: Little, Brown, 1974), pp. 640-42.
83. Greenstein, Hidden-Hand Presidency, p. 24.
84. Senator Knowland and other right-wing Republicans.
85. Greenstein, Hidden-Hand Presidency, pp. 20-24.
86. George and Smoke, Deterrence, pp. 280-81, 288-89.
87. Robert E. Hunter, Presidential Control of Foreign Policy, The Washington Papers, vol. 10, no. 91 (New York: Praeger, 1982), p. 90.
88. By Walt W. Rostow, quoted in Peter Wyden, Bay of Pigs (New York: Simon and Schuster, 1979), p. 325.
89. Theodore Sorensen, Kennedy (New York: Harper and Row, 1965), pp. 293, 294-309.
90. Quoted in ibid., p. 292.
91. New York Times, October 7, 1960; quoted in Thomas Halper, Foreign Policy Crises (Columbus Ohio: Charles E. Merrill, 1971), pp. 25-26.
92. Quoted in Sorensen, Kennedy, p. 296.
93. Wyden, Bay of Pigs, p. 325.
94. See Halper, Foreign Policy Crises, pp. 25-27, and Arthur M. Schlesinger, A Thousand Days, John F. Kennedy in the White House (Greenwich, Conn.: Fawcett, 1965), pp. 212-13.
95. Schlesinger, A Thousand Days, p. 228.
96. Sorensen, Kennedy, p. 296.
97. Theodore Sorensen, Decision-Making in the White House (New York: Columbia University Press, 1963), p. 3.
98. Alexander L. George, Presidential Decisionmaking in Foreign Policy: The Effective Use of Information and Advice (Boulder, Colo.: Westview Press, 1980), p. 157.
99. Ibid.

100. The Special Group consisted of a deputy undersecretary of state, the deputy secretary of defense, the director of the CIA, and the special assistant to the president for national security affairs.
101. Wyden, Bay of Pigs, pp. 24-25.
102. Ibid., p. 135.
103. Schlesinger, A Thousand Days, p. 225.
104. Wyden, Bay of Pigs, p. 317.
105. Quoted in ibid., p. 317. The Taylor Commission, officially known as the Cuban Study Group, was chaired by General Maxwell Taylor, former Army chief of staff. It was commissioned by President Kennedy to find out what went wrong in the Bay of Pigs affair. Parts of its report have been declassified.
106. Ibid., p. 317.
107. Sorensen, Kennedy, p. 305.
108. For an excellent discussion of Bissell's role in this affair, and his effect on the Kennedy administration, see Garry Wills, The Kennedy Imprisonment (Boston: Little, Brown, 1981), chap. 18.
109. This is an issue of staffing, because it was the fact of these figures and their relationships with Kennedy and his aides which helped to stifle any skepticism about the invasion plan. See ibid., pp. 235-39.
110. Sorensen, Kennedy, p. 305.
111. For a discussion of Taylor's analysis, with extensive quotes from Taylor, see Wills, Kennedy Imprisonment, chap. 20.
112. Wyden, Bay of Pigs, p. 317.
113. Irving L. Janis, Victims of Groupthink (Boston: Houghton Mifflin, 1972), p. 15.
114. Schlesinger, A Thousand Days, p. 228.
115. Wyden, Bay of Pigs, p. 318.
116. Ibid., p. 170.
117. Ibid.
118. Schlesinger, A Thousand Days, pp. 224-25. See also Wyden, Bay of Pigs, p. 319.
119. Janis, Victims of Groupthink, p. 34.
120. Roger Hilsman, To Move a Nation (Garden City, N.Y.: Doubleday, 1967), p. 31.
121. Wyden, Bay of Pigs, p. 100; Schlesinger, A Thousand Days, p. 227; and Hilsman, To Move a Nation, p. 32.
122. Hilsman, To Move a Nation, p. 32.
123. Wyden, Bay of Pigs, p. 149.

124. Ibid., p. 316.
125. Schlesinger, *A Thousand Days*, pp. 241-42, 276-77.
126. Ibid., p. 242.
127. Ibid.
128. Wyden, *Bay of Pigs*, p. 316.
129. Ibid., pp. 148-49.
130. Ibid., p. 316.
131. In this regard, Wills refers to Kennedy as the "prisoner of charisma." See Wills, *Kennedy Imprisonment*, chap. 19.
132. Hilsman, *To Move a Nation*, p. 32.
133. Schlesinger, *A Thousand Days*, p. 228.
134. Sorensen, *Kennedy*, p. 303.
135. Ibid., p. 302.
136. Quoted in Wills, *Kennedy Imprisonment*, p. 253.
137. Ibid., p. 252.
138. Ibid., p. 256.
139. Halper, *Foreign Policy Crises*, pp. 35-36.

3

NON-CRISIS SECURITY ISSUES

Just as the postwar period has involved a series of crises, foreign policy since World War II also has been dominated by issues of defense and security. Indeed, one of the most important policy makers in the U.S. government during this period has been the president's assistant for national security affairs, and a statutory National Security Council is the nation's highest policy-making body in the vast area of foreign affairs. The advent of nuclear weapons and Soviet-U.S. rivalry have brought security issues to the fore, and all presidents since Truman have devoted much attention to them.

Accordingly, these issues deserve a category of their own and require separate treatment from other issues. For presidents must grapple with the problems of security in a highly threatening world, and a dominant theme among these issues is the problem of arms control. Every president approaches the issue in his own way, from President Eisenhower's Open Skies proposal to President Reagan's "zero option" for reducing nuclear weapons in Europe, but all face the difficult problem of balancing security with the risk of war. Therefore, two cases of proposed arms control agreements can serve to illuminate the value of the conventional wisdom for presidential evaluation in this area: SALT I and SALT II. In the first of these cases, President Nixon was able to achieve his goal of concluding and ratifying an agreement on the limitation of strategic arms with the Soviet Union. In the case of SALT II, President Carter achieved an arms limitation agreement with the Soviet Union, but was unable to obtain its approval by the U.S. Senate.

Non-Crisis Security Issues / 73

These two cases thus provide a useful contrast of presidential success and failure in dealing with security issues, and the similar structural features of the two cases offer an important opportunity for examining the president's role in shaping foreign policy. The following studies probe the reasons for the different outcomes of these cases.

SALT I

The 1972 agreements between the United States and the Soviet Union, collectively known as SALT I, represent a presidential success in the category of non-crisis strategic issues.[1] For in this case President Nixon was able to achieve his goal of reaching an agreement with the Soviet Union on the limitation of strategic nuclear arms, and to obtain approval of this agreement in the Senate. This study will examine the reasons behind his success.

Summary of Case

The SALT process had been begun by the Johnson administration, which was concerned about nuclear stability and a potential arms race with the Soviet Union.[2] Before much progress could be made, however, President Johnson's term expired and he was replaced by Richard Nixon.
Nixon came to the issue of nuclear arms competition and SALT from a different perspective than Johnson. He had a reputation as a tough anti-Communist, and in the 1968 campaign had roundly criticized Johnson for "creating a security gap for America."[3] Nevertheless, he saw SALT as part of an overall strategy for improving Soviet-U.S. relations,[4] and thus spent considerable time during his pre-inaugural transition considering SALT and the Soviet Union.[5] He viewed arms talks in part as a political instrument to be employed for advantage in other areas of foreign policy, and in part as valuable for possible arms limitation agreements. For him, the two aspects of SALT were related, for he regarded arms talks as part of an overall strategy for linking the various components of Soviet-U.S. relations.[6]
This concept of "linkage" would be important to Nixon's strategy for pursuing his goal of a ratifiable SALT

agreement. He and Henry Kissinger, his assistant for national security affairs, believed that the Soviet Union was particularly anxious to make progress with arms talks, for whatever reason, so he would use U.S. leverage in this area to gain Soviet cooperation in other foreign policy matters (e.g., Vietnam and the Middle East).[7] At the same time, however, Nixon also wanted an agreement for its own sake, only not at the cost of U.S. defeat or undue concessions resulting from an overzealous approach to arms control.

Because of linkage and this concern for the careful handling of the arms issue, Nixon set out to establish strict White House control over SALT. He accomplished that control by using secrecy and the agency of Henry Kissinger, who was given a broad mandate in the matter of SALT.

From this beginning, the story of SALT I continued over the next two years. It is a story in two phases: the first, that of the Soviet-U.S. negotiations, would end on May 26, 1972, when President Nixon and Soviet Communist Party Chief Leonid Brezhnev signed the SALT I accords; the second phase, that of seeing those accords through approval by the Senate, ended in August of that year.

In the next phase, President Nixon sought an arms agreement through two tracks of negotiations and through pressure on the Soviet Union to reach an agreement. One track of negotiations was public, i.e., confidential but announced to the world. It involved protracted discussions between American and Soviet diplomats from November 1969 to May 1972. The U.S. delegation, led by Ambassador Gerard Smith, met its Soviet counterpart in seven lengthy sessions held in Vienna and Helsinki.[8] It was complemented by a second, secret track of direct discussions between the White House and the Soviet leadership.

This second track, known as "the Channel"[9] and consisting mostly of discussions between Kissinger and Soviet Ambassador Anatoly Dobrynin, was unknown even to Ambassador Smith and his colleagues until the middle of 1971.[10] These discussions were intended to supplement and help facilitate progress in the formal negotiations going on in Europe.[11] Sometimes Nixon would enter the Channel himself. On February 17, 1969, he met with Dobrynin to discuss Soviet-U.S. relations and help inaugurate further discussions toward improving relations.[12] Furthermore, he occasionally corresponded with Soviet Premier Alexei Kosygin (and, after August 1971, with Soviet Communist Party Chief Leonid Brezhnev), bringing these discussions to the highest level of government.

These two tracks of negotiations were accompanied by pressure on the Soviet Union to proceed with a SALT agreement. This pressure was most pronounced in the Nixon administration's pressing Congress for money to develop new strategic weapons systems, in order to spur Soviet acceptance of a treaty before it was too late. The administration pressed forward with several new programs: the Anti-Ballistic Missile defense (ABM), the Trident submarine, Minuteman III missiles, and Multiple Independently-Target Reentry Vehicle (MIRV) technology.[13] ABM was of particular concern to the Soviet Union, so "offering to limit our ABM could become the major Soviet incentive for a SALT agreement."[14] On March 14, 1969, the president approved plans to proceed with ABM development. At the same time, MIRV technology was pursued,[15] in part as further pressure on a MIRV-less Soviet Unon.[16]

The two-track negotiations and this pressure proceeded through 1969 and 1970, but in 1971 the SALT talks became deadlocked over the issue of what weapons an arms control agreement should cover: the United States insisted on linking offensive- and defensive-arms agreements, while the Soviet stand was that negotiations should be limited to ABM.[17] In order to break this deadlock, Kissinger and Dobrynin reopened the Channel and Nixon resumed correspondence with Kosygin.[18] As a result of these secret, high-level activities, on May 20, 1971, President Nixon announced a Soviet-U.S. agreement to negotiate a limit on ABM systems and to discuss measures to limit offensive strategic weapons.[19]

SALT thus moved forward to 1972, when pressure from a number of issues, including SALT, led to plans for a summit meeting between Nixon and the Soviet leaders. Kissinger was secretly dispatched to Moscow in April to prepare for the meeting, where it was hoped a SALT agreement could be finalized.[20] By this time, differences over SALT between the superpowers had been reduced considerably, so Kissinger's trip set the stage for the summit the following month. In the May 1972 summit, the two tracks of negotiations merged as Nixon and Brezhnev negotiated the conclusion of a SALT agreement. This agreement, signed on May 6 and composed of an ABM Treaty and an Interim

Agreement on Offensive Weapons, ended the first phase of the SALT I story.

The second phase did not begin at this time, but rather now came into focus. For the Senate was involved with SALT, even if only indirectly, before May 1972. Most of this involvement was in the matter of considering administration requests for the funds to develop weapons systems, and in receiving rather pro forma briefings on the progress of SALT.[21] After the agreements were signed, however, the administration had to focus more attention on getting them through the Senate.

The attention now given the Senate by the administration was great. On May 26, the same day that the SALT I agreements were signed in Moscow, the White House invited aides of two key senators to a briefing on the agreements.[22] Less than an hour after his return from Moscow on June 1, Nixon heightened this attention by addressing a joint session of Congress on SALT. Two weeks later, he and Kissinger briefed a group of 120 senators and representatives at the White House, giving a lengthy and detailed analysis of the case for the agreements.[23]

Following these high-level briefings for Congress, the months of June and July 1972 saw several administration officials testify on behalf of SALT I to the Senate Armed Services and Foreign Relations Committees.[24] At the same time, the administration lobbied Congress for money for weapons not covered by SALT I, with Secretary of Defense Melvin Laird pressing for support for the Trident submarine, the B-1 bomber, and the strategic cruise missile.[25] This two-pronged strategy, in favor of SALT I and weapons, was intended to ease the agreement's passage by linking it to a tough defense posture.[26]

After such lobbying, the administration was partially successful. On August 2, the Senate approved a military procurement bill with funds for B-1, Trident, and cruise, and on the next day it approved the ABM Treaty. Trouble for the Interim Agreement on Offensive Weapons appeared, however, when several senators said that they would offer a series of amendments to the legislation approving that agreement when it reached the Senate floor.

This group, led by Senator Henry Jackson, was critical of the Interim Agreement on the grounds that it gave the Soviet Union an advantage in nuclear throw-weight.[27] Jackson and his colleagues thus proposed an advisory amendment, which would not bind the administration, calling for numerical equality in future strategic arms agreements and a vigorous research and development program in support of a "prudent defense posture."[28] To gain passage of the Interim Agreement, on August 7 the White House announced its support for the Jackson amendment.

With this last problem out of the way, Nixon gained ratification for the Interim Agreement on September 14. On September 30, he signed it in an elaborate ceremony at the White House. He had thus achieved a success in this matter, in concluding the SALT I agreement with the Soviet Union, and then in the identical 88 to 2 votes by which the Senate passed the ABM Treaty and the Interim Agreement.

Policy Direction and Design

The first criterion of the conventional wisdom of particular relevance to this case is that of Policy direction and design. President Nixon partially met the requirements of this criterion, providing some direction and perspective for the U.S. approach to SALT, but not as predicted by the conventional wisdom.

Nixon's view of SALT revolved around the concept of linkage: he saw it as linked to his broader policy toward the Soviet Union. He did not want it divorced from that policy for his goals in the matter of arms negotiations were carefully tied to his larger goals in foreign affairs. Nixon wanted an arms agreement for its own value, but he also insisted that SALT be part of an overall improvement in East-West relations (what would be called "detente") and advancement of U.S. interests. Moreover, there was a political dimension to these goals--he wanted to use SALT to enhance his domestic political position.[29]

In line with these goals, Nixon had to develop a comprehensive framework for foreign policy to guide his administration, in order to weave together the various strands of policy. Accordingly, he and Kissinger spent a great amount of time during the transition mapping out a comprehensive policy for U.S.-Soviet relations. Indeed, this policy was part of the "grand design" they worked out in those pre-inaugural days.

Nixon and Kissinger regarded such a design as a necessary condition for the successful conduct of foreign affairs, and thus put together a "conceptual framework" for policy.[30] This framework, as it related to Soviet-U.S.

78 / THE PRESIDENT AND FOREIGN AFFAIRS

relations, was based on three principles outlined during the transition: the principle of concreteness--negotiations between the United States and the Soviet Union would deal with specific causes of tension, rather than "general atmospheric"; the principle of restraint--relations between the superpowers would be improved only if there was mutual restraint, so Soviet adventurism would be penalized by the United States; and, the principle of linkage--progress in superpower relations would have to advance on a broad front, so that SALT would proceed in relation to other issues.[31]

With this design, Nixon developed a clear notion of how SALT related to the rest of his foreign policy: it was to be an end, but also the means to an end. To that extent, Nixon refrained from becoming involved with SALT as an independent issue, rather, he was more concerned with the arms issue in the context of achieving broad foreign policy success. He thus left the details of SALT to Kissinger:

> Nixon took a keen interest in the strategy for SALT and in what channels it should be negotiated. But the details of the various plans bored him; in effect he left the selection of the options to me [Kissinger]. Yet if the bureaucracy had become aware of this, all vestige of discipline would have disappeared. I therefore scheduled over Nixon's impatient protests a series of NSC meetings where options were presented to a glassy-eyed and irritable President so that directives could be issued with some plausibility on his authority.[32]

Nixon's view of SALT was thus a political, rather than a substantive, one--he and Kissinger had developed a design for policy centered on the concept of linkage, and he concerned himself with the strategy and tactics of pursuing his goals. SALT was linked to other issues not only in the three principles of the transition, but also in Nixon's mind.

Having articulated his goals and established these principles for policy, Nixon then had to communicate his design to three relevant groups: his foreign affairs government, his domestic audience of Congress and the public, and the Soviet Union. He quickly set out to do this in a particular way.

Nixon first moved to establish his policy direction within his foreign affairs government. He was deeply suspicious of the "foreign affairs bureaucracy" in the State Department, the CIA, and at Defense, so he quickly moved to centralize control of foreign policy in the White House. The key player in this centralization was Henry Kissinger, whose abilities and shared views on policies facilitated a White House-centered foreign policy.33

Even with a centralized foreign affairs operation, Nixon still had to rely on the foreign affairs bureaucracy a great deal. Consequently, he moved to clearly impress his own design on that body. This was accomplished by not only constructing a comprehensive policy in communion with Kissinger, and by informing his subordinates of his firm support for that policy, but also by employing subterfuge to guarantee White House control.

In a February 4, 1969, letter to Secretary of State William Rogers, Defense Secretary Laird, and CIA Director Richard Helms, Nixon made it clear that linking arms talks to other issues was now official policy.34 This letter, drafted by Kissinger and his staff, was unequivocal in announcing the president's design to his foreign affairs government. For it was a clear statement of the president's acceptance of the concept of linkage. But it offered only the broad outline of Nixon's design, the details of which he and Kissinger closely guarded in order to insure its implementation.

At the same time, Nixon tried to communicate his message to his domestic audience of Congress and the public, but also in a highly guarded way. This task was more difficult, because of Nixon's clear statements to his subordinates on the issue of linkage; the State Department and the Arms Control and Disarmament Agency (ACDA) were eager for SALT to begin. Consequently, mixed signals were sent out: during a background briefing on foreign affairs on February 6, 1969, Kissinger reiterated the administration policy of linkage,35 but in the following months officials from the State Department and ACDA told Congress that arms control as an isolated issue would be eagerly pursued by the Nixon administration.36 The upshot of these contradictory efforts, and the president's guarding of most of his plans, was that Nixon's message to his domestic audience was muddled. In the beginning of the administration, this muddle would be frustrating, but as time passed White House control would grow stronger. These frustrations served as further inducements to a White House-centered handling of SALT. For over the three years of SALT I, communication of the president's design would move more firmly into the grasp of the White House. Equipped with the most complete information, and cloaked in the secrecy of the SALT negotiations and the ultra-secrecy of the Channel, Nixon would hold an advantage over the foreign affairs bureaucracy in the matter of SALT.

This advantage would be particularly pronounced in communication of Nixon's design to the third relevant party--the Soviet Union. For with the Soviet leadership, the president's design was most important. Nixon's meeting with Ambassador Dobrynin in February 1969, inaugurating the Channel, was dedicated to presenting aspects of his design to the Soviet leaders: he stressed the importance of arms talks, but only in the context of linkage.[37] In the same way, continued use of the Channel and exchanges of notes between Nixon and the Soviet leaders allowed the president to present his design to them without the mediation of the suspect bureaucracy.

In the three years of SALT I, Nixon generally adhered to the direction he and Kissinger had set during the transition. They had developed a grand design to guide policy, and used that design to develop a perspective on how SALT was related to the other aspects of this first criterion, for he had a clear idea of what he wanted in the matter of SALT, and a perspective on how it was related to other issues.

Communicating this design, however, did not conform to the predictions of the conventional wisdom. For, while the SALT-linkage policy was clearly presented to the foreign affairs government, Nixon withheld many details of his plans from the bureaucracy in order to insure White House dominance. As is clear from Kissinger's description of the handling of SALT in his memoirs, Nixon's secrecy was more a strategy designed to deceive the bureaucracy than to deceive the Soviets.[38] It was not merely a bargaining strategy. White House-centered operations helped Nixon to communicate his intentions to the Soviet leadership, but such operations were conducted at the expense of the State Department and ACDA.[39] Not only were White House tactics demoralizing to the foreign affairs bureaucracy, but they also exacerbated difficulties between the

White House and the other parts of the government. Moreover, Nixon was least successful in communicating with his domestic audience: divisions within the government sent conflicting messages to Congress and the public, and the secrecy surrounding the negotiations further served to keep this domestic audience from understanding the president's purposes. Indeed, some of the support for the Jackson amendment arose from congressional dissatisfaction with being ill-informed on the goals and progress of negotiations.[40]

Later, when the SALT I agreements were concluded, this muddling of purposes would become less significant, except in a lingering resentment among certain senators (particularly Senators Jackson and Fulbright) about the handling of SALT.[41] While the public lay largely outside of the debates over SALT I, several senators resented the rather pro forma way in which the Senate had been consulted on SALT.

Consequently, President Nixon met some of the requirements of this criterion: he developed a comprehensive framework for foreign policy and carefully outlined it to Kissinger and the NSC staff. Yet he failed to effectively communicate that design to the State Department and ACDA, Congress, or the public. In that regard, he did not meet the second requirement of Policy direction. For the president had a clear idea of what he wanted, but kept much of it to himself and his national security advisor. Moreover, because of differences between the White House and the foreign affairs bureaucracy, the message sent to Congress and the public was muddled.

The situation does not conform to policy design as conceived in the conventional wisdom. In that view, Policy direction involves having a president both know what he wants to achieve and communicate his design to the relevant parties. Nixon's complete design was not disseminated except to the White House staff. While this method of operation worked for a while, it contributed to later resentment and rebellion in the foreign affairs bureaucracy and suspicion in Congress. Eventually, the president would be strongly criticized for this method, and Congress and the bureaucracy wary of the extent of presidential control over this issue.

Nixon adopted this strategy for a particular reason. Yet, because it focuses on creating and communicating a policy design, the conventional wisdom does not address circumstances such as these: where the president guards his policy design in order to implement it, and the adverse consequences of such a strategy. In the short run Nixon's strategy worked, but in the long run it made Congress and the bureaucracy wary of presidential power. Moreover, as will be addressed below, it may be that Nixon was successful despite this strategy, and not necessarily because of it.

Organization and Staffing

Analysis of President Nixon's success in SALT I certainly requires attention to the Organization and staffing that Nixon employed. For SALT I is as much the product of Henry Kissinger and his organizational system as it is that of Richard Nixon. Indeed, in a discussion of Kissinger and his National Security Council system it is difficult to sort out the distinctions between the man and the structure.

For Nixon had given Kissinger a broad mandate: to help him devise and implement a grand design for policy, to establish and operate a White House-centered foreign policy apparatus, and to pursue a ratifiable SALT agreement. Nixon was able to give Kissinger this broad authority because they shared such similar views on policy and on the way foreign affairs ought to be conducted.[42] Both came to the White House highly suspicious of bureaucracy and its effects on policy, and so developed a system to override the permanent government and manage foreign policy from the White House.

To that end, Nixon authorized Kissinger to revive the National Security Council (NSC) as a policy body--it had been little used during the Kennedy-Johnson era, because those presidents favored informal groups for decision making. Kissinger did so, and established a group of committees and panels to integrate policy through the NSC. Each committee was chaired by Kissinger and serviced by his staff.[43] The relevant committee for SALT was the Verification Panel, established on July 21, 1969.[44] It was backed by a Working Group, directed by Laurence E. Lynn, one of Kissinger's White House men.[45] These new groups established the central White House control over SALT that Nixon wanted: by serving as panels of ultimate review on the crucial issue of verifying Soviet compliance with any

SALT agreement, the panel and its Working Group enabled Kissinger, and thus Nixon, to exercise ultimate control over arms negotiations.[46] No SALT agreement could be concluded, nor would it pass the Senate, unless Soviet compliance could be verified, so control over this panel gave the NSC, i.e., Nixon and Kissinger, an organizational device for controlling SALT.

Through this system, Kissinger acted as Nixon's agent for SALT. As noted above, the president gave his advisor considerable discretion in the substance of a SALT agreement, while maintaining a keen interest in the process of negotiations. Kissinger used this discretion to explore policy through National Security Study Memoranda (NSSM), which were policy studies for presidential review conducted by the NSC staff. NSSM numbers 3 and 28 involved strategic arms, and gave the White House the information necessary to proceed with decisions on SALT.[47] Kissinger's NSC system thus generated information and intragovernmental control over SALT.

This control was strengthened by the institution of the Channel, which Nixon and Kissinger regarded as essential to the success of their policy.[48] The Channel was indeed part of the Nixon-Kissinger organization for SALT for it was the means for conducting direct White House-Kremlin negotiations. As Kissinger has explained, the Soviet leadership soon learned that Nixon preferred to deal directly with the Soviet government through Ambassador Dobrynin, rather than through his formal negotiators. In this way the president was able to avoid confrontations and disagreements with the State Department.[49] The Channel thus sealed White House control over SALT, for it was the logical result of the Nixon-Kissinger system for policy direction. It served as part of the organizational structure for pursuing SALT, by providing Nixon with a direct link to the Soviet leadership.

The link was not only organizational, but was personal as well. Henry Kissinger was important to Nixon's success not only because of the organization he established, but because he shared Nixon's views on policy and government. Both believed in linkage, and thus in avoiding an overzealous approach to SALT. Both believed in a president-centered foreign policy. Kissinger, working closely with Nixon, brought Nixon's plans into action. Because he was able to trust Kissinger, while retaining ultimate decision for himself, Nixon was able to take full advantage of

Kissinger's intellectual and political abilities.[50] The result was that Kissinger devised and manned an organizational system that suited Nixon's needs.[51]

Yet, just as in the matter of Policy direction, the president's fulfillment of this criterion is not as has been predicted in the conventional wisdom. For Nixon's organization and staffing in this case were designed to circumvent the usual channels of government, and depended on the use of Kissinger as the president's "vicar" on SALT and other foreign policy issues. In the conventional wisdom, it is not clear what sort of Organization and staffing is best, but there is a clear implication that the president not delegate too much authority. Moreover, the conventional wisdom is also vague on whether any organizational scheme is acceptable, or whether or not one which circumvents all regular channels is legitimate.[52] In short, the conventional wisdom is unclear on the boundaries of acceptable organization and staffing strategies, i.e., whether or not "anything goes" that contributes to success.

At the same time, the conventional wisdom fails to distinguish between the long-term and short-term effects of presidential performance in this regard. As will be examined below, the Nixon-Kissinger NSC system induced bureaucratic rebellion against White House dominance. It also contributed to the "congressional revolt" against presidential foreign policy making in the 1970s, and a repudiation of Kissinger's "Lone Ranger" handling of foreign affairs by many of Nixon's critics.[53] The NSC system gave the president the control he wanted over the issue of SALT, but this scheme does not conform to the predictions of the conventional wisdom for Organization and staffing.

Management and Oversight

Closely tied to Organization and staffing in this case is Nixon's performance according to the criterion of Management and oversight. What is interesting to note is that, as with the other criteria, the president's performance according to the requirements of this standard was mediocre. For Nixon's record in this matter was quite mixed--in some respects he fulfilled the demands of this standard, but in other respects his performance was inadequate.

The first requirement of this criterion is that the president manage the mechanisms, personnel, and processes of foreign policy, in order to insure that his policy direction and design are followed. In this regard, Nixon's record was mixed: on the one hand, he did take steps to insure adherence to his preferences and design, but on the other hand these steps generated other problems.

To be specific, Nixon used a combination of secrecy and White House domination of SALT to insure adherence to his design. The NSC system and the Channel meant that only he and Kissinger "held all the cards," i.e., only they had complete information about SALT. In this way, Nixon's design was followed: the Channel provided a direct link to the Soviet leadership, so only the world of the White House really counted in SALT. Moreover, by exercising ultimate control over the content of a SALT agreement, the president was able to guarantee adherence to his design.

Besides secrecy, which kept the suspect bureaucracy from exercising much influence over policy, the Nixon-Kissinger NSC system facilitated Nixon's plans. First, this system centralized control over SALT in the White House, through the Verification Panel and its Working Group, thus increasing the chances of achieving desired goals. Second, Nixon employed Kissinger as his deputy in the matter of SALT, giving his advisor a broad mandate to seek a ratifiable SALT agreement.[54] Having little interest in the details of such an agreement, Nixon left these matters to Kissinger.

Nixon's management of the mechanisms, processes, and personnel in this case was thus largely centered on delegating power to Kissinger, who exercised his mandate as freely as possible. Where Nixon did remain most involved as a manager was in controlling the political aspects of SALT. He took a keen interest in such matters as the establishment and maintenance of the secret Channel to Moscow,[55] the political feasibility of such SALT options as limiting ABM systems to national capitals,[56] or the likely political consequences of a summit meeting with the Soviet leaders.[57] He retained the power of ultimate decision in all aspects of SALT, but given his preference for these political aspects, and his goal of a ratifiable agreement, it is safe to conclude that much of the management of SALT passed from Nixon to Kissinger.[58]

This sort of management worked in the case of SALT I, for Nixon was able to obtain the sort of agreement he wanted. It has, however, been criticized by several observers and some participants, such as Ambassador Smith, who contends that use of a secret channel and high-level involvement in negotiations led to confusion and missed opportunities for obtaining a better treaty.[59] Whether or not a better treaty could have been obtained is beyond the scope of this analysis--what is important to consider is how Nixon's management of this affair is relevant to the conventional wisdom.

This is where the factors of Organization and staffing are closely linked to Management. Nixon was able to delegate much of the responsibility for SALT, and thus concentrate on its political aspects, because he had Kissinger and the NSC system working for him. These facts made Nixon's management, while not the sort implied in the conventional wisdom, successful. For the conventional wisdom implies closer presidential management of personnel and processes than Nixon undertook.

At the same time, from another perspective, however, the conventional wisdom requires that the president exercise decisive control over his foreign affairs government, and that he may use deputies to aid him. In this regard, Nixon was more successful, but not in a way predicted by the conventional view. Through his deputy, Kissinger, Nixon did exercise decisive control, but more by subterfuge than by straightforward dominance of the executive branch. For he was

> a President who neither trusted his Cabinet nor was willing to give them direct orders. Nixon feared leaks and shrank from imposing discipline. But he was determined to achieve his purposes; he thus encouraged procedures unlikely to be recommended in textbooks on public administration that, crablike, worked privily around existing structures. It was demoralizing for the bureaucracy, which, cut out of the process, reacted by accentuating the independence and self-will that had caused Nixon to bypass it in the first place. But it worked; it achieved that elusive blend of laborious planning and crisp articulation on which successful policy depends.[60]

Kissinger acted as Nixon's agent, and by circumventing the State Department and ACDA in the management of SALT, obtained an agreement for Nixon. Again, this is not the sort of management implied in the conventional wisdom, and its price was bureaucratic demoralization and congressional rebelliousness. The conventional wisdom suggests that a president ought to dominate the executive branch through more straightforward management techniques than secrecy and subterfuge.

Therefore, in the first two aspects of Management and oversight, Nixon achieved partial and peculiar fulfillment of the conventional wisdom's standards, although the long-term effects of his performance were negative. In contrast, he did not meet the demands of the third aspect of this criterion: the five steps for effective decision making.

According to these rules, the president ought to be an active participant in each step of the decision process, at least to ensure that these steps are followed. Nixon, however, did not perform according to the demands of these standards. Fulfillment of the first three rules was left to Kissinger, with little involvement from Nixon.[61] It was Kissinger who authorized and used the analysis and options examined in NSSM numbers 3 and 28,[62] and who was allowed to choose and pursue negotiating options.[63] The president was not concerned with the analysis of choices and their consequences, except in a political sense.[64] Because of the trust he placed in Kissinger, Nixon was able to allow his advisor to ensure that such work was done. Yet, in terms of the conventional wisdom, the president at least partially abdicated his responsibilities.

As for the remaining two rules for effective decision making, Nixon was more interested in these but, again, largely in a political sense. He was keenly aware of how certain options and components of a SALT agreement would be received by the Senate, so he moved to ensure action in these areas. He was closely involved in examining the implications of a capitals-only ABM system,[65] and in the decision to pursue an ABM system as a prod to Soviet progress on SALT.[66] Therefore, while deferring to Kissinger on many details, he kept a close eye on the aspects of SALT that interested him.

Here is a fine point for assessing the conventional wisdom: it is unclear just how much responsibility a president may delegate. As has been noted in several places above, this case demonstrates the ambiguity of the conventional wisdom in the matter of delegation and control. The thrust of the criterion of Management, however, as expressed in authors such as Hunter, Lewis, and George, is that the president must not delegate as much responsibility as Nixon did. It is his responsibility to oversee the operations of the government, particularly in formation of policy. This point, however, is unclear. In any event, Nixon was successful in reaching his goals through this system. He left much of the management of SALT to Kissinger, as well as oversight of implementation. The Channel and the NSC system ensured that implementation of decisions was directed by the national security advisor, and Kissinger looked after these responsibilities as well.

The president's performance as regards this criterion was thus different from what the conventional wisdom implies. Nixon delegated much to his advisor, and exercised management and oversight only very loosely. According to this third standard, Nixon's performance was rather mediocre: his management was loose, intermittent, and focused on certain issues. Of course, this style of management arose from the degree of trust that Nixon placed in his assistant, trust based on shared policy goals and views of government. Nevertheless, the president's performance as manager in this case of presidential success was not in a form predicted by the conventional wisdom, which calls for greater direction of the government from the chief executive himself. Nixon was successful in this case, but his fulfillment of the management criterion was partial and somewhat unusual--it did not conform to expectations.

There are also some problems that may have arisen from Nixon's management style--those problems of confusion, duplicity, and demoralization which Kissinger and Smith mentioned. These problems expose the limits of the conventional wisdom for guiding evaluation, because it does not include a notion of what sort of management is acceptable. Moreover, because of the nature of the Nixon-Kissinger relationship in handling SALT, this case also raises the issue of just how much control the president is supposed to exercise, and how much responsibility he may delegate. These issues have normative implications beyond the scope of this study, but they also have a practical aspect relevant to this analysis: in this case it was possible for a president to be successful in achieving his goal by delegating most of his managerial responsibilities to a closely trusted assistant. This conclusion suggests that the conventional wisdom may be inadequate for understanding presidential performance.

Consensus-building

The final criterion of the conventional wisdom to be considered is that of Consensus-building. President Nixon met the requirements of this standard, although this factor does not serve as effectively as others for explaining his success.

An important reason why Consensus-building is less important than other factors is that building support for SALT was a task in which Nixon had quite a bit of help. Indeed, the political climate of that period contributed to the president's success with the Senate.

From the beginning of the Nixon administration in 1969, there was significant pressure from key members of Congress and in the press for arms talks and some sort of SALT agreement. Indeed, much of the journalistic and congressional "advice" offered in speeches and editorials during the transition and the early days of the administration pressed for talks to begin and agreements to be sought.[67] Moreover, even though it subsided as the SALT talks progressed in Europe, this pro-SALT feeling did not dissipate. Throughout the years 1969-72, senators such as Fulbright, Mansfield, Cooper, and Humphrey continued to press the president for an agreement and various actions to facilitate it.[68] They thus provided a willing audience for a SALT agreement when one did materialize in 1972. Even while harshly critical of the way in which the president had failed to do more than engage in a rather perfunctory consultation of the Senate regarding this agreement, Senators Fulbright and Jackson nevertheless voted to approve it.[69]

Nixon took note of this sentiment, but he was also concerned about not appearing to "sell out" to the Soviet Union. Indeed, during the course of the SALT story, this seemed to be his major worry. He knew that a SALT agreement would be well received by those who wanted to cut defense spending and improve relations with the Soviet Union,[70] such as most of the Democrats, but he did not want to lose his prodefense base of support or face a showdown with the Joint Chiefs of Staff.[71] Moreover, his own preference was for an agreement, but only a "tough" one that did not give up too much to the Soviet Union.[72] Consequently, his drive for a ratifiable SALT agreement meant attention to driving the hardest bargain possible, coupled with new weapons programs to reemphasize his interest in defense.

The Nixon policy was thus intended to present a picture of an administration searching for peace from a position of strong defense. From this position, the president worked to achieve his consensus. His consensus-building efforts came in two stages. First, before the treaty was concluded, Nixon sought a treaty and defense situation conducive to the passage of the SALT agreement. To that end, he pressed for several new weapons systems—ABM, Trident, MIRV, cruise missiles—to provide bargaining chips, reassure Congress of his dedication to defense, and to improve the U.S. defense posture.[73] While these programs infuriated several pro-SALT senators, they improved the chances of SALT I's passage. At the same time, Nixon was careful to negotiate a treaty that the Senate could accept. In general, this effort did not place any great constraints on the negotiations, for Kissinger did indeed have broad discretion over the details of SALT. Yet this effort shaped a particular aspect of the ABM treaty which formed the core of SALT I: in March 1971, the SALT negotiations were close to an agreement to limit U.S. and Soviet ABM systems to National Command Authorities (NCA), i.e., capitals; Nixon killed this idea on the grounds that Congress would never accept a plan to spend taxpayers' money to defend only Washington.[74] He thus sought, through a defense build-up and a politically feasible treaty, to make a SALT agreement as likely of passage as possible.

Once SALT I was concluded with the Soviet Union in 1972, the president undertook a three-step process to ensure ratification of the agreement. First, he engaged himself and his administration in an effort to explain the substance of the agreement to Congress. This step began dramatically upon Nixon's return from Moscow—within an hour of his arrival in Washington he appeared before a joint session of Congress to address the legislators on SALT.[75] This public explanation of SALT was backed by a more quiet effort to brief congressmen and a few aides of key senators on the substance of the agreement.[76]

The second step in this consensus-building process was to reemphasize the link between SALT and an aggressive-weapons program. Consequently, several military leaders and Defense Department spokesmen proceeded to Capitol Hill to urge acceptance of both SALT and new weapons. Secretary Laird argued before the Senate Armed Services Committee in July that SALT would enhance U.S. security, but only if tied to such programs as Trident and B-1. The understanding in the Senate was that Laird was speaking for the president.[77]

The final step toward ensuring acceptance of SALT I was to neutralize opposition to the agreement by coopting it. Specifically, Senator Jackson and some of his colleagues were concerned about imbalances between U.S.-Soviet nuclear forces in the Interim Agreement, which they felt would lock the United States into a position of inferiority.[78] To remedy this problem, and advise the administration on the conduct of future arms agreements, Jackson offered an amendment to the legislation ratifying the Interim Agreement which called for numerical equality in future agreements and "the maintenance of a vigorous research and development program" in support of a "prudent strategic posture."[79] Nixon undercut the force of Jackson's opposition by coopting it. First, Nixon had John Lehman of the National Security Council staff meet with Richard Perle, Senator Jackson's aide.[80] Eventually, the two were able to work out a compromise version of the amendment which both Jackson and the White House could support. Then, on August 7, 1972, the White House endorsed the modified Jackson amendment. With this backing, the amendment passed and SALT I's ratification was ensured.

These steps helped bring SALT I along, as is particularly evident in the story of the Jackson amendment. But, as the twin 88 to 2 votes for the ABM Treaty and the Interim Agreement suggest, the Senate was ready for a SALT agreement. Nixon's consensus-building efforts certainly helped him, but they took advantage of an existing political climate that made nearly any SALT agreement attractive. The key to SALT I lay in reassuring the advocates of strong defense, which was not difficult to do.

Consensus-building, then, was of some importance. The president was the beneficiary of a good deal of pro-SALT sentiment, anti-ABM feeling, and his own reputation as an anti-Communist.[81] Moreover, he was probably aided by the fact that SALT I was the first agreement of its kind: despite the efforts of Jackson and a few others, congressional scrutiny of the agreement was not great, nor was there much interest in halting what many hoped would be long-term negotiations by killing the first fruits of those labors.[82] The 88 to 2 margins of votes and limited debate on the agreement indicate more than effective consensus-building: they suggest a political climate hospitable to SALT.

Other Criteria, Other Factors

As the previous section noted, President Nixon and SALT I benefited from a domestic political climate conducive to passage of an arms agreement. This climate ought not to be overstated, but it must not be overlooked. SALT I came to a Senate with many vocal arms control advocates, and there was a general sentiment in the Senate against development of ABM. Indeed, a vote in 1969 on deployment of ABM passed by one vote: that of Vice-President Agnew.[83] A treaty to limit ABM systems was not going to receive rough treatment in such an environment, nor any other first attempts at arms control. With SALT I as the first agreement of its kind, facing a Senate so poised to receive such an agreement, the Nixon administration was certainly given the benefit of any doubts held in Congress.

This climate, as well as Richard Nixon's reputation as an anti-Communist and a friend of defense, helped to ensure passage of SALT I. Nixon's reputation, a well-deserved one, made it possible for him to offer such an agreement without charges of selling out to the Soviet Union. He could be trusted on this issue, and he used that trust to gain his objective.

Conclusion

The case of SALT I has identified some interesting aspects of the conventional wisdom: problems in clarifying the criteria of Organization and Management and defining what is acceptable in each, the question of delegation and presidential control, and the issue of the political climate in which the president works. Moreover, this case illuminates the problem of distinguishing short-term and long-term effects of presidential actions. In short, it exposes the incompleteness of the conventional view of presidential evaluation.

That view lacks a clear idea of what are acceptable means for fulfilling the various criteria of performance, as well as a notion of just what role the president is to play in the conduct of foreign affairs. The conventional wisdom clearly implies close presidential control of foreign affairs, and not merely delegation of his authority. It is less clear on the question of legitimate means to various ends, but this issue must be addressed. As this case has shown, certain means, whether legitimate or not, may have adverse effects in the long run.

This is not another issue excluded from the conventional wisdom. Fulfillment of the various evaluative criteria may work in the short run, but have adverse effects in the long run. Although it is beyond the scope of this study to assess all the long-term effects of presidential action in this case (and others), it is important to note that there is a relevant distinction between the near term and the long term in presidential performance. Even if it is only to note that distinction, a set of standards for evaluating presidents ought to include a notion of the short-term versus long-term effects of performance.

At the same time, a revised view of presidential evaluation ought to include an appreciation of the political climate in which a president operates. In this case, strong sentiment in the Senate against the ABM and in support of some arms control effort was part of the domestic political climate. Nixon was able to take advantage of these sentiments, even when his handling of the SALT negotiations angered such senators as Fulbright and Jackson. He did not operate in a vacuum, and his performance in this case must be viewed in light of the particular political climate.

The president's success in this case can be explained by the way in which his performance, according to the several evaluative standards, took advantage of an auspicious political climate. His methods of Organization, Management, and Policy design, as discussed above, were not what is predicted by the conventional wisdom. Nor were they necessarily effective in the long term, or even in the short term (if Smith is correct about a better treaty). Nevertheless, in this case, they enabled Nixon to exercise the control he wanted, via the Kissinger-NSC system, and thus allowed him to present the Senate with his SALT agreement. At the same time, he lured many members of the Senate with requests for more money for defense and by coopting the Jackson amendment, thus welding a coalition composed of "hawks" and anti-ABM "doves." Although, as noted above, Nixon's performance was in many ways mixed as regards fulfilling the various criteria, it was effective enough to gain passage of the agreement in the Senate.

In this respect, the case of SALT I demonstrates how even a mediocre performance according to the standards of the conventional wisdom may take advantage of a favorable political climate and yield success. To that extent, this case illuminates some important shortcomings of the conventional wisdom.

SALT II

The 1979 agreements between the United States and the Soviet Union, collectively known as SALT II, represent a presidential failure in the category of non-crisis security issues.[84] For, while President Carter was able to conclude an arms agreement with the Soviet Union he was unable to obtain its approval by the U.S. Senate. Although the agreement was submitted to the Senate in June 1979, by January 1980 the president was forced to ask that consideration of it be indefinitely delayed, and the agreement was never approved by that body. Carter did not achieve his goal of ratifying a second SALT agreement, a fact he later described as "the most profound disappointment of my Presidency."[85] It is the purpose of this study to examine the reasons behind his failure.[86]

Summary of Case

Upon his inauguration in January 1977, Jimmy Carter inherited a SALT treaty and continuing arms negotiations from his predecessors Nixon and Ford, as well as a provisional agreement on a second arms accord signed in the Soviet city of Vladivostok in 1974.[87] He and his advisors were determined, however, to alter the U.S. approach to SALT, and to break clearly with the Nixon-Ford-Kissinger handling of this issue.[88] They wanted a different approach to SALT, which they felt had been given insufficient priority under previous administrations.[89] Under Carter's predecessors, SALT was considered part of an overall political strategy for dealing with the Soviet Union. Carter and his advisors felt that this approach prevented real progress toward arms reductions, so they were determined to give SALT high status unrelated to other developments in Soviet-U.S. relations.[90]

To this end, Carter pronounced a firm commitment to reaching a new SALT agreement and also began a process of policy review with his administration. Publicly, he announced to the press that he was anxious to conclude an arms agreement with the Soviet Union, which would initially involve limits on strategic weapons and later reductions in superpower arsenals.[91] At the same time, within his administration he ordered a review of SALT and the U.S. strategic program. This review culminated in the drafting of Presidential Review Memorandum 2 (PRM 2), which outlined the president's options in the matter of SALT.[92]

From this beginning, Carter's pursuit of a second SALT agreement proceeded along two tracks: (1) negotiations with the Soviet Union, toward the goal of reaching an agreement; and, (2) efforts to gain approval of the treaty in the Senate. The negotiations took place over a period of two years, from March 1977 until June 1979, in both publicly announced diplomatic sessions between Secretary of State Cyrus Vance and Soviet Foreign Minister Andrei Gromyko, and in secret meetings between Vance and Soviet Ambassador Anatoly Dobrynin. These negotiations concluded at a summit meeting in Vienna in 1979, at which President Carter and Soviet President Brezhnev signed the SALT agreement.

This track of U.S.-Soviet negotiations was marked by difficulties. At the initial meeting in Moscow in March 1977, Secretary Vance presented the Carter administration's ambitious proposal for an agreement to include significant reductions in Soviet and U.S. strategic arsenals. This offer, as well as less ambitious variations on it, were rebuffed by the Soviet negotiators. The "March '77 proposals," as they were called, came to stand for an ambitious but disastrous attempt to shift the momentum of the SALT talks, and the Carter attempt at an aggressive approach to SALT seemed a failure.

Following this setback, President Carter sought to recover progress in SALT by moving to a less public, and less confrontational, style of bargaining. He thus authorized Vance to revive the Backchannel through Ambassador

Dobrynin which Henry Kissinger had used to negotiate the SALT I agreement.[93] Soon, this channel was being used to advance negotiations that stalled in the more visible world of diplomacy. The Channel did not, however, take on the same role in negotiations as it had had under Kissinger, when it was used to conduct a round of secret negotiations outside of regular diplomatic channels, but was employed as part of the main track of U.S.-Soviet negotiations conducted through Vance under Carter's direction.

Carter employed Vance as his key negotiator for SALT II, and the secretary met with Soviet Foreign Minister Gromyko on several occasions over the next two years: Geneva (May 1977), Washington (September 1977), Moscow again (April 1978), New York and Washington again (September-October 1978), Moscow again (October 1978), and Geneva once again (December 1978). SALT talks were also conducted by ACDA Director Paul Warnke and his Soviet counterparts, but the main avenue for negotiations was through Vance and either Gromyko or Dobrynin. These high-level talks slowly yielded the progress that the Carter administration badly wanted in the matter of SALT, as Vance and his contacts worked out the agreement which would become SALT II. Progress was difficult because of the complexity and intractability of such issues as cruise missiles, the Soviet Backfire bomber, and telemetry encryption.[94] After the December 1978 meeting in Geneva, Vance continued negotiations with the Soviet leaders via Dobrynin. These final Backchannel discussions brought SALT II to the stage where a summit meeting could be arranged for June 1979, at which Presidents Carter and Brezhnev could sign the new agreement.

The final SALT II agreement was not what Carter had originally sought, for it lacked the deep cuts in strategic weapons embodied in the March 1977 proposals. Nevertheless, it was not, as Carter once feared, an agreement which was only "validating Vladivostok."[95] SALT II thus carried the mark of Jimmy Carter.

From the order for PRM 2 to the Vienna summit of 1979, President Carter was closely involved in the effort to reach a second SALT agreement. As noted above, he was determined to break with the legacy of Nixon, Ford, and Kissinger, and was thus instrumental in shaping not only the March 1977 proposals but the ultimate SALT II agreement as well. While he acted primarily through Secretary

Vance in dealing with the Soviet Union, the president maintained close watch over both the process of negotiations and the substance of the developing agreement. Moreover, he occasionally intervened in the negotiation process himself, as in September 1977 when he met with Gromyko to discuss limits on air-launched cruise missiles and MIRVed missiles.[96] Throughout the two years of negotiations toward SALT II, the president supervised the entire U.S. effort. In this effort, he was initially frustrated but ultimately successful.

The same cannot be said for the second track of endeavors to achieve a ratifiable SALT II agreement. This track contained the Carter administration's efforts to secure approval of SALT II in the Senate, and began even before the ill-fated March 1977 proposals were presented to the Soviet negotiators in Moscow. These efforts, while broadly aimed at American public opinion and the Senate in general, were focused on those security-minded senators who might be convinced that SALT II was acceptable if they could be persuaded that the agreement did not jeopardize national security. To that end, an intense lobbying effort was undertaken. In his memoirs, President Carter describes that campaign:

> The lobbying campaign we mounted throughout the nation made the Panama Canal treaties effort pale into relative insignificance. Thousands of speeches, news interviews, and private briefings were held. The personal and political interests of each senator were analyzed as we assessed the prospects of the ultimate vote for SALT II. It was obvious that we faced formidable opposition, but we had a chance if we and the Soviets could demonstrate good faith, and if there were no obstacles to Senate confidence in the Soviet leaders.[97]

As Nixon had done in the case of SALT I, Carter returned to Washington after signing SALT II and immediately addressed Congress on the need for the treaty.[98] This dramatic gesture was followed by the formation of a SALT Task Force, composed of Vice-President Mondale and key White House aides, designed to orchestrate the administration's lobbying efforts.[99] Lloyd Cutler, a Washington lawyer, joined the group and served as coordinator for the campaign to sell SALT II.[100] Zbigniew Brzezinski, the president's national security advisor and noted for his "hard-line" attitude regarding the Soviet Union, was tapped as the principal administration briefer on SALT.[101] In addition, there were several meetings with congressional leaders, some attended by the president himself, and a campaign to heighten public interest and support for the treaty.[102]

All these efforts were accompanied by a drive to reassure key senators of the administration's concern for U.S. security. The president thus proposed a 3 percent increase in defense spending for fiscal 1980,[103] largely in response to statements by Sam Nunn and other skeptics that they could accept SALT II but only as part of an overall program of increased defense spending and more effective competition with Soviet military advances.[104] Nunn, from Carter's home state of Georgia, was of particular concern to the administration, and the president devoted special attention to courting his support of SALT II. Indeed, Carter was able to moderate Nunn's criticism of the treaty by the proposal for defense increases and by a private promise of greater increases in the future.[105]

By the fall of 1979, these efforts seemed to be making some progress for Carter's lobbying effort, which fought to overcome a general impression among critics that the Carter administration was too weak in the area of U.S.-Soviet relations. All progress soon collapsed, however, in response to events that seemed to confirm the fears of these critics. The first of these events was the discovery of a Soviet military brigade in Cuba in August 1979, which President Carter had initially demanded removed and later dismissed as insignificant. This brigade, along with the Iranian hostage crisis in November, served to compound the feeling of U.S. weakness and Soviet strength.[106] Finally, the Soviet invasion of Afghanistan in December provided SALT II's critics with further evidence of Soviet aggressiveness, and the president now feared that the treaty would not be considered on its merits, but in the context of Soviet aggression.[107] With these events on the landscape, and the 1980 presidential primary season on the horizon, President Carter came to fear that SALT II would not pass the Senate. In January 1980, he asked that consideration of it be indefinitely suspended. Although he hoped it might be later approved, Carter failed to achieve ratification of his SALT II agreement.

Policy Direction and Design

The first criterion of the conventional wisdom relevant in this case is that of Policy direction and design. It helps to explain the outcome of this case, but not in a way predicted by the conventional wisdom. For the president generally met the requirements of this standard, albeit not completely by developing and communicating a clear direction for U.S. policy, but his design was rejected by the Senate in the course of events. While not superlative in his fulfillment of this standard, the president's performance was not ineffective.

It was clear from the beginning that Carter viewed SALT as of great importance to him and to the nation, and wanted to pursue arms control regardless of what else happened in foreign affairs. In the 1976 presidential campaign he had been particularly critical of Henry Kissinger and the linkage, because he believed that linkage subjected SALT to the vicissitudes of U.S.-Soviet relations. In his inaugural address he stated his hope that "nuclear weapons would be rid from the face of the earth,"[108] a sentiment he called his "most cherished hope" and more than rhetoric at his first meeting with his staff on the matter of SALT after taking office.[109] Later, at a SALT policy meeting on March 12, 1977, he told his senior aides that he sincerely desired "real arms control,"[110] meaning significant cuts in superpower arsenals, and did not want to live in the shadow of Kissinger's Vladivostok agreement.[111] He not only wanted a "fundamentally new kind of proposal"[112] from what had gone before, but he wanted to use SALT II to make serious progress toward controlling superpower arms competition.[113] Carter believed the United States and the Soviet Union could recognize a mutual interest in "real arms control," and that there was thus no sense to the Nixon-Kissinger view of SALT as part of "linkage."[114]

The president thus viewed SALT in what was almost diametric opposition to the Nixon-Kissinger approach: where they regarded arms control as a means to reward Soviet cooperation on other issues, Carter saw it as a preliminary condition on which better Soviet-U.S. relations would be based.[115] He regarded SALT as too important to be influenced by other issues,[116] and was intent on insulating it from other issues.[117]

In pursuit of these ends, the president moved to develop a clear design for U.S. policy in the matter of SALT.

He entered office with a broad idea of what he wanted to achieve in this area, specifically, substantial arms control and ultimately arms reductions.[118] He soon developed a detailed plan for reaching those goals. In the first three months of his administration, the president and his advisors worked to develop a clear design for SALT policy. The plan that emerged from these efforts called for "deep cuts" in the U.S. and Soviet strategic arsenals (below 2,000 delivery systems for each side, down from 2,400), and alternatives for the resolution of the complex cruise missile and Backfire bomber issues.[119] This plan not only formed the basis for the March 1977 proposals in Moscow, but also guided the U.S. negotiating position throughout the effort to conclude the SALT II agreement.

Armed with a plan for SALT, Carter set out to communicate it to the relevant parties: Congress, the American public, and the Soviet Union. He was, however, more successful in presenting his design to the Soviet leaders than to Congress and the American public. He met with congressional leaders to lobby for the need for a new SALT agreement, and likewise emphasized the importance of arms control in public speeches.[120] He was also in close contact with Senator Henry Jackson early in 1977, and with Senator Nunn and other legislators as well over the next three years. Yet, the president had not been completely successful in conveying his design to Congress and the public: he did not hide his design from these groups, but was less than effective in communicating it to them.[121]

At the same time, however, he was more effective at communicating his design to the Soviet leaders, through Vance and Brzezinski, and through his own contacts with Soviet officials. In January 1977, he began correspondence with Soviet Chairman Brezhnev, seeking to convey his views on SALT and other issues of Soviet-U.S. relations.[122] This correspondence would prove useful for the exchange of ideas and for providing Carter with a direct link to the Soviet leadership. That link was augmented by his meetings with Ambassador Dobrynin, the first of which occurred in February of that year. Moreover, the president met with Soviet Foreign Minister Gromyko late in 1977, and again in May and September 1978. More than merely expressing his ideas and goals to these officials, the president engaged in bargaining with them for an agreement.[123]

President Carter, then, met some of the requirements of this first criterion. He developed a design for U.S. policy in the matter of SALT, and used that design to guide the bargaining and policy making of U.S. negotiators. Moreover, he attempted to communicate that design to the relevant parties, but with mixed results. In doing so, he partially lived up to this standard but, despite that fulfillment, he encountered significant problems regarding the direction of policy.

Many senators did not accept the president's view of the importance of SALT. Rather, they continued to view Soviet-U.S. relations in terms of linkage. They would not accept his argument that SALT II was important regardless of other aspects of U.S.-Soviet relations. Some, such as Nunn and Henry Bellmon, were concerned about the overall superpower military balance, and pressed the president for increases in defense spending. Others regarded Soviet aggressiveness, as in Afghanistan, as linked to the issue of arms control, and indicated their opposition to the treaty because of it.[124]

This linkage rejected the president's carefully constructed design. Despite the fact that the president had produced and attempted to disseminate the policy design required of him, he was rebuffed. The conventional wisdom does not account for this reaction, except to say that the president was unable to convince the requisite number of senators of the logic of his argument.

Yet that does not deny the fact that President Carter met the requirements of this first criterion, particularly as it was relevant to his administration and the Soviet leaders, and in doing so met with defeat. According to the conventional wisdom, he should not have encountered this problem.

Here is where the conventional view needs refinement. It holds that one of the most important aspects of presidential performance is Policy direction, and implies that a clear and coherent policy design will greatly aid a president's cause. Yet Carter met with problems precisely because of his design, and not because of the lack of one. To say that his problem was therefore one of consensus-building is to obscure the relevance of this case to the conventional wisdom: whatever the importance of the president's consensus-building efforts to the outcome of this case, it is still true that he met this first criterion and encounted defeat partly because of doing so. While the conventional wisdom does not suggest that fulfillment of a single criterion will lead to success, it also does not imply that fulfillment of one of the evaluative criteria will invite trouble. In short, the conventional view suggests that Carter's performance in this regard should have enhanced his chances of success.

Nevertheless, the president faced a Senate in which enough members believed in linkage, and not in the president's view of SALT, to make approval problematic. While this attitude arose for a variety of reasons, to be examined below, it indicates that the conventional wisdom is flawed as a guide to presidential evaluation. For that wisdom does not predict the problems which may arise for a president because of the fulfillment of one standard or another. It also excludes the context in which presidential performance occurs.

Consensus-building

The second criterion of relevance to this case is that of Consensus-building, but not because of any significant failings in the president's performance. Rather, Carter's record in this regard, as with Policy direction, was mixed: while not inept, it was less than a complete fulfillment of the requirements of this standard. This mix of achievement and failure can be seen throughout the course of the two years of this case.

Before the SALT II agreement was signed in Vienna, the president began to work toward its acceptance by the Senate. In the early stages of his efforts to shape SALT policy, he engaged in close consultation with Senator Henry Jackson. A leading critic of SALT I and the Vladivostok agreement, Jackson was invited to advise the president on his ideas for future arms control agreements.[125] Not only did this consultation involve meetings between Jackson and the president, but it also resulted in a lengthy memorandum from the senator outlining his views on SALT.[126] Carter gave this paper special attention, and had his staff issue a detailed response to it.[127] In his preliminary deliberations on SALT, then, the president worked closely with a key Senate figure.

Later, as the SALT negotiations dragged out over the next two years, the president acted to consult with a larger group of senators on the developing agreement. By the autumn of 1978, administration efforts had reached the point at which ". . . each of the 100 senators was kept up-to-date on the negotiations and got all the briefings by all the experts they wanted."[128] There was no shortage of contact between the Senate and the administration, yet in this period of pretreaty lobbying the administration did not dominate the SALT debate.

For, as many of SALT II's extragovernmental supporters complained, the president and his administration were not very forceful in presenting the case for SALT in this period. While the president did publicly address his goals in this area, he allowed the opposition to dominate the public debate over SALT. As National Journal noted immediately after the signing of the SALT II agreement, ". . . the Senate will begin the SALT debate with proponents somewhat on the defensive. In large part, they attribute this to the fact that opponents controlled the public debate and news stories while the treaty was being negotiated."[129] Landon Butler, a White House aide in the president's SALT Working Group, explained this opposition dominance as the result of a general administration effort not to appear too desperate to reach an agreement with the Soviets, and thus refrain from too much public comment.[130] Nevertheless, this effort lost ground for the president in' consensus-building.

Here is where Policy direction and Consensus-building touch. Part of the president's overall scheme for negotiating SALT involved maintaining a general public and congressional interest in it, while at the same time avoiding the appearance of overeagerness which might spur Soviet intransigence. Yet in adopting this strategy, and so fulfilling the criterion of Policy design, Carter and his administration encountered setbacks in their efforts at Consensus-building. The conventional wisdom, to the extent that it suggests interaction effects among criteria, does not suggest that fulfillment of one standard will hinder fulfillment of another.

At the same time, the administration invited further trouble by a tactical mistake in pretreaty dealings with the Senate. In August 1978, Carter's arms control director Paul Warnke stated that the administration might submit SALT II to Congress as an executive agreement, thus requiring the approval of a simple majority in each house rather than the two-thirds vote necessary for treaty approval in the Senate.[131] Not only did this move compound the anti-SALT feelings of several skeptical senators, whom

104 / THE PRESIDENT AND FOREIGN AFFAIRS

it was designed to circumvent, but it angered pro-SALT senators as well. This second group was furious at the administration's attempt to ride roughshod over the prerogatives of the Senate, and the fact that this plan was not abandoned for several months left a lingering skepticism about the president's judgment among many senators.[132]

This mixed record in the period before the Vienna summit was somewhat improved after the signing of the agreement, as the president mounted an elaborate lobbying campaign to build support for the treaty. This campaign began with a speech before Congress immediately upon Carter's return from Vienna, in which he argued for SALT II as beneficial to both security and arms control.[133] Coming as it did on the evening of his return from Vienna, this action, as Nixon's SALT I address had done, gave the SALT II campaign a dramatic opening.

This campaign was aimed at three groups: the Senate, journalists, and the general public. The congressional lobbying effort was directed by presidential assistants Frank Moore and Robert Beckel, and involved a host of briefings and meetings with individual senators, as well as testimony at congressional hearings. Moreover, there were continual meetings between the president, Defense Secretary Harold Brown, Vance, and Brzezinski, and key senators who might influence the vote on the treaty.[134] Vice-President Mondale also devoted considerable effort to lobbying his former Senate colleagues. Gerald Rafshoon supervised the public relations aspects of the campaign, with particular attention to reaching reporters and editorial writers.[135] Anne Wexler, the White House public liaison aide, directed an "outreach" campaign designed to educate the public about SALT issues.[136] All of these efforts were coordinated by Lloyd Cutler and Hamilton Jordan, the president's chief political aide.[137]

This campaign helped to broaden support for the treaty. Opinion polls in the summer and autumn of 1979 indicated general public support for arms control, but no clear position on the treaty itself.[138] The administration worked to translate this general support into pressure on the Senate, and to develop a strong case for the treaty to sway undecided senators. Through the summer of 1979, all these efforts seemed to be making progress, as the president worked hard to influence the Senate.

In a particularly successful aspect of this consensus-building effort, Carter managed to gain the acquiescence of

Senator Nunn. Nunn had been skeptical about SALT II because of his larger concern about the state of U.S. defenses, so he was pressing the administration for a larger defense budget. As a member of the president's party and an expert on defense issues, Nunn exercised considerable influence over security issues in the Senate. The president not only responded to his requests with a proposal for a 3 percent increase in defense expenditures, but was also able to neutralize the effect of Nunn's potential opposition to the treaty. In a private meeting with Nunn on September 13, Carter warned the senator that Nunn's overt rejection of SALT II could kill the treaty and lead to the demise of the Carter presidency. At the same time, he also promised Nunn larger defense increases in the future.[139] While he did not demand the senator's support for the treaty, he asked that Nunn not lead the attack on the treaty and the administration. With this carrot-and-stick approach, the president was able to persuade the senator to help "stem the tide against SALT."[140]

Yet the president's influence was not unbounded. For he was continually pressed by treaty opponents on the links between SALT and other issues in Soviet-U.S. relations, and was unable to convince enough senators of his view that such links should not be forged. In particular, the administration was plagued with the issue of the Soviet brigade in Cuba, which became public knowledge in August 1979. The controversy that erupted over this issue originated from an unlikely source: Senator Frank Church. The chairman of the Senate Foreign Relations Committee and a strong advocate of arms control, Church was up for reelection in 1980 and harshly criticized in his home state for his liberal views on foreign policy. Seeking to demonstrate his "toughness" on Soviet activities, he demanded the removal of the brigade and placed the issue squarely between the president and approval of SALT II.[141] Treaty opponents then used Church's position against Carter. As National Journal reported, "'Church set the tone for the whole Senate,' a foreign relations aide said. 'As a supporter of SALT, when he announced the treaty was dead unless the troops were withdrawn, he pushed the opponents to even greater rhetorical heights.'"[142]

Faced with this linkage, the president sought to defuse the brigade issue in order to save the treaty. In October he addressed the nation on this controversy. Despite his assurances that the brigade presented no threat to the United States, he was haunted by an earlier statement he had made: ". . . we consider the presence of a Soviet combat brigade in Cuba to be a very serious matter and that this [sic] status quo is not acceptable."[143] As Carter noted in his memoirs, this remark was "interpreted as a promise to remove the brigade."[144] When that did not occur, confidence in the president deteriorated and suspicion of the Soviet Union increased.[145] The treaty was in trouble.

As the autumn of 1979 wore on, Carter sought to strengthen and expand his shaky pro-SALT coalition. But once again he fell victim to linkage when the Soviet Union invaded Afghanistan in December. The result was, as Brzezinski recalled, that "SALT disappeared from the U.S.-Soviet agenda. . . ."[146]

Although he was able to exercise considerable influence, as in the case of Nunn's acquiescence, and mounted a monumental campaign to sell SALT II to the Senate and the public, Carter's consensus-building efforts were mixed at best. For he was unable to overcome the linkages imposed on him by the Senate, and made some tactical mistakes along the way: the threat of the executive agreement and the inferential promise to remove the brigade.

Yet he did not fail in all aspects of this criterion. Indeed, not only was he astute enough to neutralize Nunn's opposition, but his "come from behind" lobbying effort brought many senators and a large segment of the public to support the treaty.[147] That he could not avoid linkage was not merely the result of poor skills as a consensus-builder, but of other factors which lay outside the conventional wisdom.

Other Criteria, Other Factors

As noted above, the president's performance as regards two of the four evaluative criteria was mixed. As for the other two standards, however, his performance was clear: he fulfilled the requirements of both Organization and Management.

Carter's organizational scheme for SALT served him well, for it implemented the sorts of procedures and structures he desired. Responsibility for SALT was vested in the Special Coordination Committee (SCC) of the National Security Council, which was chaired by the president's national security advisor and brought together the senior officials of the government for defense and foreign affairs.[148] This committee allowed all issues relevant to SALT to be discussed and debated in detail by the president's senior advisors, with all recommendations (and dissenting opinions) presented to the president in writing within 24 hours of each meeting.[149] The SCC deliberations were augmented by other meetings of key officials (Vance, Brzezinski, Brown, and whomever else the president called upon) with the president, who also studied the details of SALT issues on his own.[150]

With an effective organizational scheme established, the president engaged in a close and careful management of the SALT policy mechanisms. As his national security advisor describes the president's management:

> From April [1977] on, Carter came to commit an inordinate amount of time to the SALT effort. He would meet frequently with his key advisers on a Saturday morning, in sessions lasting sometimes as much as two or three hours. He carefully monitored the work of the SCC, which met with increasing frequency, and on which I would report to him the same day a given meeting was held. He would review carefully the instructions that I sent to Paul Warnke when he was negotiating in Geneva, or to Cy Vance when he was scheduled to meet with Dobrynin or with Gromyko. He would meet with the JCS in order to solicit their support, to reduce their concerns, and to give them a sense of genuine participation in the shaping and refining of our proposals. Last but not least, he also engaged himself in direct talks with Ambassador Dobrynin, a development which both Vance and I viewed with some apprehension. We felt it was unwise for the President to become, in effect, the principal negotiator, whereas he probably thought that the issue was too important to be left to Vance or me.[151]

In short, Carter fulfilled the requirements of Management and oversight.

Yet he was unable to achieve Senate approval of his treaty. Despite fulfillment of the criteria of Organization and Management, and partial fulfillment of Policy design and Consensus-building, the president was ultimately frustrated. It is clear that the conventional wisdom does not offer a complete explanation of this case.

Such an explanation can only be accomplished by reference to three factors not included among the conventional standards, each of which contributed to Carter's defeat. The first of these involves the substance of SALT II: the issues it encompassed were complex and difficult, and the time it took to resolve them delayed the agreement and undercut its support.

SALT II involved several difficult issues: cruise missiles, the Backfire bomber, ICBM fractionation, and telemetry encryption.[152] The cruise missile issue arose from U.S. superiority in cruise missile technology, which the Soviet Union was eager to limit. At the same time, the United States wanted to limit Soviet production of the intermediate-range Backfire bomber. A more difficult problem was telemetry encryption, which term refers to the coding of data broadcast from weapons undergoing tests. Uncoded data are essential to the verification of SALT II, but the Soviet Union was reluctant to discontinue its encoding practices. Finally, there was a dispute over the rules for counting each party's ICBM arsenals, which further complicated the negotiations. Considerable time was required to resolve these differences and, as Brzezinski notes, agreement between the two superpowers proceeded about as rapidly as could be expected.[153]

Resolution of these issues dragged the SALT II negotiations into the middle of 1979, by which time the opposition had had two years in which to dominate the public debate.[154] Moreover, some supporters of arms control, such as Senators George McGovern, William Proxmire, and Mark Hatfield, were growing frustrated by the delays in producing a treaty which to them was not even a "true step toward arms reductions."[155] While delay was not the sole factor in Carter's defeat, it made him more vulnerable to his critics and to arguments for linkage.

At the same time that the issues problem was confounding the president, so was the domestic political environment. This environment had three aspects in this case. First, Carter's overall political standing was poor. From the time of the signing of SALT II in June 1979 through the autumn of that year, his public approval rating hovered around 30 percent.[156] As George Edwards had demonstrated, presidential popularity is a significant factor in a president's ability to influence Congress.[157] Carter, with a low public standing and a history of trouble with Congress, lacked a substantial base of public support with which to pressure the Senate to accept SALT II. That he could influence Nunn is, in this light, significant.

The second aspect of the domestic political environment was Carter's relationship with Congress. Both generally and in the particular matter of arms control, Congress was not willing to quietly accede to presidential demands. In the wake of the Vietnam War and the Watergate scandal, Congress had shifted away from its traditional postwar role of accommodating presidential initiatives in foreign affairs.[158] It moved rapidly during the mid-1970s to a relationship characterized by "acrimony" between the branches, with Congress asserting its powers and prerogatives in this area.[159] Carter took office during this period of "congressional upheaval," and his relations with Congress were always difficult. Moreover, this general atmosphere of discord was particularly pronounced in the area of arms control, because many senators resented the way this issue had been handled by previous administrations. The legacy of Nixon, Ford, and Kissinger was one of guarding White House prerogatives in arms control, and the Senate, particularly Henry Jackson, was wary of compromises and concessions which Kissinger had made in SALT I and the Vladivostok agreement. At the same time, even proarms control senators were reluctant to trust the president, because they felt that SALT II was inadequate as an attempt to limit or reduce strategic arsenals. Both sides were wary of this or any president.

Indeed, SALT II was examined much more carefully than had been earlier agreements, and this wariness on the part of the Senate was beyond the control of the president. In the seven years since SALT I, the "congressional upheaval" of the mid-70s had occurred, and many senators had grown increasingly concerned about Soviet compliance with arms agreements, U.S. concessions, and the overall U.S.-Soviet military balance. The executive-congressional relationship in this period certainly contributed to the difficulties of SALT II.

Finally, the impact of the upcoming 1980 elections was felt in this case. Frank Church, a vocal advocate of arms control and an admirer of Fidel Castro, was facing defeat in his reelection bid because of his liberal voting record.[160] Anxious to rebut attacks on his reputation as a "dove," Church exacerbated the controversy over the Soviet brigade in Cuba. This controversy impaired the treaty's chances of passage, which the invasion of Afghanistan eliminated. At the same time, Senate Minority Leader Howard Baker, seeking to assuage conservative critics of his support for the Panama Canal treaties, and seeking the 1980 Republican presidential nomination, attacked the treaty.[161] He had previously been a supporter of arms control.

In the same way, the international environment of the late 1970s was a factor in the president's failure. Carter did not create that environment, although many saw him as too weak to oppose it. During the Carter administration, the United States seemed to be continually reminded of the limits of its power: in the Panama Canal, which was indefensible against attack;[162] in Iran, which expelled the American presence; in Cuba, where the Soviet brigade could not be removed;[163] and, in Afghanistan, where the Soviet Union had flexed its muscle. The Carter administration often appeared weak in its response to these challenges, such as in protesting the Soviet brigade in Cuba and then discounting the matter, but it could not control all of this international environment. In this environment, SALT II was seen by many as further evidence of the decline of U.S. power.

When these international, congressional, and popular factors combined, they presented a formidable obstacle to the ratification of SALT II. No matter how effectively Carter may have worked at Consensus-building or Policy design, he would still have encountered a wary Senate, an inhospitable international environment, and the limits of his own political power. That he was less than superlative at meeting the standards of Policy design and Consensus-building insured his failure to achieve ratification of SALT II. Even without the 1980 political season looming on the horizon, SALT II was in trouble. It was surrounded by a difficult environment, and Carter's performance in relation to two aspects of the evaluative consensus did not help ease its passage through the Senate.

This combination of factors thus explains Carter's failure in the case of SALT II, but in relation to this analysis, it also helps to point out a serious deficiency of the conventional wisdom. For that wisdom does not include a sensitivity to the broader political environment in which a president operates. Rather, in establishing the relationship between fulfillment of the four evaluative criteria and success, it implies that a president has control over that larger environment. Even if Jimmy Carter had easily met all the requirements of the conventional wisdom's criteria for this case, he still would have been plagued not only with his own political standing, but with a congressional and international environment unconducive to the success of SALT II. For the conventional wisdom implies that fulfillment of the evaluative criteria strongly influences success, <u>if</u> all other things are equal. Of course, they are not, and it is extremely relevant to note that all other things are not equal. The larger political environment influences the outcome of a case.

Conclusion

The case of SALT II is important because of what it illuminates about the conventional wisdom: even if a president fulfills, or partially fulfills, its evaluative criteria, he may still fail. For the conventional wisdom does not include an understanding of the larger environment in which the president operates. Jimmy Carter's performance according to the conventional standards was not flawless, but neither was it inept. His defeat can be explained only by reference to factors outside of the conventional view.

To that extent, this case demonstrates the incompleteness and misdirection of the conventional standards for presidential evaluation. While they touch on important issues in presidential performance, they do not touch on the only issues relevant to that performance. Moreover, as the conventional wisdom stands, it suggests a degree of presidential control over events which is clearly exaggerated, perhaps dangerously so. For the president, whatever his resources, has finite powers, and thus cannot be expected to dictate all outcomes.

NOTES

1. The SALT I agreements consisted of (1) a treaty on Anti-Ballistic Missile systems; (2) an Interim Agreement

on the limitation of strategic offensive arms; (3) a protocol to the Interim Agreement, clarifying that agreement's particulars; and, (4) a set of common understandings regarding the ABM Treaty and Interim Agreement. The acronym SALT, when used alone, refers to the Strategic Arms Limitation Talks, i.e., negotiations. "SALT I" has come to stand for the 1972 agreements.

2. Roger Labrie, ed., SALT Hand Book (Washington, D.C.: American Enterprise Institute, 1979), pp. 3-8.

3. Quoted in John Newhouse, Cold Dawn: The Story of SALT (New York: Holt, Rinehart, and Winston, 1973), p. 134.

4. Labrie, SALT Hand Book, p. 8, and Henry Kissinger, White House Years (Boston: Little, Brown, 1979), p. 126.

5. Kissinger, White House Years, pp. 126-27.

6. Ibid.

7. Ibid.

8. For a thorough discussion of these talks, see Newhouse, Cold Dawn, pp. 166-72, or Gerard Smith, Doubletalk (Garden City, N.Y.: Doubleday, 1980), pp. 222-46.

9. Kissinger, White House Years, p. 138. Also known as "The Backchannel." "The Channel" is Kissinger's term.

10. Ibid., pp. 139-47, 819; Smith, Doubletalk, pp. 222-46.

11. Kissinger, White House Years, p. 139.

12. Ibid., pp. 141-43.

13. Ibid., pp. 821 passim.

14. Ibid., p. 208.

15. MIRV is a system for mounting several independently targeted nuclear warheads on a single missile.

16. See Kissinger, White House Years, p. 198, and chap. 7 in general. See also Labrie, SALT Hand Book, **pp.** 4-6; and, Tad Szulc, The Illusion of Peace (New York: Viking Press, 1978), pp. 419-26.

17. Szulc, Illusion of Peace, p. 422, and Kissinger, White House Years, p. 799.

18. Kissinger, White House Years, pp. 805-23; Szulc, Illusion of Peace, pp. 419-26.

19. Kissinger, White House Years, p. 820.

20. Ibid., p. 1,128.

21. See Alan Platt, The U.S. Senate and Strategic Arms Policy: 1969-1977 (Boulder, Colo.: Westview Press, 1978), p. 19.

Non-Crisis Security Issues / 113

22. See ibid., p. 22. Interview with John Lehman, July 27, 1976, and with Richard Perle, July 28, 1976.
23. Ibid., pp. 22-23.
24. Ibid., p. 24.
25. Ibid.
26. See Szulc, Illusion of Peace, p. 595, and ibid.
27. "Throw-weight: Maximum weight of nuclear warheads and reentry vehicles which can be carried on the powered stages of a ballistic missile. Throw-weight determines the number and size of warheads which can be carried by a missile." Defined in Smith, Doubletalk, p. 537.
28. Public Law 92-448, Approving the Interim Agreement, 30 September 1972, as amended by Senator Jackson; text in Labrie, SALT Hand Book, pp. 141-43.
29. Kissinger, White House Years, p. 126.
30. Ibid., pp. 126-30.
31. Ibid., pp. 128-30.
32. Ibid., p. 118.
33. Szulc, Illusion of Peace, p. 11.
34. Nixon letter quoted in Kissinger, White House Years, pp. 135-36.
35. Ibid., pp. 132-33.
36. See ibid., pp. 135-38.
37. Ibid., p. 143.
38. Ibid.
39. Arms Control and Disarmament Agency.
40. See Platt, Senate and Arms Policy, pp. 23-24, 26-28.
41. Ibid., p. 65.
42. For a lengthier discussion of the Nixon-Kissinger relationship, on which much has been written, see William Safire, Before the Fall (New York: Belmont Tower Books, 1975), pp. 164-65, and chap. 5 in general; Henry Kissinger, Years of Upheaval (Boston: Little, Brown, 1982), pp. 1,183-87; and, Newhouse, Cold Dawn, pp. 144-46. Each contains revealing information about the relations between a president and his chief foreign policy advisor.
43. Except one, which was not significant.
44. Newhouse, Cold Dawn, p. 162.
45. Ibid.
46. See Szulc, Illusion of Peace, pp. 12-18, 22-23; and Newhouse, Cold Dawn, p. 162.
47. See Newhouse, Cold Dawn, p. 159, and Szulc, Illusion of Peace, p. 74. See also Kissinger, White House Years, pp. 146-50.

114 / THE PRESIDENT AND FOREIGN AFFAIRS

48. Kissinger, White House Years, p. 138.
49. Ibid.
50. Kissinger's admirers and critics all recognize his phenomenal abilities as a thinker and as a political actor. For various views on Kissinger, see Marvin and Bernard Kalb, Kissinger (Boston: Little, Brown, 1974); John P. Leacacos, "Kissinger's Apparat," Foreign Policy 5 (Winter 1971-72):3-27; and, Safire, Before the Fall, chap. 5.
51. See Safire, Before the Fall, chap. 5: "Henry the K."
52. An interesting comparison is the case of Kennedy's handling of the Bay of Pigs crisis. As Garry Wills notes, Kennedy allowed Bissell to engage in "guerrilla" management in planning and executing the operation, circumventing all regular channels. For this practice, Wills had strong words of condemnation, and ultimately blames the disaster at the Bay of Pigs on Kennedy's obsession with proving that he and his antiorganizational colleagues could govern more boldly than the "bureaucratic" Eisenhower. See Wills, The Kennedy Imprisonment (Boston: Little, Brown, 1981).
53. Zbigniew Brzezinski, Power and Principle (New York: Farrar, Straus, and Giroux, 1983), p. 8.
54. See Kissinger, White House Years, p. 118.
55. Ibid., p. 148.
56. Ibid., p. 813.
57. Ibid., pp. 132, 1,135.
58. Ibid., p. 148.
59. Smith, Doubletalk, p. 466.
60. Kissinger, White House Years, p. 806.
61. See ibid., p. 118.
62. Newhouse, Cold Dawn, p. 159; Szulc, Illusion of Peace, p. 74; Kissinger, White House Years, pp. 148-49.
63. Kissinger, White House Years, pp. 148-49.
64. See ibid.
65. Ibid., p. 813.
66. Ibid., p. 209.
67. For a sampling, see Kissinger, White House Years, pp. 130-34.
68. See Platt, Senate and Arms Policy, pp. 9-10; and Kissinger, White House Years, pp. 199-215.
69. See Platt, Senate and Arms Policy, p. 10.
70. Kissinger, White House Years, p. 126.
71. Newhouse, Cold Dawn, pp. 159-62.
72. See Kissinger, White House Years, pp. 126, 132.

73. See ibid., chap. 7.
74. Ibid., p. 813. See also Newhouse, Cold Dawn, p. 205.
75. Platt, Senate and Arms Policy, p. 22.
76. Ibid., pp. 22-24.
77. Ibid., p. 24.
78. Congressional Quarterly Almanac, 1972 (Washington, D.C.: Congressional Quarterly, 1972), pp. 623-24. See also ibid., p. 26.
79. Quoted in Labrie, SALT Hand Book, pp. 141-43; Congressional Quarterly, p. 635. See also Platt, Senate and Arms Policy, pp. 26-27.
80. Platt, Senate and Arms Policy, p. 281.
81. See Kissinger, White House Years, chap. 7.
82. See Platt, Senate and Arms Policy, pp. 29-31.
83. Ibid., p. 1.
84. SALT II consists of: a treaty on the limitation of strategic offensive arms; a protocol to the treaty, which outlines common agreements and understandings regarding the text of the treaty; a memorandum of understanding on the establishment of a data base for monitoring compliance with the treaty; a joint statement of principles and basic guidelines for subsequent negotiations; and, a statement by the Soviet government on the Soviet Backfire bomber.
85. Jimmy Carter, Keeping Faith (New York: Bantam Books, 1982), p. 265.
86. The treaty is still observed by both the United States and the Soviet Union, but the failure to obtain Senate approval is interpreted as a defeat for Carter. Moreover, President Reagan, while abiding by the terms of the treaty, has repudiated the document. See Carter, Keeping Faith, p. 265; Brzezinski, Power and Principle, pp. 344-53.
87. See text of Joint U.S.-Soviet Communique, 24 November 1974, in Labrie, SALT Hand Book, pp. 281-83.
88. Ibid., p. 381; Strobe Talbott, Endgame (New York: Harper and Row, 1979), pp. 48-50.
89. Talbott, Endgame, pp. 48-50; Strobe Talbott, "U.S.-Soviet Relations: From Bad to Worse," in America and the World 1979, ed. William P. Bundy, Foreign Affairs 58 (New York: Pergamon Press, 1980), p. 522; and, Labrie, SALT Hand Book, pp. 281-83.
90. Talbott, "U.S.-Soviet Relations," p. 522.
91. Talbott, Endgame, p. 42.
92. Ibid., p. 44.
93. See ibid., pp. 78-80.

94. For a discussion of these issues, see Brzezinski, Power and Principle, pp. 322, 328-29.
95. See Talbott, Endgame, chaps. 1, 2.
96. MIRV: Multiple Independently-Targeted Re-entry Vehicle, i.e., a missile with several independent warheads. On Carter-Gromyko meeting, see Brzezinski, Power and Principle, pp. 169-71; Carter, Keeping Faith, pp. 220-21; Talbott, Endgame, pp. 127-28.
97. Carter, Keeping Faith, p. 262.
98. Congressional Quarterly Weekly Report, June 23, 1979, p. 1,221.
99. Ibid., p. 1,213.
100. Brzezinski, Power and Principle, p. 344.
101. Ibid., p. 344.
102. Ibid.
103. Congressional Quarterly Weekly Report, August 18, 1979, p. 1,738.
104. Ibid., July 28, 1979, p. 1,547.
105. Brzezinski, Power and Principle, p. 345.
106. While the Iranian hostage crisis did not involve the Soviet Union in any direct sense, it did serve to emphasize the limits of U.S. power at a time when the Soviet Union seemed to be exercising its muscle.
107. See Carter, Keeping Faith, pp. 263-65; Brzezinski, Power and Principle, pp. 352-53.
108. Talbott, Endgame, p. 39; see also Carter, Keeping Faith, p. 215.
109. Talbott, Endgame, p. 43.
110. Ibid., p. 58; Brzezinski, Power and Principle, p. 157.
111. Talbott, Endgame, p. 58.
112. Ibid.
113. Labrie, SALT Hand Book, p. 381; see also Brzezinski, Power and Principle, pp. 146-50.
114. See Labrie, SALT Hand Book, p. 382; Brzezinski, Power and Principle, p. 151.
115. Brzezinski, Power and Principle, p. 151.
116. See Talbott, "U.S.-Soviet Relations," p. 534.
117. See Carter, Keeping Faith, p. 214.
118. Brzezinski, Power and Principle, p. 147.
119. Ibid., p. 159.
120. Carter, Keeping Faith, p. 224.
121. Richard E. Cohen, "SALT II--Selling the Treaty to the Senate," National Journal, June 16, 1979, p. 995.
122. Brzezinski, Power and Principle, p. 151.

123. Ibid.
124. Carter, Keeping Faith, p. 264; Brzezinski, Power and Principle, pp. 352-53.
125. Talbott, Endgame, p. 52.
126. Ibid.
127. Ibid.
128. Congressional Quarterly Weekly Report, June 23, 1979, p. 1,213.
129. Cohen, "SALT II," p. 994.
130. Ibid.
131. Congressional Quarterly Weekly Report, June 16, 1979, p. 1,183. The act that established the ACDA also specified that congressional approval is required for all arms control agreements to which the United States is a party. Consequently, if an arms agreement is embodied in an executive agreement, it must still be approved by a majority vote of both houses of Congress.
132. Ibid.
133. Ibid., pp. 1,225-27; Carter, Keeping Faith, pp. 261-62.
134. Cohen, "SALT II," pp. 996-97.
135. Ibid.
136. Ibid.
137. Ibid.; Congressional Quarterly Weekly Report, p. 1,183.
138. William J. Lanouette, "The Senate's SALT II Debate Hinges on 'Extraneous' Issues," National Journal, September 22, 1979, p. 1,564.
139. Brzezinski, Power and Principle, p. 345.
140. Ibid.
141. Ibid., pp. 347-51; Carter, Keeping Faith, pp. 263-64; Lanouette, "Senate's SALT II Debate," pp. 1,565-66.
142. Lanouette, "Senate's SALT II Debate," p. 1,566.
143. Carter, Keeping Faith, pp. 263-64.
144. Ibid.
145. Brzezinski, Power and Principle, p. 352.
146. Ibid., p. 353.
147. After Afghanistan, much of this support evaporated. Nevertheless, before that event, Carter's efforts to build a consensus were generally effective.
148. For a discussion of the SCC, see Brzezinski, Power and Principle, pp. 57-67.
149. Ibid., p. 325.
150. See ibid., p. 166.
151. Ibid.

152. For a discussion of these issues, see Brzezinski, Power and Principle, pp. 325-31.
153. Ibid.
154. See note 129 above.
155. Cohen, "SALT II," p. 996.
156. The Gallup Opinion Index, October/November 1980, pp. 6-7.
157. George Edwards, Presidential Influence in Congress (San Francisco: W. H. Freeman, 1980).
158. Charles W. Kegley, Jr. and Eugene R. Wittkopf, American Foreign Policy: Pattern and Process, 2nd ed. (New York: St. Martin's Press, 1982), pp. 396-98.
159. Ibid.
160. Carter, Keeping Faith, p. 262.
161. Cohen, "SALT II," p. 997.
162. The irony of the Panama Canal treaties for the case of Carter and SALT II is that the very argument that made the treaties acceptable to the Senate, i.e., the indefensibility of the Canal regardless of whether the United States held it or not, helped Carter to gain passage of the treaties but contributed to the general impression of U.S. weakness later on.
163. In this case, the fact that the president loudly protested the presence of the brigade, and then later tried to minimize the brigade's importance when it was not removed, only served to underline the feeling of weakness on Carter's part.

4

NON-CRISIS NON-SECURITY ISSUES

While foreign policy in the modern era has been dominated by questions of defense and security, and while presidents have been forced to deal with an apparently endless series of crises, the foreign affairs presidency involves a host of other issues as well. These non-security issues range from matters of international trade and foreign aid to questions of normal diplomacy and international cultural relations.

Although it appears at first that these non-security issues are merely a collection of disparate topics, they do share a common fate: all the issues in this category tend to receive less attention than crises or security problems. Nevertheless, they are part of the vast realm of foreign affairs and many are growing in importance. Moreover, these issues are relevant to presidential evaluation in that some president-watchers follow issues in this category quite closely: e.g., the U.S. business and labor communities pay careful attention to international trade policy.

Indeed, trade policy is a useful topic for focusing on presidential performance in this area. For foreign trade has been a perennial issue in U.S. politics, from the long debates over the tariff in the nineteenth and early twentieth centuries, to current debates over quotas, domestic-content legislation, industrial policy, and foreign competition. Trade is one of those "intermestic" issues that, like energy and immigration issues, links foreign policy and the U.S. economy, and which promises to grow increasingly important as time passes.

Therefore, it is not only important that attention be paid to non-security issues of foreign affairs, but that evaluative standards in this area be thoughtful and realistic. For, as the United States moves into its future, presidents will be forced to devote even more time and effort to dealing with problems arising in this area.

The cases of the Trade Expansion Act of 1962 and the Trade Act of 1970 present an excellent contrast for studying presidential performance in the area of non-security issues. For in the first case, President Kennedy was able to obtain passage of a major initiative in U.S. international trade policy, which broadened presidential authority to negotiate tariff reductions and inaugurated the Kennedy Round in international trade negotiations. In the second case, President Nixon attempted to renew provisions of the Kennedy act which had lapsed, and to move toward further efforts at free trade while remaining sensitive to the situation of U.S. industry. In this effort he met defeat. The following case studies will examine the reasons behind Kennedy's success and Nixon's failure, and examine the relevance of those cases for refining the evaluative criteria of the conventional wisdom.

THE TRADE EXPANSION ACT OF 1962

The case of the Trade Expansion Act of 1962 represents a presidential success in the area of non-crisis non-security issues, for in this case President Kennedy was able to achieve his goal of passage of a new international trade bill that included broad presidential authority to negotiate tariff reductions. Not only did he achieve enactment of this bill, but he did so with what one observer called "resounding margins" in both houses of Congress.[1]

Summary of Case

The issue of international trade was high on the new president's list of economic priorities for his administration.[2] Moreover, it was an issue of national concern. For the Kennedy administration faced an important juncture in U.S. trade relations: the Reciprocal Trade Agreements Act of 1934 was due to expire in June 1962,[3] and the sagging U.S. economy was confronted by the Common External Tariff and growing power of the European Common Market.[4] Furthermore, in July 1961, Britain announced its intention of seeking membership in the Common Market, which if accepted would both broaden the reach of the Common External Tariff and increase the power of the Common Market.[5] This changing international environment presented a challenge to U.S. trade policy, for the advance of European integration presented both a threat and an opportunity to the United States. The Common Market, particularly with British membership, meant an extremely broad area of preferential treatment for member nations, from which the United States was excluded.[6] At the same time, however, if the United States could negotiate lower tariffs with the EEC,[7] it could offset the additional trade preferences the Common Market would gain from British membership, avoid a trade war with Europe and strengthen Western unity, and help boost the U.S. economy through freer trade with Europe.[8]

Even before the British announcement in July 1961, Kennedy was aware of the issue of trade, due to the upcoming expiration of the 1934 law. During his pre-inaugural transition, he commissioned George Ball, a Washington lawyer active in the antiprotectionist Committee for a National Trade Policy (CNTP),[9] to head a Task Force on Trade Policy which examined the issue and provided the president-elect with recommendations for new trade legislation to strengthen presidential tariff-negotiating authority.[10]

This attention to the trade issue continued in the first year of the Kennedy administration, as the demise of the 1934 law drew nearer. In essence, the complex question of trade policy revolved around two fundamental issues: the scope and timing of trade legislation. In the first matter, the question was whether to request merely an extension with minor modifications of the old act, as had been done in the past, or to proceed with a new initiative involving more presidential authority for a longer period to accomplish more ambitious goals.[11] On this question, Kennedy's advisors generally favored a new law, but there was concern about opposition from certain industries and their friends in Congress. The textile industry, for example, would be particularly concerned about the adverse effects of freer trade.[12]

Because of this concern, Kennedy's advisors were divided over the second issue, that of timing. Here, the question was whether to pursue the new legislation in 1962, or to wait for the new Congress in 1963. Ball, who was a firm advocate of a new bill, counseled delay until 1963 in order to avoid clashing with protectionists during an election year.[13] In this advice he was opposed by Howard Petersen, the president's special assistant for trade policy and a member of the Ball Task Force,[14] and Lawrence O'Brien, the president's chief lobbyist on Capitol Hill.[15] O'Brien and Petersen argued that a new trade bill would receive a warm welcome from some highly influential members of Congress, including Hale Boggs and Wilbur Mills. Indeed, Boggs, House Democratic Whip and member of the Joint Economic Committee, announced in October 1961 that his recent tour of Europe had convinced him that the existing act would be "grossly ineffective in dealing with the common economic front of Western Europe."[16] Mills, the powerful chairman of the House Ways and Means Committee,[17] had indicated to O'Brien that he favored a new act,[18] which served as further evidence in favor of proceeding in 1962. For his own part, the president was inclined toward an act in 1962, so that, as Sorensen noted, "the fierce fight which even a simple extension would entail might better be fought, and fought only once, for a wholly new trade instrument."[19]

Nevertheless, because of the possible strength of opposition to such an act, the president proceeded to test the political climate with a few trial balloons. On November 1, 1961, George Ball, now undersecretary of state for economic affairs, addressed the National Foreign Trade Council on the changes in the international economy wrought by the establishment of the Common Market, and argued that existing trade legislation was inadequate for meeting this challenge.[20] He avoided specific policy recommendations, but read a message from the president that concluded "It is essential that we have new tools to deal with the problems of international trade in a new and challenging world."[21] One week later, the president spoke at a news conference of the need for new tools to deal with the challenge of the Common Market.[22] In early December, Hale Boggs began hearings in the Subcommittee on Foreign Economic Policy of the Joint Economic Committee. At these hearings, former Secretary of State Christian Herter and former Undersecretary of State William Clayton testified on the inadequacy of the old Reciprocal Trade Act.[23] Finally, on November 29 the president announced that a tentative decision had been made to seek wider authority to cut tariffs, and on December 6 and 7 made a pair of speeches to the National Association of Manufacturers and the AFL-CIO advocating changes in U.S. trade law. He told the Manufacturers Association:

> The Reciprocal Trade Agreements Act expires in June of next year. It must not be simply renewed--it must be replaced. If the West is to take the initiative in the economic arena, if the United States is to keep pace with the revolutionary changes which are taking place throughout the world, if our exports are to retain and expand their position in the world market, then we need a new and bold instrument of American trade policy.[24]

After all these efforts were favorably received, a final decision was made to proceed with a new trade initiative in 1962.[25]

The Trade Expansion Act of 1962 was sent to Congress on January 25, 1962, where it was introduced into the House by Representative Wilbur Mills.[26] It contained tariff-cutting authority for the president, with particular provisions for dealing with the Common Market. Second, it included safeguards for domestic industries and labor adversely affected by tariff reductions, with provision for "adjustment assistance" to injured parties. By expanding presidential authority to cut tariffs and simplifying the procedures for so, the bill authorized a major change in U.S. trade policy.[27]

The new trade proposal now received highest priority, and the administration immediately mobilized for the campaign to sell the bill to Congress. All lobbying efforts on the bill's behalf were directed from the White House, where Petersen's trade policy staff was increased in size to handle the responsibility of orchestrating the congressional and public campaigns.[28] Petersen and congressional liaison O'Brien were equipped, inter alia, with promotional literature for the campaign, including separate brochures for each state.[29] Moreover, the White House assisted free-trade groups in their efforts on behalf of the bill, using the Committee for a National Trade Policy as coordinator for and liaison with other free-trade groups.[30]

The administration's chief spokesman for the bill was Commerce Secretary Luther Hodges, who was chosen over Ball because the undersecretary was unpopular with many members of Congress.[31] Hodges, former governor of North Carolina with friends in the textile industry, led the assault on Capitol Hill. Exhaustive hearings were held before the House Ways and Means and Senate Finance Committees, and Hodges led the lengthy parade of administration and friendly private spokesmen who testified in favor of the bill.

The president himself was also involved in this campaign. The Trade Expansion Act had received special attention in the 1962 State of the Union message, and after submitting the bill Kennedy predicted in a news conference that it would receive bipartisan support.[32] In May, he and four members of his cabinet participated in a day-long conference of 1,200 people representing 100 organizations supporting the bill.[33] He also hammered on the need for the bill in his speeches.

Beyond these efforts at lobbying, the Kennedy administration also acted to undercut opposition to the bill. It focused special attention on the textile and timber industries, but also worked on other groups as well. Textiles and timber were particularly threatened by adverse effects of reduced tariffs, so Kennedy announced a six-point plan to help the lumber industry and raised tariffs on carpets and glass.[34] Soon, support from the textile industry and legislators from affected states was forthcoming.[35]

At the same time, undercutting opposition meant acceding to congressional demands to modify the structure of executive authority for conducting trade negotiations. First, to alleviate congressional concerns that the State Department, which had previously been the agency with primary responsibility for trade negotiations, gave insufficient attention to the domestic impact of trade liberalization, Kennedy accepted Wilbur Mills's proposal for a Special Trade Representative, to be located in the executive office of the president.[36] This official would lead the U.S. delegation in all international trade negotiations, and was called upon to consult with Congress on such matters. Second, to minimize congressional concerns about misuse of the broader negotiating authority given to the president under this act, the president accepted a provision whereby two members (not of the same party) of each house would be accredited as members of the U.S. trade delegations.[37] Finally, the president accepted an amendment to make it easier for Congress to override a presidential decision on the use of the "escape clause" in the bill.[38]

With these concessions by the president, to both Congress and industry opponents, the bill was able to pass into law. Wilbur Mills's handling of the bill in the House prevented attachment of a series of protectionist amendments, and in the Senate the bill avoided any serious changes.[39] The only amendment to the administration bill forced by Congress over presidential objections forbade the granting of most-favored-nation status to Communist nations, a provision Kennedy had sought but could live without.[40]

The House passed the Trade Expansion Act on June 28, 1962, by a vote of 198 to 125.[41] Three months later, on September 19, the Senate passed the bill by a vote of 78 to 8. On October 11, the president signed the Trade Expansion Act in a ceremony at the White House, calling it ". . . the most important international piece of legislation, I think, affecting economics since the Marshall Plan. It marks a decisive point for the future of our economy, for our relations with our friends and allies, and for the prospects of free institutions and free societies everywhere."[42]

Policy Direction and Design

The first criterion of the conventional wisdom relevant to this case is that of Policy direction and design. For it was President Kennedy's skill in meeting the requirements of this standard which contributed to his success in this case.

Specifically, the president met the requirements of this criterion for articulating not only a direction in which he wanted national policy to go, but he also integrated this policy into a larger national policy scheme and explained how the Trade Expansion Act fit that design. To do this, he outlined his policy direction both within his administration and outside of it.

As noted above, Kennedy knew that trade was an issue which demanded attention. Not only was the 1934 act nearing expiration, but the changes in the international economy wrought by the Common Market meant that this matter would have to be confronted soon. Accordingly, the president made it a high priority for economic policy, along with the recession and the balance of payments, which he listed in his first State of the Union message.[43] His attention to the issue would grow over the next year, as events progressed, until the Trade Expansion Act was labeled the highest legislative priority of 1962.[44]

Kennedy's view of the trade issue was essentially a political one. While he understood the economic reasons for the trade bill, he tended to view it as a political device to revive and strengthen the Atlantic alliance of the United States and Western Europe. As his senior aide, Theodore Sorensen, noted in this regard, "The President was never intimately interested, in my opinion, in the economics of trade, certainly not as much as he was interested in the politics of trade."[45] The president was keenly interested in strengthening the alliance, and understood trade as an important part of the overall trans-Atlantic relationship, for "the concept of a unified democratic Europe as part of a freely trading Atlantic community had been a basic element of Kennedy's world strategy."[46] This strategy included a ". . . vision of North America and Western Europe happily joined by policies and institutions in common pursuit of economic expansion and military defense."[47]

This vision would be an important part of the policy design that the president laid out in proposing the trade act, for it reflected his goals and also provided a clear picture of how the bill fit into his larger foreign policy scheme. He would use it in communicating his policy direction to his administration, Congress, the nation, and America's allies.

The president communicated his intentions to his administration through two key figures: George Ball and Howard Petersen. The two had served together on the pre-inaugural Task Force on Trade Policy, and recommended to the president an initiative for new trade legislation. Ball became undersecretary of state, and Petersen special assistant to the president. Together, the two dominated the administration's trade policy deliberations. Indeed, it was Petersen who was responsible for drafting the new legislation.[48]

Within the administration, it was not particularly difficult for the president to convey his design. Not only did he use Ball and Petersen, two firm advocates of free trade, as his chief aides on this issue, but he also kept responsibility for drafting the new legislation in Petersen's White House office.

Outside the administration, Kennedy conveyed his policy design to Congress and the nation, and indirectly to European allies, through an intense lobbying program. The bill's introduction to Congress was preceded by statements from Ball, former Secretary of State Herter, former trade administrator Clayton, and the president himself, on the need for "a new and bold instrument of American trade policy."[49] Later, in sending the bill to Congress on January 25, 1962, the president outlined "five fundamentally new and sweeping developments" that justified a new trade law: the growth of the Common Market; growing pressures on the balance of payments; the need to accelerate economic growth; the Communist aid and trade offensive; and the need to expand trade with Japan and developing nations.[50]

The five points outlined in the president's message that would be repeated and reemphasized throughout the campaign to pass the Trade Expansion Acts, clearly tied the bill to the larger aspirations of Kennedy's foreign policy, and, indeed, his presidency: strengthening the Western alliance, standing up to the Communist threat, improving the balance of payments and economic growth, and expanding U.S. trade with the whole world.[51] Attentive to his interest in the political aspects of trade, the president clearly identified the bill with U.S. leadership of the Free World:

> At rare moments in the life of this nation an opportunity comes along to fashion out of the confusion of current events a clear and bold action to show the world what we stand for. Such an opportunity is before us now. This bill, by enabling us to strike a bargain with the Common Market, will "strike a blow" for freedom.[52]

With such words the president articulated both his intentions in the matter of the Trade Expansion Act and the act's role in his larger design for U.S. policy. By doing so, and by drafting the new bill in the White House he fulfilled the demands for Policy direction, and even contributed toward the effort at Consensus-building which passage of the bill entailed. For the stress in Kennedy's campaign for the bill on its benefits to other economic issues, and to the strength of the anti-Communist alliance, helped to make the bill more appealing to Congress and the public.[53] It was, he said, more than a trade bill, it was a blow for freedom.

In this way, Kennedy used clear Policy direction to explain exactly what he wanted, in the substance of the bill, and why it was important. Clarifying these issues also helped in the drive for a consensus, thus illuminating a link between the criteria of the conventional wisdom.

A further link between these standards can be seen in the use of Ball and Petersen. For the president's use of them not only helped to identify his Policy direction, but it is linked to the criterion of Organization and staffing as well. By skillful organization and staffing, i.e., selection of the two men and assignment to them of chief responsibility for the bill to Petersen, the president facilitated the advancement of his policy design. The links between issues of the common wisdom, mentioned elsewhere, are important here as well.

Organization and Staffing

As noted in the previous section, President Kennedy's performance as regards the criterion of Organization and staffing helps to explain his success in this case. While not the single most important element of that success, this criterion was important to it.

First, skillful use of Ball and Petersen helped the president to maintain control over the trade issue within his administration. Rather than using the State Department as the chief agency for handling trade issues, as had been done in the past, Kennedy established in the White House the special assistant for trade policy. This organizational move increased his ability to direct events in the drive for a new trade bill, both in its inception and in the campaign for its passage.

Beyond these actions, which have also been discussed above, the president carefully chose his chief spokesman for the administration's lobbying of Congress. Luther Hodges, the secretary of commerce, had close connections with the key interest group of concern to the administration: the textile industry.[54] Moreover, Hodges was popular in Congress, a distinction that George Ball did not share.[55] The selection of Hodges as chief spokesman increased the chances of the bill's success by demonstrating an administration attentiveness to the concerns of the textile industry and the business community in general.

Therefore, by employing particular individuals in sensitive positions, i.e., effective staffing, and by centralizing authority over the trade initiative in the White House, the president met the requirements of the criterion of Organization and staffing.[56] In doing so, he contributed to his own ultimate success in this case.

Management and Oversight

The president's performance as regards the third criterion of the conventional wisdom also helps to explain his success in this case. For in his Management and oversight of the trade initiative he moved closer to achieving passage of the Trade Expansion Act.

In terms of Management and oversight, this case occurred in two stages. The first was the decision stage, lasting from the transition period to the submission of the new act to Congress. The second stage, that of selling the bill, began even before the bill's submission in January 1962.

The president managed the decision stage carefully. Before his inauguration he had the Ball Task Force look into the issue of trade policy, and it offered him assessments of that issue independent of the State and Commerce departments' bureaucracies. Indeed, Ball and Petersen each offered the president individual memoranda containing their policy recommendations, and there was disagreement between them on exactly how to proceed. On the one hand, Ball favored a new trade act, to be introduced to Congress in 1963.[57] Petersen, however, counseled renewal of the 1934 act, to be undertaken immediately.[58]

Kennedy leaned toward a new act with wider presidential authority because such an act would be consistent with his larger goals. Nevertheless, he only wanted to propose such an act if he thought it might pass Congress, since he knew that even a renewal of the existing act would involve a difficult struggle.[59] Accordingly, he consulted with Lawrence O'Brien, his congressional liaison, on the probable reception a new act would receive in Congress. O'Brien, encouraged by a favorable response from Wilbur Mills, advised the president that a new act could pass in

1962.[60] This advice, combined with Hale Boggs's call for a new act in the near future, helped convince Kennedy that he could succeed.

Even with this encouragement, Kennedy remained cautious. Through the months of November and December 1961, he floated several trial balloons--the Ball speech to the National Foreign Trade Council, presidential press conference remarks, speeches before labor and business groups. In taking all these precautions, the president was examining not only the question of good policy but of how his policy would be received by the various interests and parties to which it would be relevant.

In this way, President Kennedy moved through the stages of the decision process, consulting a variety of sources on the likely course of action. Moreover, in testing the political climate of labor and business, he was also allowing the relevant values and interests affected by this policy to be considered. Finally, by announcing in December 1961 a tentative decision to pursue a new trade act, he was leaving the door open to reconsideration of his decision should this initiative be rebuffed. Not only were all these actions politically savvy, but they facilitated an effective decision process as well.

Once the decision was made, the president exercised oversight of the administration of that decision. Petersen, now in the White House, had come around to favoring a new act for which he was now responsible. By keeping the drafting of the bill in the executive office, Kennedy was able to effectively oversee implementation of his decision.

In the second stage of this case, the president also fulfilled the requirements of the Management and oversight criterion. This stage began in 1961 when Petersen became the special assistant for trade policy. Not only did this action facilitate presidential oversight of the bill's drafting, but it provided the president with a means for directing the campaign on the bill's behalf. That campaign was run from the White House, through Petersen's enlarged staff and O'Brien's lobbying efforts. Not only was the administration's effort directed from there, but nongovernment groups supporting the bill were as well. Petersen's office maintained close contact with the Committee for a National Trade Policy,[61] which coordinated the efforts of several free-trade groups.[62] In this way, the president could oversee the entire effort in support of the bill.

In these two stages, Kennedy exercised effective management and oversight by moving carefully through the decision process and then using a White House deputy to facilitate his oversight. In doing so, he made it much more likely that he would achieve his goal of a new act, for he skillfully cleared the way for such an act and then insured that his plans were implemented. Management and oversight alone cannot explain the president's success, but they do help to explain how he heightened his chances for that success.

Consensus-building

The final criterion of the conventional wisdom, Consensus-building, also helps to explain the president's success in this case, although like the other factors addressed in this study it does not stand alone. For Kennedy's work at building a coalition in support of his trade initiative, while it met the requirements of this standard, could not have overcome all odds to achieve the bill's passage.

In this case, consensus-building had three facets. The first of these was the intense lobbying effort of the administration and various free-trade groups, much of which has been described above.[63] There were speeches by the president and other administration officials, press conference statements, testimony before the Senate Finance and House Ways and Means committees,[64] a special presidential message to Congress,[65] meetings with congressional leaders and members, and special lobbying efforts by O'Brien and Petersen.

Indeed, with the Trade Expansion Act as Kennedy's top legislative priority for 1962, administration lobbyists went all-out to sell the bill.[66] They were equipped with literature demonstrating the benefits of the bill to each state,[67] and legislators from states likely to be adversely affected were carefully courted.[68] While coordinating the efforts of several free-trade groups through the Committee for a National Trade Policy, the White House also carefully cultivated important legislative leaders. It already had the highly significant support of Wilbur Mills, but was able to obtain backing from Senate Finance Committee Chairman Harry Byrd and the powerful Senator Robert Kerr (who was also on the Finance Committee).

These efforts were built around two themes that the president and his lobbyists stressed. First, they focused on the economic benefits that would accrue from passage of the act: greater exports, coping with the Common Market, and rectifying the balance of payments deficit. On this last point, the bill's virtues were greatly oversold. The president had been warned that the act would probably not affect the balance of payments to any significant degree, but he continued to press the point. For the promise of a better balance for the United States was an appealing selling point for the bill.[69] At the same time, the administration also focused on noneconomic advantages of the act--to strengthen Western unity, and thus provide a more solid West with which to confront the Communists. The bill would "strike a blow" for freedom. With these arguments in tandem, economic growth and Western unity, Kennedy and his administration made their case for the new law.

All of this lobbying, both public and private, contributed to the success of the Trade Expansion Act. But it was not the only aspect of Kennedy's consensus-building, which also included a strategy of undercutting opposition and one of accommodating Congress.

Undercutting opposition was an important part of the Kennedy strategy, and perhaps a crucial one as well. For the bill was opposed by some powerful interests, particularly the textile and timber industries. The president sought to mollify these industries with assistance programs that were designed to silence their complaints about adverse effects of freer trade. This effort began even before the bill was submitted to Congress, when on May 2, 1961, the president announced a seven-point program to aid the textile industry. This plan promised negotiations leading to voluntary export restraints and greater access for foreign textiles to the Common Market.[70] A seventeen-nation textile conference was held later that year, and in February 1962 an agreement was reached that lived up (at least in part) to Kennnedy's promises.[71] Moreover, in March the president announced a tariff increase on carpets and glass, to protect them from imports.[72] As a result of both these actions, on March 31, 1962, the American Cotton Manufacturers Institute, the major cotton textile group, endorsed the Trade Expansion Act.[73] As for the lumber industry, which also felt threatened by the bill, the president offered it a six-point program of aid that included preferential procurement of U.S. timber by the Defense Department and an export agreement with Canada.[74]

By these actions, and by the bill's promise of "adjustment assistance" to other affected businesses or labor, the president was able to significantly undercut opposition to his trade initiative. He coopted the support of his strongest opponents with aid programs, and thus eased the way for the success of his congressional lobbying efforts.

The final aspect of the president's consensus-building was accommodation to congressional concerns about the broad scope of executive power provided for in the bill. These concerns reflected an uneasiness in Congress over the history of trade negotiations and policy, which many legislators felt was one of executive action with insufficient attention to the views of Congress or congressional constituencies. Specifically, there was concern that the State Department, which had been responsible for trade negotiations in the past, paid far too little attention to the domestic impact of trade negotiations because it pursued only foreign policy goals.[75] Likewise, members of Congress were upset that a presidential refusal to invoke the escape clause (i.e., raise tariffs on affected products and "escape" a tariff reduction agreement) was too difficult to overturn, since it required a two-thirds vote in each house.[76] In order to deal with these concerns, the Senate Finance and House Ways and Means committees insisted on changes in the administration bill. First, responsibility for trade negotiations would be vested in a special trade representative, to be located in the executive office of the president. This officer would be expected to consult with Congress on trade issues, and would also chair a new interagency Trade Information Committee.[77] Second, two members of each house of Congress (from different parties) would be accredited to the U.S. delegation to international trade negotiations.[78] Finally, override of a presidential "escape clause" decision would now be accomplished by a simple majority vote in each House.[79]

The president openly supported these changes, because they decreased congressional fears about the expansion of executive power. He opposed, however, a congressional insistence that most-favored-nation status be withheld from all Communist countries. While the Senate was willing to give the president the authority to grant such status, the House prevailed in conference.[80] Despite his opposition to this provision, Kennedy was unwilling to veto the bill because of it and ultimately accepted it.

Therefore, by accommodation to congressional demands, of which only the prohibition on most-favored-nation status altered the substance of the bill, the president facilitated his ultimate success in this case. This accommodation, combined with the administration lobbying effort and the strategy of diffusing opposition, certainly help to explain Kennedy's success in the case of the Trade Expansion Act.

These three aspects of consensus-building not only aid in that explanation, but they point to links between the conventional wisdom's criteria as well. For the fact of effective direction and design helped in the effort at consensus-building, as the administration was able to justify the act in terms of larger foreign policy goals. Moreover, effective organization, staffing, and management also aided this effort to achieve consensus, for the president maintained White House control over the campaign for the bill and employed a deputy (Hodges) who was well received by oppositon groups and on Capitol Hill.

Nevertheless, the criteria of the conventional wisdom do not provide a complete explanation for Kennedy's success. For there are important factors outside of that consensus that complete the explanation of his victory.

Other Factors

The outcome of this case can be explained in part by the president's fulfillment of the four criteria of the conventional wisdom, so it does demonstrate the relevance of those standards to his success. Nevertheless, these criteria do not provide a complete explanation for the outcome of this case, which must include an understanding of the political environment in which it occurred.

That environment had two aspects: international and domestic. The international environment aided the president by giving a particular relevance to his call for new trade legislation. No matter what the success of the Common Market had been in the previous years, it was the 1961 British application for membership in that community that gave urgency to his request for broader powers in negotiating tariff reductions.[81] For the British application was a precipitous event--not only did it provide focus and support for all the existing reasons why a new law for freer trade was necessary, but it also demanded U.S. response before too long. It presented both a threat and an opportunity: at that time, British membership in the EEC was expected to be quickly followed by that of several other European nations, so the British announcement heralded a wide expansion of the Common Market.[82] On the one hand, such an expansion, because it excluded the United States from this European trade preference area, threatened to spark a trans-Atlantic trade war. At the same time, however, if the United States could negotiate tariff reductions with the Common Market, conflict could be avoided and Western unity enhanced.

It was this event that made the president's case a compelling one. While the administration bill, as drafted by Petersen, was eventually structured to respond to the challenge of a larger Common Market, interest in new legislation predated the British announcement. Not only had George Ball recommended a new act in his Task Force memorandum, but his appointment as undersecretary of state can be attributed to his views on trade.[83] As for the president, he was keenly interested in strengthening the ties of the Western alliance, and concerned about dealing with trade barriers that made that difficult.[84] The British application precipitated both the decision to pursue a new act and helped make the case for it. Without that event, whatever the other reasons for a new law, Kennedy's case for broader power would have been much less compelling.[85]

Accordingly, the international economic environment of 1961-62 must be factored into a complete explanation of Kennedy's success.[86] At the same time, the domestic environment is also relevant.

The domestic political environment of this case had two facets, friendly congressional leadership and the attitude of U.S. business and labor communities. First, Kennedy's bill was likely to receive a favorable welcome from two important members of Congress, Wilbur Mills and Hale Boggs, no matter the effectiveness of the president's efforts at consensus-building. Boggs had independently called for new legislation in 1961, and Mills indicated to O'Brien that same year his receptiveness to a new bill. With this support, particularly that of the powerful Ways and Means Committee chairman, passage of the president's initiative was greatly facilitated.[87]

Beyond this support, the attitude of the business community was likewise significant. In this regard, the activities of the Committee for a National Trade Policy were particularly important. This committee, composed of executives from several large corporations and such other figures as George Ball and Charles Taft (brother of the late senator), had worked for years to promote the idea of freer trade with the U.S. business community. Throughout the 1950s, it waged a public relations war for freer trade, disseminating information and evidence in support of its cause and helping to coordinate the efforts of other like-minded groups.[88] It participated in the battle over the extension of the Reciprocal Trade Act in 1954-55, and maintained its publicity campaign after that. While it was not a powerful organization in the sense of being able to sway a large number of votes in Congress, it was effective in bringing many business leaders around to the cause of free trade.[89] Indeed, in their exhaustive study of American Business and Public Policy, Bauer, Pool, and Dexter traced the activities of the committee and concluded: "But for the basic changes in business attitudes generated in the 1950s [at the impetus of the committee], the Trade Expansion Act would not have passed in 1962, no matter what deals were made in its favor."[90] In sum, then, the committee helped to make Kennedy's domestic audience more receptive to his initiative.

Business and labor, then, largely supported the Kennedy bill, with the notable and temporary exceptions of the textile and timber industries.[91] The U.S. Chamber of Commerce, the National Association of Manufacturers, AFL-CIO, and even the American Cotton Manufacturers Institute all supported the bill. Had the domestic political environment been hostile to the very idea of free trade, the president would probably not have been able to sell the bill to Congress. The domestic attitude in favor of such an act could not be obtained overnight: it existed before President Kennedy took office.

In both its domestic and international aspects, then, the political environment certainly contributed to the president's success in this case. Indeed, the two facets complemented one another: the domestic attitude was receptive to a move toward freer trade, which the British application to the Common Market made more urgent. The political environment thus facilitated Kennedy's effort at consensus-building by providing an impetus for a new law and a domestic audience acceptant of such a proposal. It is a factor outside of the conventional wisdom and one that must be considered in order to explain the outcome of this case.

Conclusion

This case, as the case of SALT II, demonstrates the incompleteness of the conventional wisdom for explaining presidential success or failure. For that wisdom implies the ability of the president to control or influence all events and circumstances, yet it is obvious from this case that such an implication is erroneous. The president may benefit from factors outside the conventional wisdom, and take advantage of them, as Kennedy did in this case, or may be impeded by such factors. In either event, success or failure can only be explained by reference to factors external to the conventional wisdom.

THE TRADE ACT OF 1970

The case of the Trade Act of 1970 represents a clear presidential failure in the area of non-crisis non-security issues, for in this case President Nixon's attempt to achieve passage of his international trade proposals was frustrated in Congress. He was thus defeated in his first major initiative in the area of international trade policy, and it is the purpose of this case study to examine the reasons behind that failure.

Summary of Case

Richard Nixon had long been an advocate of freer international trade, but at the same time was sensitive to political pressures which moderated that view. In his 1968 campaign for the presidency, he had reaffirmed his commitment to free trade as a matter of principle, but cited textiles as a "special case" to be given special treatment.[92] The textile industry, concentrated in the South, had been hardest hit by Japanese competition, and Nixon sought to win southern votes by promising that aforementioned special treatment. Consequently, he stated in the campaign that he would take steps toward an expansion of free international trade, while at the same time clearly promising to do something about textile imports.[93]

The result of this combined pledge of free trade and help for textiles was the Trade Act of 1970,[94] sent to Congress on November 18 of that year.[95] The bill had three broad purposes: to reestablish presidential authority to reduce tariffs, which had lapsed in 1967,[96] and to grant the president the power to eliminate the American Selling Price (ASP) system of evaluating imports for calculation of duties;[97] liberalization of the current criteria for providing relief and assistance to industries, firms, and workers adversely affected by imports; and greater presidential authority to retaliate against unfair trade practices by other nations.[98] In general, it sought to enhance free trade by renewing the lapsed tariff-cutting authority of the 1962 Trade Expansion Act, modify and expand presidential control over trade barriers and retaliation to barriers, and protect domestic industry. In his accompanying message, the president said of the bill: "It is modest in scope, but significant in its impact."[99]

The bill was soon caught up in a whirl of protectionist trade proposals submitted to the Ninety-first Congress. Responding to a poor balance-of-trade and pressure from domestic interests, over 300 members of the House had introduced some sort of import quota legislation. The Ways and Means Committee had before it 59 bills related to steel imports, 47 to textiles, 40 to dairy imports, 24 to footwear, and 55 that authorized the president to set ceilings on imports threatening U.S. industries.[100] Of great importance was the fact that among this crowd was Wilbur Mills, chairman of the committee and long an advocate of free trade. At the administration's request he introduced a textile-import quota bill, although he preferred adjustment assistance as a means for coping with the adverse effects of trade on domestic industry.[101]

The Mills bill was part of an overall strategy for dealing with the complex problem of trade--by dealing with an issue closely related to the Nixon trade proposal. That issue was an administration effort to negotiate a voluntary agreement with Japan to reduce textile exports by that country, which the Mills bill was intended to facilitate. Honoring his campaign pledge, and interested in the 1970 congressional elections, Nixon sought an agreement with the Japanese in order to aid the domestic textile industry through Japanese restraint. In pursuit of this

Non-Crisis Non-Security Issues / 139

goal, the administration conducted extensive negotiations with Japanese officials. These efforts were both public, in talks conducted by either Commerce Secretary Maurice Stans or presidential assistant Peter Flanigan,[102] and private, in Backchannel discussions between presidential assistant Henry Kissinger and an emissary of the Japanese prime minister.[103] In this strategy, a quota bill from the Ways and Means chairman was intended to put pressure on Japan to agree to self-restraint or face statutory quotas. Nevertheless, despite extensive secret and public discussions, meetings between President Nixon and Japanese Prime Minister Eisaku Sato, and Mills's proposal, no agreement was ever reached.[104]

Yet the Mills bill was not dead, for it was endorsed by the administration following the collapse of yet another effort to reach an agreement with Japan.[105] After a June 1970 meeting between Commerce Secretary Stans and his counterpart in the Japanese government once again failed to produce an agreement, the president "reluctantly" endorsed textile quota legislation as a further prod to Japanese concurrence.[106] He did not, however, endorse the bill's provision for footwear quotas, and explicitly stated his opposition to quotas on any items other than textiles.[107] Consequently, the administration supported both the original bill and the Mills bill.

After these actions, and exhaustive hearings conducted in May and June 1970, the Ways and Means Committee drafted a "clean bill" incorporating most of the Nixon proposals and the Mills quota on textiles, but also including provisions that the administration opposed.[108] Specifically, it retained oil import quotas, and implemented mandatory quotas for footwear and restrictions on imports of other products.[109] Furthermore, it failed to include two provisions that Nixon had proposed: tax advantages to U.S. exporting firms[110] and continuation of U.S. participation in the International Coffee Agreement.[111]

Nevertheless, the Nixon administration still hoped for ultimate success. It was counting on changes in the bill to be negotiated in a conference committee in the Senate. To that end, the president declared on July 20 that he would veto any law containing mandatory quotas on products other than textiles: "I would not be able to sign the bill because that would set off a trade war."[112] He feared that these other quotas would stimulate even more quotas, and so pressed his "special case" argument for textiles.[113] This veto threat, along with congressional lobbying and pressure on the Japanese to reach an export agreement, were all part of Nixon's effort to achieve passage of his trade proposals and avoid protectionist legislation.

On the floor of the House, Mills defended the "clean bill," quotas and all. He argued that these quotas were only temporary, and pointed to the failure of the Japanese to submit to a voluntary agreement as evidence of the need for new barriers. On November 19, 1970, Nixon suffered the first half of his defeat as the House passed the committee bill by a vote of 205 to 165.[114]

Meanwhile, in the Senate, trouble was mounting for the president. Aware that time was running out for the Ninety-first Congress, the Finance Committee began working on the trade bill in October. It held two days of hearings, and then the committee began its markup of the bill.[115] Unfortunately for the president, the committee was chaired by Senator Russell Long, who favored protection of U.S. industry because he felt that the United States was not being treated fairly by its trading partners.[116] Under Long's influence, the committee voted on October 13 to attach the trade bill to the Social Security Amendments Act of 1970, which had been passed by the House and was scheduled to go to the Senate floor before the end of the session. This action not only moved the bill closer to floor action, but nullified the threat of a presidential veto: the Finance Committee's version of the trade bill was not to the administration's liking, but that bill was now protected by the Social Security Act, to which the administration was already committed.[117]

The administration now made its last efforts to prevail. The White House stepped up efforts to reach an agreement with Japan, and drew attention to its consideration of a November 15 proposal by the Japanese government.[118] William Timmons, chief of congressional liaison in the White House, tried unsuccessfully to delay a vote on the bill in the House,[119] and was equally unsuccessful in trying to persuade Long to separate the trade bill from the Social Security bill.[120]

On November 20, the Finance Committee reported the combined trade and Social Security bill to the Senate. Not only was it caught up in the controversy over free trade and protection, but over welfare and provisions in the Social Security bill as well.[121] By the time the Senate convened on December 28 to consider the combined bill, the chance of agreement with Japan appeared dim once again, and the bill was wrapped in a tangle of parliamentary maneuvers. At the urging of Senator Long, the Senate deleted the trade provisions of the combined bill and thus killed what remained of the Trade Act of 1970.[122]

Policy Direction and Design

The first criterion of the conventional wisdom, that of Policy direction and design, helps to explain the outcome of this case, but not in a way predicted by the evaluative consensus. For President Nixon met the requirements of this first standard, yet in doing so helped to create problems for his efforts to achieve his goal.

From early on, the president made it clear what he wanted in this case: he wanted to uphold his long commitment to the principles of free trade, and at the same time to deal with the "special case" of the textiles industry. As noted above, in both his campaign statements and his initial message to Congress on trade policy, he laid out these combined goals.

Not only was this direction for trade policy articulated on its own, but also as part of a comprehensive design for foreign policy. In his 1970 foreign policy report to Congress, dubbed Nixon's "State of the World" message, the president made it clear how his trade policy fit into the larger aspects of his foreign policy:

> Peace has an economic dimension. In a world of independent states and interdependent economies, failure to collaborate is costly--in political as well as economic terms. Economic barriers block more than the free flow of goods and capital across national borders; they obstruct a more open world in which ideas and people, as well as goods and machinery, move among nations with maximum freedom.
> Good U.S. economic policy is good U.S. foreign policy. The pre-eminent role we play in the world gives us special responsibility. In the economic sphere, more than in almost any other area, what we do

> has a tremendous impact on the rest of the world. . . . Our continued support of a stronger world monetary system and freer trade is crucial to the expansion of world trade and investment on which the prosperity and development of most other countries depend.
>
> <u>Trade Policy</u>. Freer trade among all nations provides greater economic benefits for each nation. It minimizes potential frictions as well. . . .
>
> But growing interdependence also means greater reliance by each nation on all other nations. Each is increasingly exposed to its trading partners. In today's world, all major countries must pursue freer trade if each country is to do so. The principle of true reciprocity must lie at the heart of trade policy--as it lies at the heart of all foreign policy.[123]

With such words, he clearly linked trade policy to other issues, and integrated them into an overarching design.

This design was conveyed to the administration by the president's statements and through officials sympathetic to the president's views. The office of the special trade representative, traditionally pro-free trade, was given chief responsibility for drafting the Trade Act, but only through concurrence with the State and Commerce departments.[124] While the State Department was also traditionally in favor of free trade, Commerce Secretary Stans, who had the president's ear on this issue, adopted Nixon's view of combining free trade with the concerns of domestic industry.[125] Overall, the administration was clear on the president's design for policy, which it in turn conveyed to Congress.

This design was thus conveyed to Congress in messages such as the "State of the World" report and the trade policy proposals of 1969, and in extensive Nixon administration lobbying of Congress. The exhaustive hearings on the trade bill before the House Ways and Means Committee allowed the administration yet another opportunity to explain its goals and policy direction for international trade,[126] as did countless other informal contacts between administration lobbyists and Congress.[127] Moreover, the president made several public statements to reiterate the position he expressed more formally in written statements, as in a press conference on July 21, 1970.[128] On that occasion, he repeated his basic position of free trade and the "special case" of textiles, and threatened to veto mandatory quotas on other goods.[129]

Consequently, it is clear that the president met the requirements of the criterion of Policy direction and design. He stated a clear direction he intended for trade policy, integrated it into a comprehensive scheme, and conveyed it to the relevant parties. Yet he was unsuccessful. Indeed, it was his fulfillment of this criterion which helped to bring on some of the problems that led to his failure.

Specifically, the policy direction articulated by President Nixon invited trouble. He quite openly wedded free trade to defense of the textile industry, as per his campaign promise. Not only was this marriage of convenience a difficult one, but it generated problems for the president. Other domestic industries and members of Congress wanted to know why textiles should be a special case, when there were other industries or firms adversely affected by foreign competition. The shoe industry in particular had been affected by imports, and many members of the Ways and Means Committee felt it deserved as much protection as textiles.[130] Indeed, Mills argued in the House debate on the trade bill that the president had been either oversold by the textile industry or undersold by the shoe industry: "If there is a difference in the import problems of the textile industry and the shoe industry, it is that those of the shoe industry are greater."[131] Moreover, those members who had introduced bills to protect steel or dairy products or who, like Senator Long, wanted to see broader protection of U.S. industry, did not like the idea of the "special case" approach.

This problem illustrates an interesting shortcoming of the conventional wisdom. The president met all the requirements of the criterion of Policy direction and design, yet it was in doing so that he invited trouble. The conventional wisdom suggests nothing of this sort. Rather, it implies that it is the clear articulation and integration of policy which is important and good. It does not show sensitivity to the problems which a clear articulation might engender. Nor does it allow for the fact that a clear and comprehensive policy may not be popular or well received. In ignoring these counterproductive aspects of Policy design, the conventional wisdom demonstrates its shortcomings as a tool for evaluation.

Consensus-building

The other criterion of the conventional wisdom of particular relevance to this case is that of Consensus-building. For this standard, like that of Policy direction, presents an interesting problem for the conventional wisdom: while the president's performance according to the demands of this criterion may have contributed in part to his frustration in late 1970, it was not so inept as to explain the ultimate failure of Nixon's Trade Act. The president was never able to build a consensus in support of his proposals, but he was not without influence.

Nixon's relations with Congress were rocky. On October 11, 1969, he sent a formal message to each member admonishing Congress for failing to take speedier action on his legislative proposals.[132] On several other occasions, he publicly criticized the legislature for its handling of his legislative requests. While these acts did not foreclose any chance of his achieving passage of desired legislation, they certainly did not help to predispose Congress in Nixon's favor.

In the case of the Trade Act, the president's consensus-building efforts met with mixed results. As noted above, the awkward marriage of free trade and protection for textiles did not sit well with many members, so the structure of Nixon's proposals impeded his coalition-building effort. As the course of events progressed, and the president attempted to coerce Congress by the threat of a veto, he did not win additional supporters. Instead, as noted above, the Senate Finance Committee nullified the effect of that threat by attaching the trade bill to a Social Security bill.

Here is where the criteria of Policy direction and Consensus-building touch. The very shape of Nixon's policy design interfered with his work toward a consensus, and when he continued to press for the realization of that design, was further frustrated. Perhaps accommodation to the demands of some, such as Wilbur Mills and the shoe industry, would have offset the problem of the "special case," but Nixon seriously feared that giving in to broader protectionist legislation would usher in a trade war.[133] Adherence to his design brought Nixon trouble.

Nevertheless, the conduct of the Nixon consensus-building operation showed the administration's influence and skill. The effort to sell the trade bill to Congress was directed by the president's chief of congressional liaison, William Timmons, with help from Secretary Stans, Deputy Assistant Secretary of Commerce Stanley Nehmer, and Counsellor to the President Bryce Harlow.[134] This group was notable in its exclusion of Special Trade Representative Carl Gilbert. Gilbert, unpopular on Capitol Hill because of his career as a free trade advocate, had little influence in the Nixon administration and was seldom used in the assault on Congress to sell the trade bill.[135] On the other hand, Harlow, who had served in the Eisenhower administration, was the original chief of Nixon's congressional liaison operation and highly regarded on Capitol Hill.[136] Moreover, Stans also enjoyed a measure of good will in Congress, because he was seen as sensitive to the problems of U.S. industry.[137]

Not only was this team generally well received in Congress, but it was effective in certain aspects of its task as sales team for the trade bill. One particular incident which demonstrated that effectiveness was the battle over the repeal of the American Selling Price System (ASP) in the Ways and Means Committee. The president had made repeal of ASP an important part of his trade proposals, because ASP acted as a significant nontariff barrier to trade which both angered America's trading partners and embarrassed U.S. trade negotiators. Yet the committee initially voted to retain it. At that point, the sales team sprang into action.

Harlow, Stans, and Nehmer moved to have the committee's decision reversed by placing pressure on the committee through industry groups. They threatened these groups that the president would veto any trade bill that did not include a repeal of ASP, and thus kill quotas important to those groups. They contacted the textile, chemical, and oil industries, all of whom had stakes in quotas in the bill, and delivered the veto warning.[138] As Stans described their activities, "We called the chemical companies, and we told the textile industry very flatly that they would not get their quotas unless the President got a bill he could sign. We talked to both the mill people and the apparel people and let them know that they should go to work on it. . . . We did the same to a lesser extent with the oil companies."[139] As a result of this action, the chemical and textile industries agreed to accept repeal of the ASP, and on August 11 the Ways and Means Committee produced a trade bill authorizing the repeal.[140]

Nixon and his administration were thus able to exercise the requisite skills to build support for certain aspects of the trade proposals, but to achieve only a partial success in fulfilling this criterion. For the president was unable to see his proposals pass through Congress as he wanted them, and the bill that died in the Senate was already judged unsatisfactory to him.[141] As the preceding analysis demonstrates, while the Nixon relationship with Congress was not unblemished, it was not unworkable. Moreover, in this case the president employed as his agents such men as Harlow and Stans, who were not only well received on Capitol Hill, but skillful in their approach to dealing with Congress.

The record of President Nixon according to this criterion was thus mixed, and cannot explain the ultimate defeat of the Trade Act of 1969/70. For there was another factor that made it impossible for even such skillful lobbyists as Harlow, Timmons, Stans, and Nehmer to achieve a bill acceptable to the president and for the president to win passage of such a bill. That other factor lies outside of the conventional wisdom.

Other Criteria, Other Factors

The president's failure in this case does require analysis of a third factor outside of the conventional wisdom, but before that analysis is undertaken, it is important to note the role of the remaining criteria of the conventional wisdom in this case. For President Nixon's performance according to these standards seemed to make no real contribution to his defeat.

The first of these criteria is Organization and Staffing, and the president's performance in this area satisfied the requirements of this standard. First, his organizational system for handling trade policy enhanced his efforts to sell his proposals to Congress. Since trade policy was not accorded the same status by the president as matters of national security, his organizational scheme for this policy area was less centralized than it was for other aspects of foreign policy. The office of Special Trade

Representative (STR) was overshadowed by the National Security Council, which acquired a small staff of international economists to handle trade and economic issues, but this body did not exercise complete control over trade policy.[142] Rather, the president employed the STR's office, the NSC, and the State and Commerce departments all for handling this policy area.[143] Responsibility for drafting the Trade Act was vested in the STR, but on consultation with State and Commerce. The Secretary of Commerce conducted the negotiations with Japan, assisted in the Backchannel by Kissinger. The congressional lobbying effort has been discussed above, and worked effectively on those issues over which it had influence. In sum, then, organization did not contribute to Nixon's failure.

Nor did staffing contribute to it. All of the personnel employed in the congressional liaison operation were well received in Congress, and none of the administration presented any real problems for the president in this case. Indeed, Special Trade Representative Carl Gilbert was given a minor role in the lobbying operation, but because of his standing in Congress this was probably wise.

At the same time, the president fulfilled the requirements of the criterion of Management and oversight. He employed trusted deputies to carry out his policies and programs, such as Harlow, Stans, and Kissinger, and both the production of the trade proposals and the lobbying of Congress operated fairly smoothly. In one negative incident, on June 18, 1970, Assistant Secretary of Commerce Kenneth Davis sharply attacked the administration's trade proposals because he supported statutory quotas instead of voluntary agreements. The next day his remarks were repudiated by Secretary Stans, and he resigned from office.[144] Other than this single incident, which was so quickly resolved, there were no other apparent problems or failures of management. Attention has been drawn to the fact that there were differences of opinion within the Nixon administration over exactly how to proceed--Commerce favoring more protection, State and STR less of it--yet, except for the Davis incident, administration spokesmen presented a united front on the president's proposals.[145] There were no serious problems of management or oversight to disrupt the president's initiative.

Because these two criteria were fulfilled, and because the first two standards of the conventional wisdom cannot completely explain the outcome of the case, attention

148 / THE PRESIDENT AND FOREIGN AFFAIRS

must now be directed to a factor outside of that evaluative consensus. That factor is the force of domestic politics.

Congress was keenly sensitive to the force of domestic opposition to free trade in 1970, because it generally pushed in one direction and because of the congressional elections that year. As the National Journal noted in describing the domestic political scene that year:

> Pressure on Congress for protective legislation has been building for several years as increased imports, foreign barriers to U.S. exports and now rising unemployment have gradually won converts from the free trade camp.
>
> Almost 300 members of the House have introduced quota legislation of one sort or another in the 91st Congress--among them 20 or 25 members of the key Ways and Means Committee, which generally initiates all trade legislation.[146]

In the late 1950s and early 1960s, domestic political pressure for protection was much weaker. At the time of the 1962 Trade Expansion Act debate, much of the business community and the major labor organizations favored free trade, and there were no strong regional interests uniting to defeat the bill. In 1970, however, strong pressure for protection now dominated the political scene. It was this same sort of domestic political pressure that had moved candidate Richard Nixon to promise help for the southern textile industry, and was now pressing for protection of other industries as well.

Throughout the 1960s there was growing sentiment in the United States that, as Senator Long had expressed it, the United States was not being treated fairly by its trading partners. Increases in industrial and agricultural imports led to a declining balance of trade surplus, down from $7.1 billion in 1964 to $300 million in 1968 and $1.3 billion in 1969.[147] In this environment, with concern that unfair trade practices by the Japanese were injuring U.S. enterprise, even traditionally pro-free trade labor unions shifted to a protectionist stance.[148] The AFL-CIO called for import quotas to protect U.S. jobs, and the resulting labor-management coalition favoring protection created a powerful force, keenly felt in Congress.[149]

This general labor-management coalition was especially pronounced in certain areas and industries, such as the textile industry in the South and the shoe industry in Massachusetts, Pennsylvania, and New York.[150] The result was strong pressure on Congress to do something about imports.

The Nixon administration, honoring the president's campaign pledge and interested in wooing southern voters in the upcoming congressional elections, sought to help the textile industry through both the "special case" argument and negotiations with Japan for a voluntary export agreement. Yet the pressure on Congress came from more than just the textile industry--the shoe, dairy, steel, and oil industries were all clamoring for jobs, and both the South and New England were areas particularly concerned about imports. In the Ways and Means hearings in May and June 1970, there was a parade of witnesses from affected industries and labor groups asking for quotas and other forms of aid, to be implemented in response to the protectionist practices of Japan and other nations.[151] In the Senate, where similar pressure was likewise exerted, Senator Long was not alone in favoring protection. In such an atmosphere of domestic politics, the president's Trade Act was doomed.

Domestic politics, then, was a major factor in President Nixon's failure in this case. That factor, combined with the adverse effect of the president's policy design and his generally rocky relations with Congress, served to defeat his proposals and consign the Trade Act of 1969/70 to memory.

Conclusion

It is interesting to note in this case that President Nixon generally fulfilled the four criteria of the conventional wisdom, and yet he failed. He failed because fulfillment of one criterion actually backfired on him, and because a significant factor outside of the evaluative consensus defeated him. Both these facts point to the limitations of the conventional wisdom as a tool for presidential evaluation, in that it ignores a factor such as domestic politics and implies that any fulfillment of the policy design criterion is good. These limitations suggest areas in which the evaluative criteria must be revised.

NOTES

1. Lawrence F. O'Brien, No Final Victories (Garden City, N.Y.: Doubleday, 1974), p. 131.
2. After the recession and the balance of payments problem. See Robert A. Pastor, Congress and the Politics of U.S. Foreign Economic Policy 1929-1976 (Berkeley: University of California Press, 1980).
3. For a thorough discussion of the background of U.S. trade policy, see ibid. or Congressional Quarterly Weekly Report, January 5, 1962, p. 918.
4. See Pastor, Congress and Politics; CQ Weekly Report, January 5, 1962, p. 918; John Evans, The Kennedy Round in American Trade Policy (Cambridge, Mass.: Harvard University Press, 1971), chap. 7; and, Ernest H. Preeg, Traders and Diplomats (Washington, D.C.: The Brookings Institution, 1970), chap. 3.
5. Evans, The Kennedy Round, p. 137.
6. Ibid.
7. European Economic Community, the official name of the Common Market.
8. Evans, The Kennedy Round, pp. 137-38; and, Preeg, Traders and Diplomats, pp. 41-43.
9. Raymond Bauer, Ithiel deSola Pool, and Lewis Anthony Dexter, American Business and Public Policy, 2nd ed. (Chicago: Aldine-Atherton, 1972), p. 378.
10. On the Ball report, see Evans, The Kennedy Round, p. 139.
11. Pastor, Congressional Politics, p. 105; O'Brien, No Final Victories, p. 131; Preeg, Traders and Diplomats, p. 44.
12. Preeg, Traders and Diplomats, p. 44.
13. Arthur M. Schlesinger, A Thousand Days: John F. Kennedy in the White House (Greenwich, Conn: Fawcett, 1965), p. 773; ibid.
14. Petersen, a Philadelphia banker, had joined the White House staff in August 1961.
15. O'Brien, No Final Victories, p. 131.
16. New York Times, October 7, 1961, quoted in Evans, The Kennedy Round, p. 139, n. 21.
17. Tariffs are taxes, so all legislation relevant to tariffs must originate in the House, and thus pass first through the Ways and Means Committee.
18. O'Brien, No Final Victories, p. 131.
19. Sorensen, Kennedy, p. 411.

20. See Pastor, Congress and Politics, p. 106.
21. Quoted in ibid.
22. See Evans, The Kennedy Round, p. 140.
23. Pastor, Congress and Politics, p. 107; Evans, The Kennedy Round, p. 141.
24. Quoted in Pastor, Congress and Politics, p. 107, n. 9: "New Perspectives on Trade Policy: Address by President Kennedy to the National Association of Manufacturers, New York, December 6, 1961."
25. Preeg, Traders and Diplomats, p. 46.
26. Congressional Quarterly Weekly Report, January 26, 1962, p. 98.
27. It is beyond the scope of this study to describe in any detail the substance and importance of the act, but several excellent discussions of it are available. See Evans, The Kennedy Round, chap. 7; Pastor, Congress and Politics, chap. 4; Preeg, Traders and Diplomats, chap. 3; CQ Weekly Report, January 26, 1962, p. 98; CQ Weekly Report, June 1, 1962, pp. 927-30; and CQ Weekly Report, October 5, 1962, pp. 1803-6.
28. Pastor, Congress and Politics, p. 108.
29. Preeg, Traders and Diplomats, p. 49.
30. Pastor, Congress and Politics, pp. 110-11.
31. Ibid., p. 108.
32. CQ Weekly Report, January 26, 1962, p. 127.
33. Preeg, Traders and Diplomats, p. 50.
34. Pastor, Congress and Politics, p. 114.
35. Bauer, Pool, and Dexter, American Business, p. 362.
36. Preeg, Traders and Diplomats, p. 49; Pastor, Congress and Politics, p. 112. In truth, this provision strengthened the hand of the president vis-à-vis the State Department bureaucracy.
37. Preeg, Traders and Diplomats, p. 49.
38. Pastor, Congress and Politics, p. 113. The "escape clause" allows the United States to withdraw or modify a previously made tariff concession that results in serious injury to a domestic industry. It was under authority granted him by the escape clause of the existing law that Kennedy raised the tariff on glass and carpets in 1962. See Evans, The Kennedy Round, pp. 16-18, 167-69.
39. See Pastor, Congress and Politics, pp. 111-17; Evans, The Kennedy Round, pp. 144-58; and, Congressional Quarterly Almanac 1962 (Washington, D.C.: Congressional Quarterly, 1963), p. 276.

40. Pastor, Congress and Politics, p. 113.
41. CQ Weekly Report, June 29, 1962, p. 1,083.
42. CQ Weekly Report, October 12, 1962, p. 1,915.
43. Pastor, Congress and Politics, p. 105.
44. Sorensen, Kennedy, pp. 410-11.
45. Quoted in Lewis J. Paper, The Promise and the Performance (New York: Crown, 1975), p. 270.
46. Schlesinger, A Thousand Days, p. 769.
47. Ibid.
48. Pastor, Congress and Politics, p. 105.
49. Quote from President Kennedy's speech to the National Association of Manufacturers, found in Pastor, Congress and Politics, p. 107.
50. CQ Weekly Report, January 26, 1962, pp. 122-23.
51. Several of Kennedy's advisors told him that he was overselling the bill's probable impact on the balance of payments, a particularly pressing issue of the time. See Preeg, Traders and Diplomats, p. 51.
52. Quoted in ibid., p. 47.
53. Ibid., p. 45.
54. See Pastor, Congress and Politics, pp. 108-9.
55. Schlesinger, A Thousand Days, p. 126.
56. This centralization was not complete, for the departments still had some say on this issue. Nevertheless, Petersen's White House office went a long way toward coordinating and centralizing the administration's trade initiative.
57. Schlesinger, A Thousand Days, p. 773.
58. Ibid.
59. For a more cynical view of Kennedy's strategy, see Bauer, Pool, and Dexter, American Business, p. 422.
60. O'Brien, No Final Victories, p. 131.
61. CQ Weekly Report, March 9, 1962, p. 404. See also Bauer, Pool, and Dexter, American Business, chap. 26.
62. CQ Weekly Report, p. 404.
63. For a thorough discussion of the nongovernment groups involved in the debate on this bill, see CQ Weekly Report, March 9, 1962, pp. 403-8.
64. For a report on the hearings, see U.S. Congress, House Committee on Ways and Means, Trade Expansion Act of 1962, Hearing before the Committee on Ways and Means, 6 vols., 87th Cong., 2d. sess., 1962; and, U.S. Congress, Senate Committee on Finance, Trade Expansion Act of 1962, Hearing before the Committee on Finance, 2

Non-Crisis Non-Security Issues / 153

vols., 87th Cong., 2d. sess., 1962. For a summary of these hearings, see Evans, The Kennedy Round, pp. 144-56.
    65. For a text of the president's message, see CQ Weekly Report, January 26, 1962, pp. 122-26.
    66. Sorensen, Kennedy, p. 410.
    67. Preeg, Traders and Diplomats, p. 49.
    68. Ibid., p. 412.
    69. Ibid., p. 51.
    70. Pastor, Congress and Politics, p. 109.
    71. Ibid.
    72. Preeg, Traders and Diplomats, p. 53.
    73. Pastor, Congress and Politics, p. 109.
    74. Ibid., p. 114.
    75. Ibid., p. 112.
    76. Ibid., p. 113.
    77. Ibid.
    78. Ibid.
    79. Ibid.
    80. Ibid.
    81. Evans, The Kennedy Round, p. 138.
    82. Ibid., pp. 137-38.
    83. Preeg, Traders and Diplomats, p. 44. See also Bauer, Pool, and Dexter, American Business, p. 74.
    84. See Schlesinger, A Thousand Days, p. 769; Sorensen, Kennedy, pp. 410-11; Evans, The Kennedy Round, p. 135; and, Pastor, Congress and Politics, pp. 105-6.
    85. Evans, The Kennedy Round, p. 138.
    86. Some have also suggested that, after the disappointing year of 1961, with its Bay of Pigs and Berlin Wall crises, Kennedy saw the Trade Expansion Act as a possible success in foreign affairs to be pursued intently. While this explanation is possible, it does not eliminate the fact of the international economic situation just described. See Bauer, Pool, and Dexter, American Business, p. 422.
    87. Of course, this support was a factor in the decision to seek new legislation, but it was certainly not the only factor. The support of Boggs and Mills was indeed relevant to Kennedy's ultimate success.
    88. For a fuller discussion of the committee, see Bauer, Pool, and Dexter, American Business, chap. 26.
    89. See ibid.
    90. Bauer, Pool, and Dexter, American Business, p. 387.

91. There were some grumblings in the oil community, but it was primarily concerned about import quotas rather than tariffs. For a discussion of this issue, see Pastor, Congress and Politics, p. 114, and CQ Almanac 1962 (Washington, D.C.: Congressional Quarterly, 1963), pp. 288–89.

92. Gerald M. Meier, Problems of Trade Policy (New York: Oxford University Press, 1973), p. 102; CQ Weekly Report, July 18, 1969, p. 1,292.

93. Meier, Problems of Trade, p. 102.

94. Nixon's proposal was originally entitled the Trade Act of 1969, but it was not taken up in Congress until the following year, when the designation was changed.

95. For a complete text of President Nixon's trade policy message to Congress, see CQ Almanac 1969 (Washington, D.C.: Congressional Quarterly, 1970), pp. 95A–97A.

96. The Trade Expansion Act's tariff reduction provisions expired in 1967, and President Johnson unsuccessfully attempted to have them revived. For details of the Johnson administration proposals in this area, see CQ Almanac 1968 (Washington, D.C.: Congressional Quarterly, 1969), pp. 728–32.

97. ASP was a provision, dating from a 1923 law, which required that duties for certain imports be based not on the actual price of the good, but on the (higher) U.S. selling price of the item. This device allowed stiff duties at an objectively low tariff rate, and was a particularly contentious point with America's trading partners. For further details, see Frank V. Fowlkes, "House Turns to Protectionism Despite Arm-Twisting by Nixon Trade Experts," National Journal, August 22, 1970, p. 1,815.

98. CQ Almanac 1970 (Washington, D.C.: Congressional Quarterly, 1971), p. 1,051.

99. CQ Almanac 1969, p. 96A.

100. Pastor, Congress and Politics, pp. 124–25. See also CQ Weekly Report, March 27, 1970, p. 861.

101. CQ Weekly Report, July 18, 1969, pp. 1,292, 1,296. Mills would later change his view and support quotas, as will be mentioned below.

102. Meier, Problems of Trade, pp. 105–10; National Journal, October 31, 1970, p. 2,409.

103. Kissinger, White House Years, pp. 330–39. Kissinger does not name the emissary, who he states was a mutual friend of the prime minister and him.

104. It is noteworthy that throughout the period 1969-71, the special trade representative and his office were pushed into the background. For greater discussion of this matter, see Anne H. Rightor-Thornton, "An Evaluation of the Office of the Special Representative for Trade Negotiations: The Evolving Role, 1962-1974," in U.S. Commission on the Organization of the Government for the Conduct of Foreign Policy, Report, vol. 3, Appendix H: Case Studies in U.S. Foreign Economic Policy: 1965-1974, pp. 88-104 (Washington, D.C.: Government Printing Office, 1975), pp. 96-97 in particular.

105. CQ Almanac 1970, p. 1,051.

106. Ibid.; National Journal, August 29, 1970, p. 1,885; Henry Kissinger, Years of Upheaval (Boston: Little, Brown, 1982), p. 338; and, New York Times, June 26, 1970: cited in Meier, Problems of Trade, pp. 110-11, n. 2.

107. CQ Almanac 1970, p. 1,051.

108. For excerpts from these hearings, see ibid., pp. 1,052-58.

109. Ibid., p. 1,059.

110. By identifying them as Domestic International Sales Corporations (DISC), which would make them a class of firms eligible for tax benefits. This proposal was intended to encourage greater exports to enhance a favorable balance of trade.

111. CQ Almanac 1970, p. 1,059.

112. Ibid., p. 1,060. See also Fowlkes, "House Turns to Protectionism," pp. 1,815-16.

113. Fowlkes, "House Turns to Protectionism," p. 1,817.

114. Pastor, Congressional Politics, pp. 126-27; CQ Almanac 1970, pp. 1,062-64; and, CQ Weekly Report, November 27, 1970, pp. 2,847-49.

115. CQ Almanac 1970, p. 1,064.

116. Frank V. Fowlkes, "White House May Lose Gamble; Protectionist Bill is Emerging," National Journal, November 21, 1970, p. 2,555.

117. In an election year, Nixon was strongly pressured against vetoing a bill that included an increase in Social Security benefits. Ibid., pp. 2,555-56; CQ Almanac 1970, pp. 1,064-65.

118. Fowlkes, "White House," p. 2,556. See also Kissinger, Years of Upheaval, pp. 338-40.

119. Pastor, Congress and Politics, p. 127.
120. Fowlkes, "White House," p. 2,556.
121. CQ Almanac 1970, p. 1,066.
122. Ibid.
123. CQ Weekly Report, February 20, 1970, pp. 533-34.
124. Rightor-Thornton, "Evaluation of Office," pp. 88-104. See also Pastor, Congress and Politics, p. 124.
125. CQ Weekly Report, July 18, 1969, p. 1,293.
126. See CQ Almanac 1970, pp. 1,052-58.
127. See Fowlkes, "House Turns to Protectionism," pp. 1815-16.
128. New York Times, July 21, 1970: quoted in Meier, Problems of Trade, p. 113, n. 24.
129. See quote from Nixon above: "I would not be able to sign the bill . . ."
130. Fowlkes, "House Turns to Protectionism," p. 1,817.
131. CQ Almanac 1970, p. 1,063.
132. Dom Bonafede and Andrew Glass, "Nixon Deals Cautiously With Hostile Congress," National Journal, June 22, 1970, p. 1,356.
133. Fowlkes, "House Turns to Protectionism," pp. 1,816-17.
134. Ibid., pp. 1,815-16.
135. Rightor-Thornton, "Evaluation of Office," pp. 88-104.
136. For a profile of Harlow, see Bonafede and Glass, "Nixon Deals Cautiously," p. 1,356.
137. See Rightor-Thornton, "Evaluation of Office," pp. 88-104.
138. Fowlkes, "House Turns to Protectionism," p. 1,816.
139. Ibid.
140. Ibid.; Pastor, Congress and Politics, p. 126.
141. Fowlkes, "White House," p. 2,555.
142. Rightor-Thornton, "Evaluation of Office," pp. 88-104.
143. Ibid. See also Pastor, Congress and Politics, p. 124.
144. CQ Almanac 1970, p. 1,058.
145. By Congressional Quarterly, National Journal, and Robert A. Pastor.

146. Frank V. Fowlkes, "Pressure Mounting on Congress to Enact Import Quota Legislation," National Journal, May 16, 1970, p. 1,034.
147. Ibid.
148. Ibid.
149. Ibid.
150. Fowlkes, "House Turns to Protectionism," p. 1,817; Fowlkes, "Pressure Mounting," p. 1,036.
151. CQ Almanac 1970, pp. 1,056-58.

5

TOWARD A NEW WISDOM

This book began by posing two questions: By what standards are presidents evaluated in the area of foreign affairs; and, How useful are those standards for effective presidential evaluation? These issues are important, for they concern the nature of the presidential ordeal and the value of its instruments.

Yet these issues have never been sufficiently examined by scholars. Although evaluation is important to democracy, historical understanding of presidents, and the making of foreign policy, it is a subject that receives little explicit attention from president-watchers. Rather, it has usually been treated only incidentally, even by those scholars and commentators who focus their attention on presidential policy making.

Nevertheless, presidential evaluation warrants careful study. For there is a conventional wisdom on how it ought to be conducted, one which guides assessments of presidents and subtly influences presidential action. Moreover, as the case studies undertaken here have demonstrated, this conventional wisdom is seriously flawed. Accordingly, it is time for a new wisdom on presidential evaluation.

In order to begin moving toward that new wisdom, this final chapter will examine the results of the case studies, propose a means for more effective evaluation of presidents, consider some implications of this study for the presidency itself, and outline a program for developing a more general theory of presidential evaluation.

RESULTS OF THE CASE STUDIES

The six case studies provide some interesting results as regards the conventional wisdom and these results are summarized in Table 5.1. As is clear from this table, presidential performance according to the conventional wisdom does not generally explain the outcomes of the cases. Except in the Bay of Pigs crisis, there is little significant difference between cases of success and failure. Consequently, while the conventional wisdom focuses on important and perhaps necessary criteria for presidential achievement, fulfillment of those criteria is insufficient for producing success.

Yet the outcome of these cases cannot be explained as merely due to chance. Rather, there is a pattern to the conditions affecting success and failure: outcomes can be explained as the results of the complex interaction of presidential performance with certain external circumstances.

In the cases of success, the president generally fulfilled the conventional criteria, and in doing so took advantage of auspicious circumstances. President Eisenhower's performance in the Taiwan Strait crisis met the requirements of the conventional wisdom, but his success can be explained only by reference to U.S. power predominance over China. In the same way, Nixon and Kennedy each took advantage of a domestic political climate conducive to the sort of legislation each was proposing (Nixon: SALT I; Kennedy: Trade Expansion Act), and Kennedy was also aided by an international political climate that made his case for free trade more compelling. Performance did not dictate outcomes.

In the cases of failure, only one case can be attributed to the president's failure to fulfill criteria of the conventional wisdom: the Bay of Pigs. Kennedy's failure to meet the requirements of the Organization and staffing and Management and oversight criteria ushered in disaster: he established a collegial system for decision making, but failed to properly manage that system and oversee his subordinates. Moreover, his fulfillment of the criterion of Consensus-building, at least in terms of his advisors, actually contributed to his failure. Kennedy's ability to achieve an easy consensus among his advisors underscores the ambiguity of this standard--in living up to the demands of this standard, he achieved the opposite of what he wanted.

TABLE 5.1

Results of the Case Studies

Criterion Case	Policy Direction & Design	Organization & Staffing	Management & Oversight	Consensus -building	Other Factors
Success — Taiwan Strait Crisis	yes	yes	yes	mixed	U.S. power predominance
Success — SALT I	mixed	yes, w/ reservations	yes, w/ reserv.	yes	domestic political climate
Success — Trade Expansion Act	yes	yes	yes	yes	domestic and international political climates
Failure — Bay of Pigs Crisis	yes	no	no	yes, w/ reserv.	bureaucratic "slippage"
Failure — SALT II	yes	yes	yes	mixed	issues of SALT domestic & intl. climates
Failure — Trade Act of 1970	yes	yes	yes	mixed	domestic politics

160

The other two failures demonstrate the insufficiency of the conventional criteria for explaining outcomes, for in these cases presidential performance was generally good. To explain the president's failure requires reference to the circumstances of each case. In the case of SALT II, the complexities of arms control delayed conclusion of the treaty, which in turn undermined the president's consensus-building efforts. Moreover, the domestic and international political environments were important to the outcome: at home was a Senate wary of presidential secretiveness in arms negotiations; abroad, the Soviet invasion of Afghanistan emphasized the uncertainty of the international environment. In the case of the Trade Act of 1970, President Nixon's bill fell victim to domestic politics in the form of a wave of protectionism in Congress. Nixon and Carter both performed at a level on par with the levels of performance in cases of presidential success. With some reservations, it is possible to say that they met the demands of the conventional wisdom. Yet they failed.

These results reveal that the process-outcomes relationship posited by the conventional wisdom is wrong. Therefore, they point to a number of changes that ought to be made in the "calculus" of presidential policy-making performance. Indeed, these cases suggest how the whole concept of evaluation might be changed.

If presidential evaluation is to be effective, it must separate evaluation of process from evaluation of outcomes. For, as the case studies show, the connection between these elements is tenuous. Performance according to the process criteria alone cannot explain outcomes because such factors as power predominance, domestic politics, and bureaucratic "slippage" are all relevant to presidential achievement. Therefore, a more effective scheme than the present one would employ a two-stage system for presidential evaluation, one which separates effectiveness from achievement. In the first stage, presidential effectiveness should be assessed according to the four-process criteria and an additional criterion to be described below. In the second stage, presidential achievement should be assessed with outcomes measured in light of such contextual factors as affect achievement. The next section will examine this new conceptual scheme more closely.

As for the conventional wisdom, its flaws do not end with the error of the process-outcomes relationship. Rather, it is plagued with two other fundamental drawbacks.

First, the cases have exposed several significant conflicts and trade-offs among the criteria of the conventional wisdom. These conflicts and trade-offs not only affect how a president will be assessed, but also his ability to achieve his goals or to make policy.

One conflict arises from the divergent demands of consensus-building and the requirements for effectivenesss in the management of the decision process. As Kennedy learned in the Bay of Pigs case, the cultivation of a consensus among a president's advisors may undermine the analysis and reflection necessary for effective decision making. Because he pressed for and quickly achieved a consensus, the president impaired the process for realistically examining the CIA's invasion proposal. Outside of the advisory circle, there can still be this conflict: as Lyndon Johnson learned, an easy congressional consensus in support of the Gulf of Tonkin Resolution and the escalation of the Vietnam War did not make for better decision making, but instead intensified opposition to the war when the policy seemed to fail. Building a consensus may actually undermine the decision process.

Next, as the cases of SALT II and the Trade Act of 1970 demonstrate, there is a trade-off between Policy design and Consensus-building. A president's carefully wrought design, whether it be goal-oriented or strategic, may inhibit his chances of developing a coalition to support his proposals. Sorting out this conflict for the purpose of evaluation may alter an assessment of a president's performance: is priority to be given to "being right" in designing policy, as Carter's defenders argued in the case of SALT II, or should the president have modified his design to achieve consensus? There is a balance to be struck here, between design and consensus, or even between design and success, and striking it may alter an initial evaluation of a president's performance.

Related to this conflict is the trade-off between success or failure in one case and a president's grand design. In the case of his Trade Act, President Nixon regarded southern votes as so important to future elections (1970 and 1972) that he would not drop the "special case" argument regarding textiles. His overall design subordinated one trade bill to political gains for the president and his party. A president may not even have political goals in mind when constructing a design (although he probably will), but that design may accept losses on some issues to increase the chance of success on others.

The third trade-off in evaluating process performance arises from the conflicting demands for a president's time, attention, resources, political capital, or whatever. Examining a president's performance in a particular case may or may not uncover this problem, but it did arise in the case studies undertaken here. As his national security advisor noted, Carter spent an "inordinate" amount of time on SALT II: Brzezinski meant not only time, but effort and political capital as well. This extreme effort detracted from his performance in other cases, just as Nixon's troubles with his Trade Act can be explained in part by the attention, effort, and resources he was expending on other issues (particularly U.S.-Soviet relations). While this study focuses only on individual cases, and such a conflict as this one is more readily apparent in a view of entire presidencies, even the small set of cases examined here reveal the difficulties this conflict creates.

Aside from these conflicts and trade-offs, the conventional wisdom exhibits a second major shortcoming: it does not include any consensus on the importance of democratic accountability. Yet it is clear from the cases that accountability is a relevant issue. Nixon's broad delegation of SALT issues to Kissinger, as well as his circumvention of Congress and the State Department in policy making, raises this issue. Moreover, Kennedy's actions in the Bay of Pigs crisis, stifling dissent and preventing relevant experts and congressional leaders from participating in or influencing his decision, also raise this question. Clearly, foreign policy making involves accountability as well as effectiveness and achievement, but this issue is not supported by a consensus of the observers of the conventional wisdom.

The results of the case studies, then, are significant in that they reveal the fundamental error of the conventional wisdom, expose conflicts and trade-offs among the various criteria for evaluation, and point to the absence of any consensus on the need for democratic accountability. Consequently, the cases emphasize the need for a more effective scheme of presidential evaluation in foreign affairs.

TOWARD MORE EFFECTIVE EVALUATION

As noted above, the principal requirement for a scheme for more effective evaluation is to separate assessment of process performance (effectiveness) from assessment of outcomes performance (achievement). Such a scheme will provide a more accurate picture of presidential performance and the context in which it occurs, thus enhancing the value of assessments made by president-watchers.

In the first stage of this scheme, effectiveness should be evaluated according to the four process criteria plus an additional criterion of Democratic accountability. These standards, tempered by a sense of the president's need to balance the conflicting demands and trade-offs of the policy process, will yield better evaluations of presidential effectiveness.

The four process criteria of the conventional wisdom are still quite useful since they focus on important elements of presidential performance, but they must be refined. First, observers employing these standards ought to be sensitive to differences between the short-term and long-term effects of presidential behavior under each criterion. As the case studies have demonstrated, such differences are important. Nixon's secretive "crablike" management of SALT negotiations worked for him in the short term, but over time contributed to bureaucratic resistance and congressional dissatisfaction with his handling of foreign policy, as well as creating difficulties for his successors, Ford and Carter. Conversely, while Kennedy's collegial decision-making system worked well for him in the long term (as Alexander George argues),[1] in the short term (i.e., until Kennedy learned how to use it) it had disastrous effects. So evaluators must be mindful of this distinction, as must presidents. In the daily press of events, it is easy to seek the short-term answer to a problem, yet that approach may backfire in the long run.

A second refinement would be to distinguish between the normative and instrumental aspects of each criterion. For the comments of the observers in the conventional wisdom imply that the various process criteria are important in both aspects, e.g., Consensus-building is seen as important because "Presidential power is the power to persuade"[2] and because the president is a democratic official who ought to seek consensus because it is good. In each of the four process criteria are these aspects: each is seen as an element of effectiveness because fulfillment of each standard will enhance presidential success, but each standard is also seen as part of a president's responsibilities as a democratic officeholder. He must have a policy design in order to succeed, but many observers want that design to be articulated publicly so it may be debated. The president must effectively organize and manage his foreign policy government, but there is concern among many president-watchers about secretiveness, deal making, congressional consultation, and other normative questions of the decision process (e.g., Nixon and SALT I).

This distinction between normative and instrumental aspects of performance underscores the need for a new criterion of Democratic accountability. Indeed, such a standard could help to clarify the different aspects of Policy direction, Organization, Management, and Consensus-building: with a Democratic accountability standard as part of the "calculus" of presidential effectiveness, assessments according to the other four process criteria could focus on the instrumental requirements for Policy design, Staffing, Management, and Consensus-building. In other words, this additional standard could make the idea of presidential effectiveness more comprehensive: effectiveness as performance according to certain instrumental standards which is balanced with the need for presidential accountability.

While there is no consensus in the conventional wisdom for what this new criterion would mean, several observers have considered the meaning of accountability. From their remarks, and from the lessons of the case studies, it is possible to articulate this new standard. It would be added to the four process criteria of the conventional wisdom.

Democratic accountability: The president's performance in foreign affairs is to be judged according to his ability and willingness to act in a manner consistent with the requirements of democratic government. These include adherence to constitutional ethics, public discussion and debate of policy and actions, and consultation with executive, congressional, and other public leaders.

This criterion is most succinctly stated in Richard Pious's call for presidents to work toward "placing presidential power and accountability in better constitutional balance."[3] It is a standard based on the fact that presidents can and do act in ways contrary to the principle of democratic accountability. Sometimes it is the limits of presidential power which encourage such behavior: Nixon sought to overcome the power of the bureaucracy through subterfuge, "crablike" management, and extensive delegation of power over SALT to Kissinger. At other times, when the president's discretionary power is extensive, he may avoid the processes of consultation and consensus-building to minimize leaks or inhibit dissent.

Just as Pious sees presidential power, which is nevertheless limited, as tempting to unaccountability, so do Louis Koenig and Erwin Hargrove insist that a president be judged according to this standard. Koenig is particularly concerned about those cases, such as crises, in which the president may act without the approval of Congress. But he is also interested in the broader accountability of the president as a democratic leader and so insists that the chief executive promote democratic principles and the role of Congress, public opinion, and the foreign affairs bureaucracy in policy making.4 In short, the president must not only be held accountable by those who evaluate him, but he must also act in a manner consistent with democratic discussion, debate, and persuasion.

What does this mean? For Pious, it means that:

> Presidents do their part when they invite full and timely consultation within the executive branch, permitting careerists to work closely with political executives in formulating options. They act in the spirit of the system when they give advance notice of their intentions to legislative leaders, provide them with adequate and relevant information, and allow congressional thinking to influence their deliberations.5

In the same vein, accountability is described by Hargrove as "open politics":

> Presidents and prime ministers who are prudent will soon learn that the best resource for firm acceptance of policy is the favorable opinion of those in government whose assent is needed step by step as policy develops. Presidents should look on Congress as a resource by means of which Presidential policies can be given solid footing. But in order for this to be so Presidents must be willing to persuade, to make

a public case, and to suffer defeat in some
respects. Policy that prevails in this way
is incorporated into the prevailing opinion
of national leadership and actually strength-
ens the President when he needs support.
Other things being equal it is also likely to
be better policy if it has been subjected to
a process of debate and criticism. A President in a democracy must be required to go
through the exercise of persuading other
power holders to accept his views or else
we have no democracy. This process of persuasion and bargaining keeps democratic
norms alive. If a President is free to do
as he wishes, in what sense can we say
that we have a democracy, and why will a
President be concerned at all about his accountability for what he does?[6]

This "open politics," like the discussions of democratic accountability in Pious and Koenig, relates directly
to the lessons of the case studies. Those studies noted
that, even when the president was able to act toward
achieving his goal, the criterion of Consensus was too ambiguous to give a thorough assessment of presidential performance. Rather, that vague criterion begged the question
of whether the president's performance fulfilled the implied
normative aspects of consensus-building, i.e., the requirements of democratic accountability.

Accountability is thus an important factor in framing
a complete and effective evaluation of performance, and
these three observers have indicated what it means. Of
course, it does not mean that presidents should never act
decisively on their own initiative, or should never have
recourse to secrecy in policy making, but it does mean
that presidents must be accountable for what they do.
While it may appear obvious to the reader that the president must be accountable for his actions, it is interesting
that accountability does not appear to be worthy of mention by most observers of the conventional wisdom. Perhaps
the fundamental lesson of the case studies in this regard
is that presidential accountability is not to be taken for
granted.

With this additional standard, the evaluation of
presidential effectiveness becomes more complex. It now

includes five criteria, each with its own requirements, and involves a number of conflicts and trade-offs. Consequently, in order for effectiveness to be assessed, president-watchers must engage in a conceptual "calculus" of presidential effectiveness based on how well a president reconciles these competing demands. In other words, presidential evaluators must be sensitive to the need to strike a balance between the different requirements of effectiveness. The conventional wisdom is misleading in suggesting that presidential evaluation is an easy checklist of duties that will lead to success, when in fact evaluation is a much more difficult process. It is instead a thoughtful calculation of how well a president copes with the many demands of his job, determined according to a set of guidelines for asking the right questions.

Effectiveness is thus the first concern for president-watchers, but it is more involved than the conventional wisdom implies. But so is the final concern of evaluators, i.e., presidential achievement.

Achievement means presidential performance according to outcomes, but it is now clear that outcomes involve more than merely asking whether the president succeeded or failed. Rather, achievement involves outcomes in context: what the president achieved in the circumstances of the case.

In this sense, evaluation of presidential achievement ought to be, like the assessment of effectiveness, a "calculus"; what the president accomplished in light of the circumstances involved. As the case studies have shown, explanations of presidential success or failure ultimately depend on the circumstances of individual cases: who has power predominance, the president's power vis-à-vis Congress and/or the bureaucracy, the influence of domestic politics, the international political climate, and other such contextual factors. For all these factors limit the president's power to shape outcomes and must therefore be included in any calculus of achievement.

In the future, evaluators of presidential foreign policy performance must be mindful of these factors. Their attention should not be directed to a simple success/failure outcome, but rather to how well the president works within the context of his ability to influence outcomes. This is why evaluation must inevitably be a "calculus": it can only be fair and accurate if all major relevant factors are considered. Of course, this makes presidential evaluation an involved process, but not an impossible one.

Foreign policy is too important to be approached simplistically. So it is not unreasonable to demand a two-stage evaluative scheme if that scheme will yield more effective assessments of performance. Evaluation must be accurate to be useful: it should be conducted without the illusion that good process will guarantee good outcomes; it should be sensitive to the conflicting demands of the president's job; it should be attentive to the need for accountability in office; and, it should include the various contextual factors that affect outcomes. If president-watchers were to reflect on how well presidents coped with circumstances, whether taking advantage of suspicious ones or avoiding dangerous ones, then their evaluations would be more reliable.

IMPLICATIONS OF THIS STUDY FOR THE PRESIDENCY

If foreign policy demands better evaluations by president-watchers, it also demands high levels of performance by presidents. Once again, the case studies offer some important lessons: four suggestions to presidents to help them cope with their responsibilities.

Hedge your bets. The case studies all serve as evidence of the factors which influence presidential achievement. Consequently, they suggest that the president should be sensitive to the amount of influence he has in any given situation. Because president-watchers, even if employing the evaluative scheme outlined above, focus on outcomes, the president must think in terms of "hedging his bets." He should capitalize on auspicious circumstances, when he can find them, and avoid risky ones. Despite the various legends that "great presidents" are the ones who take big chances in order to achieve big successes,[7] the evidence is clear that the president is more likely to fail in a big way. Rather than being cautious by increasing the size of the invasion force or abandoning the Bay of Pigs operation, Kennedy undertook what he knew would be a big gamble and lost.[8] There is little benefit to playing "long shots."

Pay attention to the process. The case studies reveal that the four process criteria are not an easy checklist of duties for the president, but are instead a rather demanding set of responsibilities. The president must take extreme care in establishing and operating the foreign policy decision process, for it can fail him when he needs it most.

Specifically, the cases illuminate problems in the decision-making models that presidents employ. Nixon's hierarchical, White House-dominated NSC system enhanced his ability to control foreign policy in all its phases, but it triggered resistance from the State Department and Congress. Indeed, the hierarchical system failed to truly serve Nixon's purpose, because bureaucratic resistance undermined his ability to implement his policies: the State Department tried to circumvent presidential authority, while Congress attacked detente and presidential war making. The hierarchical model of policy making thus lends itself to excessive centralization, is prone to bureaucratization, and can isolate the president from potentially useful advisors (e.g., Congress, State Department officials). It may also undermine consensus-building (because of wariness of deal making and secretiveness).

As for the collegial decision-making system, which Kennedy employed in order to avoid the problems of hierarchy, it is plagued with its own problems. When not properly employed, as was the case in the Bay of Pigs crisis, it fails to provide for serious consideration of policy proposals. This system lacks measures for the routine oversight of the president's subordinates and, as the influence of Kennedy and Bissell demonstrates, it is susceptible to the influence of personality and charisma. Moreover, considering the amount of time and effort the president was forced to devote to this one problem, it is possible that the collegial model places inordinate demands on the president.

As Sorensen noted, "Procedures do, of course, affect decisions."[9] Good processes and management techniques cannot necessarily save a president from failure, but inattention to the problems of process may guarantee it.

Long-term versus short-term outcomes. The president should pay careful attention to distinguishing between the short-term and long-term effects of his policies and actions. As noted above, what works in the near term may not work in the long term, or may even increase future problems. Too little attention is now paid to this distinction, and the result has been serious trouble for the president.

The timing of proposals. Just as Paul Light[10] has noted the importance of timing to presidential success in domestic policy proposals, so the case studies confirm the same for foreign policy. This finding is particularly relevant in those foreign policy matters that require congressional action, but applies to all foreign policy cases. Carter encountered significant problems with SALT II because of timing, while Kennedy's Trade Expansion Act was the beneficiary of good timing. There are no magic rules for timing proposals, but it is yet another factor to be taken into consideration when presidents design their foreign policies.

MANIFESTO FOR A GENERAL THEORY OF PRESIDENTIAL EVALUATION

While this study has demonstrated the need for a refined approach to presidential evaluation, it is nevertheless only the beginning of a new view of evaluation. What is needed now is a larger effort, involving citizens as well as scholars, to develop a more general theory of presidential assessment. Such an effort must be grand in its conception and execution: its goal is no less than the creation of a more coherent way of thinking about how to evaluate presidents. What follows constitutes a manifesto for evaluation theorists: not a theory itself, but the groundwork for one.

<u>Principles</u>. The purpose of a presidential evaluation is threefold: the democratic evaluation of incumbents by citizens; historical understanding of the presidency and U.S. government; and, insight into the policy processes of the presidency. Each of these is related to the others, for effective democratic evaluation depends on accurate understanding of policy and history, while insights into policy making depend on an understanding of past experience and citizen expectations, and historical studies can be guided by the questions raised by citizens and policy makers.

The goal of evaluation is to serve these purposes through fair and accurate assessments of presidential performance. Because the purposes of evaluation are so important, the watchword for presidential evaluators should be honesty. While evaluation may be employed for partisan, scholarly, or whatever ends, evaluators must be concerned about honesty in clarifying their assumptions, their use of information and evidence, attention to contrary interpretations, and the reasonability of conclusions drawn. In short, whatever the motivation of a particular presidential assessment, the evaluator must strive for accuracy and honesty in his work. For there is an inherently political element in presidential evaluation, even if it is undertaken for reasons of scholarship: assessments of presidents will always have political ramifications (how president is interpreted, whether a president was effective or not). So honesty is vital to this effort. Unfortunately, many attempts at presidential evaluation are colored by hidden assumptions, misinterpretations of evidence, and fallacious reasoning in arriving at conclusions. A better theory of presidential evaluation is impossible without an honest approach to the subject.

At the same time, the tone of an evaluative theory ought to be one of ideals tempered by reality. Presidential evaluation, in the present conventional wisdom and in the future, will always reflect some notion of what is expected of the president. These ideals are essential, else evaluation has no meaning for without some yardstick for measuring performance, all presidential performance is equal. Yet these ideals must be tempered by reality: as the case studies have demonstrated, ideals out of touch with the realities of the presidency yield inaccurate and potentially dangerous assessments of presidents. As this study has undertaken to modify the ideals of the conventional wisdom by a brush with historical experience, so should a general theory of evaluation combine these elements.

Finally, evaluation must be seen as an open-ended process. It cannot be static because changing circumstances over time, whether of presidential power, the international environment, or whatever, may alter the standards for presidential assessment. Moreover, as new evidence comes to light or new questions are asked, evaluations of individual presidents may change. This does not mean that evaluation is to be altered capriciously, thus being of extremely limited value, but that a general theory of evaluation will allow for changes over time.

While these principles are rather general in nature, they are nevertheless important. For they touch on points that will affect the ultimate value of presidential evaluation.

<u>Structure</u>. While the presidency is in one sense a seamless garment, its individual threads are not indistinct. It is both possible and beneficial to disaggregate the

presidency into a variety of substantive areas, as well as to regard it as a whole.

In this regard, theory-building ought to be directed toward the development of evaluative models in a number of areas: substantive policy areas (e.g., foreign affairs, as in this study, or economic policy, domestic policy, etc.); intergovernmental relations (executive-congressional relations, presidential-bureaucratic relations, the presidency and state and local governments); overall presidential management; and, public leadership. Models in each of these areas, integrated through an overarching theory of evaluation, can provide more detailed and potentially informative assessments than some attempt to give a measure of overall presidential performance. While these overall assessments are quite popular, as in the number of attempts to rank presidents, they are of little value: they do not offer any insights into what makes for "great" presidents or what the president is expected to do.

Evaluation, then, is to be built on a structure of evaluative models in several substantive areas, integrated through a larger theory of evaluation. This overarching theory, which should be developed from some general conception of the role of the presidency in the political system, can ultimately provide a framework for future evaluation. It will guide by indicating the purpose of the presidency (i.e., its role in the system), defining the components of the institution relevant to fulfillment of that purpose (i.e., substantive areas), and reasonable standards for presidential performance. In short, an integrated theory of presidential evaluation will identify the right questions to ask in order to assess performance.

Who will ask these questions? The evaluators can be seen as falling into different "evaluation communities": the general public, scholars, and commentators are the main ones, as in this study. This is not to say that others will not or should not offer assessments, such as interest-group leaders, but that the most important general evaluation communities will be the ones mentioned above: the public, for obvious reasons; scholars, because of their role in contributing to understanding of the presidency and U.S. politics; and commentators, because of their highly visible place between the public and the president.

Each of these evaluation communities can be expected to engage in different types of evaluations. The public, which has the least time and resources for in-depth evaluations, will rely heavily on its sources of news information in order to make informed assessments. These assessments will be less complex than scholars or commentators might be expected to make, but that does not mean they will necessarily be simplistic. For the public is clearly capable of sophisticated evaluation of public affairs, but must be provided with the information necessary to make those evaluations.[11] One does not have to believe that every citizen is a perfectly informed intellectual to expect some sophistication in public evaluations, only that citizens are capable of analysis and reason.[12] It is not unrealistic to expect the public to understand the importance of process, or to accept the fact that the president cannot control events. If the public now holds an unrealistic expectation of what presidents can do, that should not be surprising: the conventional wisdom reveals that scholars and commentators do so as well. It is therefore imperative that the public be better informed.

Scholars should engage in research into all aspects of the topic of presidential evaluation. Such work will be particularly important to developing realistic standards for assessment in policy areas, intergovernmental relations, and other areas of performance. Accordingly, evaluation scholarship itself must be held to the highest standards. For the influence of scholars on politics, indirect as it may be, is not insignificant: scholars affect commentators' perceptions,[13] presidential behavior,[14] the views of nearly anyone who attends college, and the opinions of the "attentive public" that participates so extensively in U.S. politics.

Commentators can be expected to continue the evaluations they have always undertaken, but they ought to be more explicit in the standards they employ for these assessments. They must also focus their attention on the sorts of information the public needs for evaluations: presidential policy making, factors affecting outcomes, and other substantive topics.

The evaluations of these three groups will not be perfect, but they can be improved. Moreover, the importance of presidential evaluation is such to make the effort at improvement worthwhile, for it is clear that conventional understanding of presidential assessment is seriously flawed.

The context of evaluation. Presidential evaluation, like presidential performance, exists in a particular context. Understanding that context is important to developing a better understanding of presidential evaluation.

First, the presidency is a political office, but that does not mean that evaluation can only serve partisan ends. Indeed, it is imperative that assessments not be considered merely partisan. For each of the three purposes of evaluation requires that it go beyond partisanship, in order to provide for fairness in assessments and an improved understanding of policy making. Notable works such as Fred Greenstein's collection, <u>The Reagan Presidency: An Early Assessment</u>, have demonstrated that nonpartisan evaluation is not only possible, but can also be truly informative.[15]

Second, evaluation is and will continue to be conducted in a situation of imperfect information. This fact is particularly relevant to current evaluations, but also often plagues historical ones. Nevertheless, evaluations must be conducted, because not doing so is an unreasonable option. Consequently, just as presidents must often cope with the problem of imperfect information, so must their evaluators. That is one reason why evaluation is an open-ended process: new information may come to light, or time may give a different perspective to old evidence. Perfect information will usually not be available, but that does not mean that attempts at evaluation are futile. The choice is not between all or nothing--it is coping with what is available.

Third, evaluation is reflective rather than predictive. It is conceptually and qualitatively distinct from efforts to predict presidential performance by means of character assessment, political experience, or any other tests. The point of evaluation is not to anticipate what a candidate might do, but to assess what actual officeholders have done. While attempts to predict presidential behavior have their value, they cannot and should not be confused with performance evaluation, nor should they be seen as substitutes for reflective evaluations. Prediction deals with potentials, but evaluation must deal with the record. In this respect, evaluation is constrained by the limits of information and is only possible after the fact, but so does it offer more than prediction in that it deals with the realities of the presidency. If presidential evaluations are built on a solid historical foundation, and undertaken through thoughtful standards of performance, they will yield more usable information about the presidency than any attempts to anticipate how candidates might behave in office.

The context of evaluation, then, is a reminder of its limits. It serves as a caution to those who seek to develop a theory of evaluation and those who engage in presidential evaluations.

<u>An agenda for the future</u>. If a general theory of presidential evaluation is to be developed, it will be built on the answers to questions only suggested here. What follows, then, is a brief look at the agenda for the future.

The agenda will involve investigations into the presidency, policy making, the U.S. political system, the international system, and other topics which touch on presidential performance. It is not for scholars alone, but includes issues that can only be answered through public discussion and debate.

A fundamental issue on this agenda is to determine the purpose of the presidency and its role in the U.S. political system. This issue implies research into the Founding period, the historical development of the presidency, and the current roles of the presidency in the political order. But it also implies public debate over what the purpose and role of the presidency should be, as well as philosophical efforts such as Kenneth Thompson's <u>The President and the Public Philosophy</u>.[16] All these efforts will contribute to a definition of the presidential purpose and what is to be expected of presidents, which definition can then guide evaluations. Assessments of presidents must be rooted in some clear notion of the reasons for the office.

Likewise, the nature of presidential accountability is an issue for study. The discussion above offered a preliminary view of accountability, but this question deserves far greater consideration. It is a topic that bears on the U.S. constitutional order,[17] the nature of U.S. democracy, and the requirements for presidential accountability.[18]

Related to this question is the matter of the nature and limits of presidential power. There has been extensive work on this topic, from Neustadt's <u>Presidential Power</u>[19] to Cronin's <u>The State of the Presidency</u>,[20] but much of it has not been directed to the question of evaluation. As noted in Chapter 1, even scholars who deal directly with presidential power often fail to explicitly address the question of how presidential power should affect evaluations. Cronin and Neustadt have been notable exceptions to this failure, but there is still a gap in the literature between presidential power and presidential evaluation.

Finally, a general theory of evaluation demands further research on presidential assessment. The work begun here must be expanded to develop a more comprehensive understanding of presidential foreign policy performance, but research cannot stop there. It must branch out into other substantive issues, from policy areas to intergovernmental relations. What is the conventional wisdom on presidential performance in economic affairs? in executive-congressional relations? How realistic are these expectations?

Other research should look at the linkages among these different factors, such as in how presidential performance in one area influences performance in others. How does personality affect performance?[21] How does our constitutional system influence presidential behavior? An overarching theory to integrate evaluation will require an understanding of these linkages in order to be useful to president-watchers.

This book has moved from the conventional wisdom toward some guidelines for developing a new wisdom on presidential evaluation. In doing so, it has demonstrated the problems and errors of the contemporary view of presidential performance, while pointing to ways in which that view can be revised.

That view must be revised. For the president is always on trial and the judgments rendered affect him, the nation, and potentially the world. This work begins the effort to sharpen the instruments of the presidential ordeal.

NOTES

1. See Case Study: The Bay of Pigs Crisis in Chap. 2.

2. Richard E. Neustadt, Presidential Power, rev. ed. (New York: John Wiley and Sons, 1980).

3. Richard M. Pious, The American Presidency (New York: Basic Books, 1979).

4. Louis Koenig, The Chief Executive, rev. ed. (New York: Harcourt, Brace, and World, 1968), p. 236.

5. Pious, American Presidency, p. 421.

6. Erwin C. Hargrove, The Power of the Modern Presidency (New York: Alfred A. Knopf, 1974), p. 167.

7. For a discussion of these legends, see Bruce Buchanan, "Assessing Presidential Performances: Can We Do Better" (Paper presented to the American Political Science Association, New York, N.Y., 1981).

8. See Peter Wyden, *Bay of Pigs* (New York: Simon and Schuster, 1979), p. 318, and Garry Wills, *The Kennedy Imprisonment* (Boston: Little, Brown, 1981), chap. 19.

9. Theodore C. Sorensen, *Decision-making in the White House* (New York: Columbia University Press, 1963), p. 3.

10. Paul Light, *The President's Agenda* (Baltimore: Johns Hopkins University Press, 1982), pp. 203-4.

11. George C. Edwards, *The Public Presidency* (New York: St. Martin's Press, 1983), see chap. 5 for a discussion of the public's ability to engage in analysis.

12. After all, that is the fundamental assumption of democracy.

13. As a cursory reading of the columns of Hugh Sidey, George F. Will, or David Broder will demonstrate.

14. In this regard, witness America's "government by professors" in recent years: Kissinger, Brzezinski, Moynihan, Kirkpatrick, and others all occupying positions of influence, not to mention their influences on the thinking of presidents.

15. Fred I. Greenstein, ed., *The Reagan Presidency: An Early Assessment* (Baltimore: Johns Hopkins University Press, 1983).

16. Kenneth W. Thompson, *The President and the Public Philosophy* (Baton Rouge: Louisiana State University Press, 1981).

17. For important work on this topic, see Joseph M. Bessette and Jeffrey Tulis, eds., *The Presidency in the Constitutional Order* (Baton Rouge: Louisiana State University Press, 1981).

18. In the wake of Watergate, quite a bit of literature appeared on this question, but much of it was marred by excessive partisanship. Much work remains to be done.

19. Neustadt, *Presidential Power*, chap. 1.

20. Thomas E. Cronin, *The State of the Presidency*, 2nd ed. (Boston: Little, Brown, 1980), p. 2.

21. Notable in this area is Bruce Buchanan's *The Presidential Experience* (Englewood Cliffs, N.J.: Prentice-Hall, 1978), but more work must be done.

APPENDIX

STEP 1: THE EVALUATIVE CRITERIA OF PRESIDENTIAL OBSERVERS

Author	Criteria
Scholars	
Bailey, T. A.	Overall tests: Achievements; Administrative capacity; Appointees and advisors; Blunders; Congress; Crises; Dignity; Eloquence; Enemies; Ethics; Executive; Foreign affairs (how effective and how much his own secretary of state); Growth; Impact; Industriousness; Integrity; Leadership; Military (ensure national security); National interest; Prestige; Program; Public opinion; Scandals; Sensitivity (to domestic and international political climate); Veto Additional tests (for modern presidents): Activist; Congress (leadership of); Executive agreements; Press conferences; Radio and television; World leadership [Thomas A. Bailey, Presidential Greatness, reissued with a new preface (New York: Irvington, 1978).]
Barber, J. D.	1. Whether the president is able to exhibit the characteristics that are most likely to bring him success, i.e., the traits of the active-positive character: drive for results, emphasis on rational mastery of difficult situations, and flexibility in style used to achieve results. 2. Whether the president is able to provide public leadership: "remind

Author	Criteria
	the people that their past was not without achievement and their future is not yet spoiled." [James David Barber, The Presidential Character, 2d ed. (Englewood Cliffs, N.J.: Prentice-Hall, 1977).]
Burns, J. M.	1. How well the president performs as "master-broker" in the foreign affairs government: judging among and/or reconciling conflicting claims, interests, groups, pressures, and ideas. 2. Whether the president serves as a source of foreign policy leadership: propose new ideas, and develop plans and programs for the future. [James MacGregor Burns, Presidential Government: The Crucible of Leadership (Boston: Houghton Mifflin, Sentry edition, 1973).]
Cowhey and Laitin	1. How well the president exercises oversight of his foreign affairs government: make sure that all necessary work is done, and done properly. 2. Ability of the president to adopt and fulfill the appropriate role in the policy-making process, according to the structure of an international situation: computation (when there is general agreement on situation structure and policy goals); judgment (agreement on goals, but not structure); bargaining (agreement on structure but not goals); inspire/withdraw (disagreement on structure and goals). [Peter F. Cowhey and David D. Laitin, "Bearing the Burden: A Model of Presidential Responsibility in Foreign Policy," International Studies Quarterly 22 (June 1978):267-96.]

Author	Criteria
Corwin, E. S.	1. Ability of president to act in his capacity as the organ of foreign relations: shaping policy within conditions set by Congress; giving direction to government. 2. Ability of president to act in his capacity as commander-in-chief: control armed forces; serve as the "steward" of national power in wartime and in emergencies. 3. Ability of president to act in his role as the chief executive, as that role pertains to foreign relations: supervise the day-to-day conduct of foreign relations. 4. Ability of the president to exhibit leadership of the nation and its allies. [Edward S. Corwin, The President: Office and Powers, 4th ed. (New York: New York University Press, 1957).]
Cronin, T. E.	The president is to be judged in light of the limits on his power to fulfill his "job description": 1. Crisis management; 2. Symbolic and morale-building leadership; 3. Priority setting and program design; 4. Recruitment leadership; 5. Legislative and political coalition building; 6. Program implementation and evaluation; 7. Oversight of government routines and establishment of early-warning system for future problem areas. [Thomas E. Cronin, The State of the Presidency, 2nd ed. (Boston: Little, Brown, 1980).]
Destler, I. M.	The president is to be judged according to a concept of his position as overseer of the foreign affairs government. Specifically, judgment of performance in this position involves three tasks: 1. ability of the president to see to it that U.S. foreign policy is coherent and

Author	Criteria
	integrated; 2. ability of the president to choose an organization scheme, and personnel to fill it, which will maximize policy coherence and serve his needs while minimizing problems; 3. ability of the president to oversee his aides in their conduct of his affairs and responsibilities. [I. M. Destler, "National Security II: The Rise of the Assistant (1961-1981)," in <u>The Illusion of Presidential Government</u>, ed. Hugh Heclo and Lester M. Salamon (Boulder, Colo.: Westview Press, 1980), pp. 263-85; Destler, <u>Presidents, Bureaucrats, and Foreign Policy</u> (Princeton: Princeton University Press, 1974); and, Destler, "The Evolution of Reagan Foreign Policy," in <u>The Reagan Presidency: An Early Assessment</u>, ed. Fred I. Greenstein (Baltimore: Johns Hopkins University Press, 1983), pp. 117-58.]
George, A. L.	1. Ability of the president to reconcile three conflicting values in making foreign policy: search for high-quality decisions; need for acceptability, consensus, and broad support of decisions; and, prudent management. 2. To the extent possible in reconciling these three values, whether the president works to ensure that the five procedural tasks for effective decision making are carried out: ensure that sufficient information about a situation is obtained, that it is adequately analyzed, and that a valid diagnosis of the problem is produced; facilitate consideration of all major values and interests affected by the situation; assure a search for a relatively wide range of options, and a consideration of the consequences of each; provide for a careful consideration of the problems that may arise in

Author	Criteria
	implementing options; and, maintain receptivity to indications that current policies are not working out well, and cultivate an ability to learn from experience. 3. Whether the president develops an organizational scheme that will enhance effective decision making. [Alexander L. George, "The Case for Multiple Advocacy in Making Foreign Policy," <u>American Political Science Review</u> 66 (September 1972):751-85; George, <u>Presidential Decisionmaking in Foreign Policy: The Effective Use of Information and Advice</u> (Boulder, Colo.: Westview Press, 1980).]
<u>Greenstein, F.</u>	1. Ability of the president to direct policy making and decision making toward ". . . the grand contours of policies and project their consequences in order to weigh their substantive and political costs and benefits" and to provide "general conceptions of the direction that public policy should take." 2. Ability of the president to organize and coordinate his "foreign policy team" for policy making, as well as to choose effective personnel for it. 3. Ability of the president to balance the need for formal structures in policy making with more informal, collegial modes of consultation in decision making. 4. Ability of the president to cope with the limits of his power imposed by the context of the presidency (Congress, bureaucracy, other nations, etc.). 5. Ability of the president to employ political and interpersonal skills for persuasion, bargaining, and compromise. [Fred I. Greenstein, <u>The Hidden-Hand Presidency</u> (New York: Basic Books, 1982); Greenstein, <u>The Reagan Presi-</u>

Author	Criteria
	dency: An Early Assessment (Baltimore: Johns Hopkins University Press, 1983).]
Hargrove, E.	1. How well the president fulfills his role as originator of foreign policy. 2. Whether the president structures the decision process for effective decision making. 3. Whether the president is able to develop and implement a management strategy for dealing with bureaucratic politics. 4. Whether the president is able to bargain and persuade others to go along with him, appealing to the opinions of Congress, the public, and elites (engage in open politics, i.e., democratic policy making, by trying to gain real support of these groups). [Erwin C. Hargrove, The Power of the Modern Presidency (New York: Alfred A. Knopf, 1974).]
Hilsman, R.	1. How well the president performs in his capacity as "ultimate decider" in foreign policy: decide which policies will be pursued, decide what will be done or not done. 2. How well the president performs in his capacity as "ultimate coordinator" of foreign policy. 3. How well the president performs in his capacity as "ultimate persuader" of foreign policy. [Roger Hilsman, The Politics of Policy Making in Defense and Foreign Affairs (New York: Harper and Row, 1971).]
Hoxie, R. G.	1. Whether president performs effectively in meeting the requirements of presidential staffing: select top aide whose career includes experience with more than one political figure; aides must avoid publicity; president must avoid emotional

Author	Criteria
	dependence on top aide; and, a central staff figure should emerge. 2. How well president carries out his responsibility formulation. 3. How well president carries out his responsibility for policy execution. 4. Whether president is able to exercise leadership. 5. Whether president is able to build a consensus for his programs and policies in Congress and the nation. 6. Ability of president to make command decisions. [R. Gordon Hoxie, "The Not So Imperial Presidency: A Modest Proposal," Presidential Studies Quarterly 10 (Spring 1980):194-210; Hoxie, Command Decision and the Presidency (Pleasantville, N.Y.: Readers' Digest Press, 1979).]
Hughes, E. J.	"What shapes and makes an effective Presidential style?" (p. 107.)--This question revolves around six specific political senses: (1) Sense of confidence; (2) Sense of proportion; (3) Sense of drama; (4) Sense of timing; (5) Sense of constancy; (6) Sense of humanity. [Emmett John Hughes, The Living Presidency (New York: Coward, McCann, and Geoghegan, 1972).]
Hunter, R.	1. Who governs? (Whether president asserts his primacy and his choices within government.) 2. Education. (Whether president has prepared himself for foreign affairs before his election.) 3. Management. (Whether president effectively manages the mechanisms of foreign policy. 4. Domestic policies. (Whether the machinery of foreign policy is tied to that of domestic policy, and both to politics.)

Author	Criteria
	5. Lines of authority. (Whether they are clear, and the organizational scheme workable.)
6. World view. (Whether president and administration have a world view to organize foreign policy.)
7. NSC advisor. (Whether he is used to effectively coordinate foreign policy.)
8. Policy coordination. (Whether it is effective.)
9. Secretary of state. (Whether he is chief spokesman after the president, is compatible with him, and is a key figure in policy formation.)
10. Coordinating outreach. (Whether speeches, press contacts, and public contacts are coordinated.)
11. Economic policy. (Whether president develops mechanisms for coordinating international and domestic economic policies.)
12. Striking a balance. (Whether president steers a middle course between overmanaging and undermanaging system.)
[Robert E. Hunter, *Presidential Control of Foreign Policy*, The Washington Papers, no. 91 (New York: Praeger and The Center for Strategic and International Studies, Georgetown University, 1982).]
Janis, I. L.	1. Whether the president seeks out a broad range of ideas, analyses, and alternatives in decision making, and avoids an easy consensus.
2. Whether president develops organizational or managerial mechanisms to facilitate his oversight.
[Irving L. Janis, *Victims of Groupthink* (Boston: Houghton Mifflin, 1972).]
Kissinger, H. A.	1. Whether the president is able to establish an overall design for foreign policy making, which includes a conception

Author	Criteria
	of national interests, goals, priorities, and how they fit together, and which can serve as a "moral compass" and as a basis for "moral leadership."
2. Ability of the president to provide "moral leadership" in foreign affairs.
3. Ability of president to pursue and reconcile two conflicting imperatives: maintenance of security and the avoidance of nuclear war.
4. Whether the president is able to establish and oversee an effective decision-making machinery that is compatible with his personality and style, leads to action, gives the president real choices without causing feuds or burdening the president with too many decisions, and gives scope to presidential discretion without fostering megalomania.
5. Ability of president to build and proceed from a consensus behind his foreign policy.
[Henry A. Kissinger, "First, Coherent Policy," New York Times, January 18, 1982, p. A35; Kissinger, White House Years (Boston: Little, Brown, 1979.)]
Koenig, L. W.	1. How well the president is able to maintain a high "quality of counsel" in his administration through effective subordinates and advisors.
2. Whether the president makes effective use of the "organs of debate and criticism" on which national consensus is built (press, Congress, policy elites).
3. Whether president is able to build a consensus in support of his policies.
4. Whether president is able to foster "creativity" in foreign affairs, i.e., balance clarity and contradiction, principle and expediency.
5. Whether the president is able to exercise control over his foreign affairs

Author	Criteria
	government (secretary of state, decision process, military) and its decision processes.
6. Whether president is able to develop a means for long-term planning.
7. Whether president is able to achieve certain national policy goals: better relations between nations, security and strength, balance between security and other interests, and arms control.
8. How well the president arranges for and conducts crisis management.
[Louis W. Koenig, The Chief Executive, rev. ed. (New York: Harcourt, Brace, and World, 1968); and Koenig, The Chief Executive, 4th ed. (New York: Harcourt, Brace and Jovanovich, 1980).]
Laski, H. J.	1. Ability of president to act as the "central motive force" of policy: be in control, be active, and be the source of policy direction.
2. Whether president is able to establish and operate an effective system for organization and management of foreign affairs.
3. Ability of the president to speak in "world terms."
4. Whether president is able to mobilize public opinion in support of his policies.
5. Ability of the president to exhibit leadership of the nation in foreign affairs.
[Harold J. Laski, The American Presidency, An Interpretation, reissued with a new introduction by James McGregor Burns (New Brunswick, N.J.: Transaction Books, 1980).]
Lynn and Whitman	1. Ability of president to communicate a sense of how the policy or issue in question relates to the "larger aspirations of his presidency."

Author	Criteria
	2. Whether president is able to maintain effective use of his executive office advisors and associates. 3. Whether president is able to recognize and resolve conflict within his administration. 4. Ability of president to be an effective political leader: build consensus in government and among public for his policies, be sensitive to positions and strength of political opposition, be able to develop a strategy for overcoming or neutralizing opposition. [Laurence E. Lynn, Jr., and David P. Whitman, The President as Policymaker: Jimmy Carter and Welfare Reform (Philadelphia: Temple University Press, 1982).]
Neustadt, R.	1. What were his purposes, and did these run with or against the "grain of history," and how relevant were they to the times? 2. What was his "feel" for the nature of his power? (As described by Neustadt, an issue of organization, management, and oversight of the president's foreign affairs government, i.e., "operating style.") 3. What was his stance under pressure in office, his response to it, and how did his "peace-making with himself" affect the style and content of his decision making? 4. What was his legacy for his office, the party system, public policy, and the U.S. position in the world? 5. Because presidential power is the "power to persuade," a president must be judged in light of the limits on his power. [Richard E. Neustadt, Presidential Power, rev. ed. (New York: John Wiley and Sons, 1980).]

Author	Criteria
Pious, R.	1. Whether president is able to effectively organize and staff his foreign affairs government. 2. Whether president is able to manage the foreign affairs government and coordinate his advisory system for effective decision making. 3. Whether president is able to build a consensus in support of his policies. 4. How effectively president works toward "placing presidential power and accountability in better constitutional balance." [Richard M. Pious, The American Presidency (New York: Basic Books, 1979).]
Reedy, G. E.	1. President must resolve the policy questions that will not yield to quantitative, empirical analyses. 2. President must convince enough of his countrymen of the rightness of his decisions so that he can carry them out without destroying the fabric of society. [George E. Reedy, The Twilight of the Presidency (New York: World, 1970).]
Rossiter, C.	Standards for achievement: The times; Forceful and imaginative leadership; Possess a philosophy of greatness; Technical administrative mastery; Quality appointments; Legendary character; Legacy for presidency; Sense of direction of history and historical legacy. Qualities for effectiveness: Bounce; Political skill; Affability; Cunning; Sense of history; The "Newspaper Habit"; Sense of humor. [Clinton Rossiter, The American Presidency, 2nd ed., Time Reading Program Special Edition (New York: Time, 1963).]
Sapin, B. M.	1. How well president performs his function as the tone-setter of foreign

Author	Criteria
	policy (tone: democratic, prerogative, etc.). 2. How well president performs his function as <u>goal-setter</u> of foreign policy. [Burton M. Sapin, "Isn't It Time for a Modest Presidency in Foreign Affairs?" <u>Presidential Studies Quarterly</u> 10 (Winter 1980):19-27.]
<u>Sorensen, T. C.</u>	1. Whether president exhibits political self-knowledge (knows his own priorities and interests, his power and limitations). 2. Whether the president exercises prudent political judgment (deals effectively with public opinion, press, interest groups, Congress, and bureaucratic politics). 3. Whether president exercises effective oversight of his subordinates. 4. Whether the president is able to build a bipartisan consensus in support of his policies. 5. Whether president exhibits leadership (self-confidence, self-assertion, inspiration). 6. Whether the president is willing and able to make the "ultimate decisions." [Theodore C. Sorensen, <u>Decision-Making in the White House</u> (New York: Columbia University Press, 1963); Sorensen, <u>A Different Kind of Presidency</u> (New York: Harper and Row, 1984).]
<u>Spanier and Uslaner</u>	1. Presidential responsibilities: dealing with crises, maintaining national security. 2. Presidential objectives: to seek national security and the best foreign policy for the nation, and to reconcile the command and hierarchy demands created by this search with the need for consensus in a democratic society. [John Spanier and Eric M. Uslaner, <u>Foreign Policy and the Democratic Dilemmas,</u>

Author	Criteria
	3rd ed. (New York: Holt, Rinehart, and Winston, 1982).]
Tugwell, R. G.	1. General criteria: How well president performs according to the "rules" of presidential behavior--Restraint: whenever possible, president should exercise restraint in his use of power; Necessity: whenever nation is confronted with crises or unexpected situations for which there exist no prearranged solutions, the president should act to meet the demands presented; Responsibility: president should grasp and project what is necessary to secure nation's future. 2. Modern foreign policy: How well president performs according to the example and standard set by President Franklin Roosevelt for achieving those goals. [Rexford G. Tugwell, Off Course, From Truman to Nixon (New York: Praeger, 1971); Tugwell, The Enlargement of the Presidency (Garden City, N.Y.: Doubleday, 1960).]
Vinyard, D.	1. Whether president properly fulfills his presidential responsibilities: communicate with governments, formulate policy, recognize governments, oversee the daily operation and management of foreign policy, serve as commander-in-chief. 2. Whether president is sensitive to public relations. 3. Whether president is willing and able to make the ultimate decisions. [Dale Vinyard, The Presidency (New York: Charles Scribner's Sons, 1971).]

Author	Criteria
Commentators	
Broder, D.	1. President is responsible for setting the goals for foreign policy, including development of a grand design. 2. President must have effective organization and staffing. 3. President is responsible for effectively managing his foreign affairs government, including being in charge himself. 4. President is responsible for building a bipartisan consensus behind his foreign policy. 5. President is to be judged according to his policies and in pursuing particular policy goals (human rights), and the success he achieves in handling his job and foreign affairs. (David Broder, columns in Washington Post, January 1980-January 1984.)
Donovan, H.	Ideally, presidents should have the following characteristics: Body ("look like a president," have physical stamina, be outdoorsman or athlete); Character and temperament (exhibit and possess integrity, perseverance, and healthy ambition, be and "look" fair and compassionate, possess a sense of humor, be an optimist, have dignity and distance combined with quality of being "human," be steady and stable); Brains (superior intelligence but need not be an intellectual, be a simplifier, possess sense of judgment and proportion, possess sense of history, possess political philosophy that is realistic and coherent, and possess a foundation of religious values); president must be a communicator; president must be able to think in terms of contingencies; president needs "an ever fresh curiosity about this big and complicated

Author	Criteria
	country"; president should be flexible and pragmatic, but firm and decisive; president must be perceptive about people; president must be able to exercise management, oversight, and control of his administration; president needs a sense of priorities. President should also be judged by results he can achieve (legislative success, administrative expertise, firmness, and prudence in crisis). (Hedley Donovan, "Fluctuations on the Presidential Exchange," Time, November 9, 1981, pp. 121-22; Donovan, "Job Specs For the Oval Office," Time, December 13, 1982, pp. 20-29.)
Kraft, J.	1. President is responsible for charting a course for foreign policy, which includes: setting goals and priorities; developing a comprehensive design for policy; and, providing coherence for individual issues, cases, and national interests. 2. President is responsible for effective organization and staffing of his administration and foreign policy government. 3. President is responsible for effective management of his foreign policy government, including effective crisis management. 4. President is responsible for building a consensus in support of his policies. 5. President is to be judged according to what he is able to achieve with his limited resources: the president's power is limited by events (e.g., Watergate) and conditions (e.g., War Powers Acts), so he is to be judged according to that which he can control (management, policy making, organization, and staffing); it is possible to judge a president's performance as a whole of his presidency, and according to individual events, policies, cases.

Author	Criteria
	6. President is also to be judged according to how effectively he pursues particular policy goals (arms control). (Joseph Kraft, "The Post-Imperial Presidency," New York Times Magazine, November 2, 1980, pp. 31-95; Kraft, columns in Washington Post, January 1980-January 1984.)
Lewis, F.	1. President is responsible for seeing to it that the foreign affairs government is organized, coherent, and effective in its operation.
	2. President is responsible for developing a coherent and overarching design for foreign policy, which includes a sense of objectives, goals, and priorities. This design should educate and assure the public as well as inform policy making. It should also contribute to continuity in policy making, which is a quality the president ought to foster.
	3. President is responsible for effectively managing his foreign affairs government.
	4. President is also to be judged according to how effectively he pursues particular policy goals (reconciling Western security and prevention of nuclear war, balancing the U.S. stance between Soviet Union and China, promoting Allied cooperation, preserving a steady policy for the Mideast and Persian Gulf, producing a policy for SALT and Euromissiles, and sincerely pursuing arms control).
	(Flora Lewis, columns in New York Times, January 1980-January 1984.)
Reston, J.	1. President is responsible for seeing to it that the government develops a coherent, consistent, integrated foreign policy which can proceed from a basis of bipartisan support.

Author	Criteria
	2. President is responsible for effectively managing his foreign affairs government on a day-to-day basis. 3. President is responsible for being decisive in his handling of foreign affairs. (James Reston, columns in New York Times, January 1980–January 1984.)
Sidey, H.	1. President is responsible for setting goals for foreign policy and charting a course, which includes a "grand design" of where he wants to go and how to get there, a "grand strategy," and a sense of coherence for how various policies, problems, and issues are related to one another. 2. President is responsible for marshalling support for his policies. 3. President must be decisive. 4. President must demonstrate leadership, which includes elements of dignity, eloquence, majesty, poetry, power, a sense of history, courage, decision. 5. President is also to be judged according to the results he achieved. (Hugh Sidey, "Assessing a Presidency," Time, August 18, 1980, pp. 10-15; Sidey, regular column, "The Presidency," Time, January 1980–January 1984.)
White, T. H.	1. President must be strong, dynamic, and in control of foreign affairs and his foreign affairs government. 2. President must effectively staff and manage his foreign affairs government. 3. President must deal with the media and the influence of television in his conduct of foreign affairs. 4. President is particularly to be judged according to the results he is able to achieve, and the policies he pursues ("open up the government"),

Author	Criteria

but in light of limitations on his power. [Theodore H. White, *America in Search of Itself, The Making of the President, 1956-1980* (New York: Harper and Row, 1982).]

Will, G. F.
1. President is responsible for setting goals for foreign policy and for giving it coherence.
2. President is responsible for controlling and managing foreign policy.
3. President is responsible for building a consensus in support of his foreign policy.
4. President should inspire and demonstrate leadership.
5. President is to be judged on how effectively he pursues particular policy goals (support of allies, maintenance of national security).
(George F. Will, columns in *Newsweek*, January 1980-March 1984; Will, columns in Washington *Post*, January 1980-January 1984.)

Public Expectations/Judgments.

1. The president has primary responsibility for handling foreign affairs and making foreign policy.
2. The president is to be held responsible for the outcomes he is able to achieve in foreign policy: he is to be held accountable for setbacks and rewarded for successes.

[Compiled from: John E. Mueller, *War, Presidents, and Public Opinion* (New York: John Wiley and Sons, 1973); Samuel Kernell, "Explaining Presidential Popularity," *American Political Science Review* 72 (June 1978):506-22; and, Stephen J. Wayne, "Great Expectations: What People Want from Presidents," in *Rethinking the Presidency*, ed. Thomas E. Cronin (Boston: Little, Brown, 1983).]

STEP 2: OBSERVERS' CRITERIA AS GENERAL CONCEPTS

Complete List of Generalized Criteria/
Concepts Found in Observers

Goal-setting/priorities	Comprehensive design
Achievement/outcome	Intangibles
Circumstances	Leadership
Philosophy of power	Executive management
Oversight	Staffing/appointments
Organization	Crisis management
Political skills	Activity/forcefulness
Preparation	Policies
Democratic government	Physical characteristics
Intelligence	Character
Decisions/decisiveness	Policy coherence
Consensus-building	Mediation
Policy formation/initiation	Long-term planning
Coping	Limits of power

Criteria of Individual Observers Generalized

Bailey: Achievements/outcomes; Executive management; Consensus-building; Crisis management; Intangibles; Activity; Leadership; Policies; Policy initiation/formation; Political skills.

Barber: Mediation; Policy initiation/formation.

Cowhey and Laitin: Oversight; Executive management.

Corwin: Policy initiation/formation; Goal-setting/priorities; Executive management; Crisis management; Leadership.

Cronin: Crisis management; Leadership; Goal-setting/priorities; Policy initiation/formation; Staffing/appointments; Consensus-building; Executive management; Oversight; Limits of power.

Destler: Oversight; Policy coherence; Comprehensive design; Organization; Staffing/appointments; Executive management; Limits of power.

George: Consensus-building; Executive management; Goal-setting/priorities; Oversight; Organization.

Greenstein: Policy coherence; Organization; Staffing/appointments; Comprehensive design; Executive management; Coping; Limits of power; Political skills.

Hargrove: Policy initiation/formation; Organization; Executive management; Consensus-building; Democratic government.

Hilsman: Decisions/decisiveness; Executive management; Oversight; Consensus-building; Goal-setting priorities.
Hoxie: Staffing/appointments; Policy initiation/formation; Executive management; Leadership; Consensus-building; Decisions/decisiveness.
Hughes: Intangibles; Political skills.
Hunter: Activity/forcefulness; Preparation; Executive management; Policy coherence; Organization; Comprehensive design; Oversight; Staffing.
Janis: Oversight; Organization; Executive management.
Kissinger: Comprehensive design; Goal-setting/priorities; Policies; Organization; Executive management; Oversight; Leadership; Consensus-building.
Koenig: Staffing/appointments; Democratic government; Consensus-building; Policy coherence; Long-term planning; Oversight; Executive management; Crisis management; Policies.
Laski: Activity/forcefulness; Policy initiation/formation; Organization; Executive management; Leadership; Consensus-building.
Lynn and Whitman: Policy coherence; Oversight; Executive management; Mediation; Consensus-building; Political skills.
Neustadt: Goal-setting/priorities; Organization; Executive management; Oversight; Coping; Achievement/outcomes; Policies; Limits of power.
Pious: Organization; Staffing/appointments; Executive management; Oversight; Consensus-building; Democratic government.
Reedy: Goal-setting/priorities; Consensus-building; Democratic government.
Rossiter: Circumstances; Leadership; Philosophy of power; Executive management; Staffing/appointments; Character; Achievement/outcomes; Intangibles; Political skills; Preparation.
Sapin: Goal-setting/priorities; Intangibles (tone-setting).
Sorensen: Goal-setting/priorities; Political skills; Oversight; Consensus-building; Leadership; Decisions/decisiveness.
Spanier and Uslaner: Crisis management; Executive management; Policies; Consensus-building; Democratic government.
Tugwell: Goal-setting/priorities; Crisis management; Political skills; Policies.

Vinyard: Policy initiation/formation; Executive management; Political skills; Decisions/decisiveness.
Broder: Goal-setting priorities; Comprehensive design; Organization; Staffing/appointments; Executive management; Consensus-building; Policies; Achievement/outcomes.
Donovan: Physical characteristics; Character; Intangibles; Intelligence; Philosophy of power; Political skills; Executive management; Oversight; Goal-setting/priorities; Achievement/outcomes.
Kraft: Goal-setting priorities; Comprehensive design; Organization; Staffing/appointments; Executive management; Policy coherence; Crisis management; Consensus-building; Achievement/outcomes; Policies; Limits of power.
Lewis: Organization; Policy coherence; Oversight; Comprehensive design; Goal-setting/priorities; Executive management; Policies.
Reston: Policy coherence; Comprehensive design; Executive management; Decisions/decisiveness.
Sidey: Comprehensive design; Goal-setting priorities; Policy coherence; Consensus-building; Decisions/decisiveness; Activity/forcefulness; Leadership; Achievement/outcomes.
White: Activity/forcefulness; Oversight; Staffing/appointments; Executive management; Political skills; Achievement/outcomes.
Will: Goal-setting priorities; Policy coherence; Executive management; Consensus-building; Leadership; Policies.
Public Expectations: Achievement/outcomes; Goal-setting/priorities.

STEP 3: SYNTHESIS OF THE CONVENTIONAL WISDOM

Policy Direction and Design

    Goal-setting/priorities (17)
    Comprehensive design (9)
    Policy coherence (10)
    Policy initiation/formation (8)
    Long-term planning (1)

Organization and Staffing

    Organization (12)
    Staffing (11)

Management and Oversight

    Executive management (27)
    Oversight (18)
    Crisis management (7)
    Mediation (2)
    Decisions/decisiveness (7)

Consensus-building

    Consensus-building (18)
    Political skills (10)

Achievement/Outcomes

    Achievement/outcomes (9)

Other Criteria Left Out of Conventional Wisdom

    Leadership (11)--no consensus on what this means.
    Policies (10)--no consensus on what policies are good.
    Intangibles (5)--no consensus.
    Activity/forcefulness (5)
    Democratic government (4)
    Limits of power (5)
    Character (4)
    Preparation (2)
    Coping (2)
    Physical characteristics (1)
    Intelligence (1)

BIBLIOGRAPHY

The sources in this bibliography are divided into two groups. The first group contains those works which were used to develop the "conventional wisdom" analyzed in this book. It is a comprehensive list of works consulted, representing both contemporary thought on presidential evaluation (as in the writings of the various commentators and such works as Greenstein's The Hidden-Hand Presidency and Cronin's The State of the Presidency) and older works that are still influential (such as Laski's 1940 book on the presidency, which was reissued in 1980 with a new introduction by James MacGregor Burns). The second group contains a selected list of sources used for the case studies, methodology, analysis, and general context. Because all works consulted in this group were not equal in importance, the list below contains only the most important of these sources. Not listed, but nevertheless important, were archival materials, newspaper articles, and the extremely helpful reporting provided by National Journal and the publications of Congressional Quarterly, the Weekly Report, and Almanac.

THE CONVENTIONAL WISDOM

Bailey, Thomas A. Presidential Greatness. Reissued with a new preface. New York: Irvington, 1978.

Barber, James David. The Presidential Character. 2nd ed. Englewood Cliffs, N.J.: Prentice-Hall, 1977.

Broder, James S. Columns in Washington Post, January 1980–January 1984.

Burns, James MacGregor. Presidential Government: The Crucible of Leadership. Boston: Houghton Mifflin, 1973.

Cowhey, Peter F., and David D. Laitin. "Bearing the Burden: A Model of Presidential Responsibility in

Foreign Policy." *International Studies Quarterly* 22 June 1978):267-96.

Corwin, Edward S. *The President: Office and Powers.* 4th ed. New York: New York University Press, 1957.

Cronin, Thomas E. *The State of the Presidency.* 2nd ed. Boston: Little, Brown, 1980.

Destler, I. M. "Altering the Security Job." *New York Times*, March 25, 1980, p. A19.

_____. "The Evolution of Reagan Foreign Policy." In *The Reagan Presidency: An Early Assessment*, edited by Fred I. Greenstein, pp. 117-58. Baltimore: The Johns Hopkins University Press, 1983.

_____. "National Security II: The Rise of the Assistant (1961-1981)." In *The Illusion of Presidential Government*, edited by Hugh Heclo and Lester M. Salamon, pp. 263-85. Boulder, Colo.: Westview Press, 1981.

_____. *Presidents, Bureaucrats, and Foreign Policy.* Princeton: Princeton University Press, 1974.

Donovan, Hedley. "Fluctuations on the Presidential Exchange." *Time*, November 9, 1981, pp. 121-22.

_____. "Job Specs for the Oval Office." *Time*, December 13, 1982, pp. 20-29.

Edwards, George C., III. *The Public Presidency.* New York: St. Martin's Press, 1983.

George, Alexander L. "The Case for Multiple Advocacy in Making Foreign Policy." *American Political Science Review* 66 (September 1972):751-85.

_____. *Presidential Decisionmaking in Foreign Policy: The Effective Use of Information and Advice.* Boulder, Colo.: Westview Press, 1980.

Greenstein, Fred I. *The Hidden-Hand Presidency.* New York: Basic Books, 1982.

———, ed. *The Reagan Presidency: An Early Assessment*. Baltimore: The Johns Hopkins University Press, 1983. (Introductory and concluding chapters written by Greenstein.)

Hargrove, Erwin C. *The Power of the Modern Presidency*. New York: Alfred A. Knopf, 1974.

Hilsman, Roger. *The Politics of Policy Making in Defense and Foreign Affairs*. New York: Harper and Row, 1971.

Hodgson, Godfrey. *All Things to All Men: The False Promise of the Modern Presidency*. New York: Simon and Schuster, 1980.

Hoxie, R. Gordon. "The Not-So Imperial Presidency: A Modest Proposal." *Presidential Studies Quarterly* 10 (Spring 1980):194-210.

Hughes, Emmet John. *The Living Presidency*. New York: Coward, McCann, and Geoghegan, 1972.

Hunter, Robert E. *Presidential Control of Foreign Policy*. The Washington Papers, vol. 10, no. 91. New York: Praeger and The Center for Strategic and International Studies, Georgetown University, 1982.

Janis, Irvin L. *Victims of Groupthink*. Boston: Houghton Mifflin, 1972.

Kernel, Samuel. "Explaining Presidential Popularity." *American Political Science Review* 72 (June 1978):506-22.

Kinder, Donald R. "Presidents, Prosperity, and Public Opinion." *Public Opinion Quarterly* 45 (Spring 1981): 1-21.

Kissinger, Henry A. "First, Coherent Policy." *New York Times*, January 18, 1982, p. A35.

———. *White House Years*. Boston: Little, Brown, 1979.

———. *Years of Upheaval*. Boston: Little, Brown, 1982.

Koenig, Louis W. *The Chief Executive*. Rev. ed. New York: Harcourt, Brace and World, 1968.

―――. *The Chief Executive*. 4th ed. New York: Harcourt, Brace and Jovanovich, 1980.

Kraft, Joseph. Columns in Washington *Post*, January 1980–January 1984.

―――. "The Post-Imperial Presidency." New York *Times Magazine*, November 2, 1980, pp. 31–95.

Laski, Harold J. *The American Presidency: An Interpretation*. Reissued with a new introduction by James MacGregor Burns. New Brunswick, N.J.: Transaction Books, 1980.

Lewis, Flora. Columns in New York *Times*, January 1980–January 1984.

Lynn, Laurence E., Jr., and David F. Whitman. *The President as Policymaker: Jimmy Carter and Welfare Reform*. Philadelphia: Temple University Press, 1982.

Mueller, John E. *War, Presidents, and Public Opinion*. New York: John Wiley and Sons, 1973.

Neustadt, Richard E. *Presidential Power*. Rev. ed. New York: John Wiley and Sons, 1980.

Pious, Richard M. *The American Presidency*. New York: Basic Books, 1979.

"Poll Cites Qualities of Ideal President." New York *Times*, October 9, 1983, p. 32.

Reedy, George E. *The Twilight of the Presidency*. New York: World, 1970.

Reston, James. Columns in New York *Times*, January 1980–January 1984.

Rossiter, Clinton. *The American Presidency*. 2nd ed. Time Reading Program Special Edition. New York: Time, 1963.

Sapin, Burton M. "Isn't It Time for a Modest Presidency in Foreign Affairs?" *Presidential Studies Quarterly* 10 (Winter 1980):19-27.

Sidey, Hugh. "Assessing a Presidency." *Time*, August 18, 1980, pp. 10-15.

──────. "The Presidency." Regular column in *Time*, January 1980-January 1984.

Sigelman, Lee. "Dynamics of Presidential Support: An Overview of Research Finding." *Presidential Studies Quarterly* 9 (Winter 1979):206-16.

Sorensen, Theodore C. *Decision-making in the White House*. New York: Columbia University Press, 1963.

Spanier, John, and Eric M. Uslaner. *Foreign Policy and the Democratic Dilemmas*. 3rd ed. New York: Holt, Rinehart, and Winston, 1982.

Tugwell, Rexford G. *The Enlargement of the Presidency*. Garden City, N.Y.: Doubleday, 1960.

──────. *Off Course: From Truman to Nixon*. New York: Praeger, 1971.

Vinyard, Dale. *The Presidency*. New York: Charles Scribner's Sons, 1971.

Wayne, Stephen J. "Great Expectations: What People Want from Presidents." In *Rethinking the Presidency*, edited by Thomas E. Cronin, pp. 185-99. Boston: Little, Brown, 1982.

White, Theodore H. *America in Search of Itself: The Making of the President, 1956-1980*. New York: Harper and Row, 1982.

Will, George F. Columns in *Newsweek*, January 1980-March 1984.

──────. Columns in Washington *Post*, January 1980-January 1984.

SELECTED OTHER WORKS

Brzezinski, Zbigniew. *Power and Principle*. New York: Farrar, Strauss, and Giroux, 1983.

Buchanan, Bruce. "Assessing Presidential Performance: Can We Do Better?" Paper presented to the American Political Science Association, New York, New York, 1981.

Carter, Jimmy. *Keeping Faith*. New York: Bantam Books, 1982.

Divine, Robert A. *Eisenhower and the Cold War*. New York: Oxford University Press, 1981.

Eckstein, Harry. "Case Study and Theory in Political Science." In *The Handbook of Political Science*, vol. 7, edited by Fred I. Greenstein and Nelson W. Polsby. Reading, Mass.: Addison-Wesley, 1975.

Eisenhower, Dwight D. *Mandate for Change, 1953-1956*. Garden City, N.Y.: Doubleday, 1963.

Evans, John. *The Kennedy Round in American Trade Policy*. Cambridge, Mass.: Harvard University Press, 1971.

George, Alexander L. "Case Studies and Theory Development: The Method of Structured, Focused Comparison." In *Diplomacy: New Approaches in History, Theory, and Policy*, edited by Paul G. Lauren. New York: Free Press, 1979.

George, Alexander L., and Richard Smoke. *Deterrence in American Foreign Policy: Theory and Practice*. New York: Columbia University Press, 1974.

Hilsman, Roger. *To Move a Nation*. Garden City, N.Y.: Doubleday, 1967.

Hoopes, Townsend. *The Devil and John Foster Dulles*. Boston: *Atlantic Monthly* and Little, Brown, 1974.

Labrie, Roger, ed. *SALT Hand Book*. Washington, D.C.: American Enterprise Institute, 1979.

Leacacos, John P. "Kissinger's Apparat." Foreign Policy 5 (Winter 1971):3-27.

Light, Paul. The President's Agenda. Baltimore: The Johns Hopkins University Press, 1982.

Lyon, Peter. Eisenhower: Portrait of the Hero. Boston: Little, Brown, 1974.

Meier, Gerald M. Problems of Trade Policy. New York: Oxford University Press, 1973.

Newhouse, John. Cold Dawn: The Story of SALT. New York: Holt, Rinehart, and Winston, 1973.

Pastor, Robert A. Congress and the Politics of U.S. Foreign Economic Policy, 1929-1976. Berkeley: University of California Press, 1980.

Platt, Alan. The U.S. Senate and Strategic Arms Policy, 1969-1977. Boulder, Colo.: Westview Press, 1978.

Preeg, Ernest H. Traders and Diplomats. Washington, D.C.: The Brookings Institution, 1970.

Rightor-Thornton, Anne H. "An Evaluation of the Office of the Special Representative for Trade Negotiations: The Evolving Role, 1962-1974." In Report, vol. 3, Appendix H: Case Studies in U.S. Foreign Economic Policy: 1965-1974, pp. 88-104. U.S. Commission on the Organization of the Government for the Conduct of Foreign Policy. Washington, D.C.: Government Printing Office, 1975.

Rushkoff, Bennett. "Eisenhower, Dulles, and the Quemoy-Matsu Crisis of 1954-1955." Political Science Quarterly 96 (Fall 1981):465-80.

Safire, William. Before the Fall. New York: Belmont Tower Books, 1975.

Schlesinger, Arthur M. A Thousand Days: John F. Kennedy in the White House. Greenwich, Conn.: Fawcett, 1965.

Smith, Gerard. *Doubletalk*. Garden City, N.Y.: Doubleday, 1980.

Sorensen, Theodore C. *Kennedy*. New York: Harper and Row, 1965.

Talbott, Strobe. *Endgame*. New York: Harper and Row, 1979.

_____. "U.S.-Soviet Relations: From Bad to Worse." In *America and the World 1979*, edited by William Bundy, pp. 515-39. New York: Pergamon Press, 1980.

Thompson, Kenneth W. *The President and the Public Philosophy*. Baton Rouge: Louisiana State University Press, 1981.

U.S. Congress. House Committee on Ways and Means. *Trade Expansion Act of 1962, Hearings before the Committee on Ways and Means*, 6 vols. 87th Cong., 2d. sess., 1962.

U.S. Congress. Senate Committee on Finance. *Hearings on the Trade Expansion Act of 1962, before the Committee on Finance*, 2 vols. 87th Cong., 2d. sess., 1962.

Wills, Garry. *The Kennedy Imprisonment*. Boston: Little, Brown, 1981.

Wyden, Peter. *Bay of Pigs*. New York: Simon and Schuster, 1979.

INDEX

ABM (Anti-Ballistic Missile defense) (see SALT I)
ACDA (see Arms Control and Disarmament Agency)
achievement, presidential, 168
Afghanistan (see SALT II)
AFL-CIO, 122, 136, 148
American Cotton Manufacturers Institute, 132, 136
American Selling Price, 138, 145, 146, 154
Anderson, Robert, 34
appointments and staffing, 13, 54-55
Arms Control and Disarmament Agency (ACDA), 79, 80

B-1 bomber (see SALT I)
Backchannel, the (see Channel)
Backfire bomber (see SALT II: issues)
Bailey, Thomas, 6
Baker, Howard, 110
Ball, George, 121, 122, 126, 128, 129, 135
Bay of Pigs crisis, 25, 31-32, 49-65; Escambray Mountains, 51, 64; invasion force, 50, 51, 56; planning, 49-50, 51, 64
Beckel, Robert (see SALT II: administration lobbying effort)
Bellman, Henry (see SALT II: Senate and)
Berle, Adolph, 61
Bissell, Richard, and Bay of Pigs, 51, 53, 56, 57, 58; and Kennedy administration, 54
Boggs, Hale, 122, 129, 135
Bowie, Robert, 34-35
Bowles, Chester, 58
Brezhnev, Leonid, 74, 96, 100
"brinkmanship" (see Eisenhower, D.)
Broder, David, 5, 13
Brown, Harold, 106
Brzezinski, Zbigniew, 96, 100
Bundy, William, 58

Burke, Arleigh, 60
Burns, James MacGregor, 7
Butler, Landon (see SALT II: administration lobbying effort)
Byrd, Harry (see Trade Expansion Act of 1962: administration lobbying effort)

Carter, Jimmy, 94-110; decision making, 106-7; "March 1977 proposals," 96, 100; relations with Congress, 109; view of arms control, 94, 99-100
case-study methodology: advantages of, 24; comparability and variety, 24; "disciplined-configurative" mode, 24; theory and, 23, 24
Castro, Fidel, 49, 50, 56, 109
Central Intelligence Agency (CIA), 41, 49, 54, 56, 58, 64
Chamber of Commerce, U.S., 136
"Channel, the," 74, 95, 96 (see also Kissinger, H.)
Chiang Kai-shek, 34, 36, 40, 42
Chinese Nationalists (see Taiwan Strait crisis)
Chou En-lai, 35
Church, Frank, 105-6, 109-10
Churchill, Winston, 41, 45, 46
CIA (see Central Intelligence Agency)
Clayton, William (see Reciprocal Trade Act of 1934)
collegial model of policymaking, 52, 58, 59, 164
Commerce, Department of, 142, 147
Committee for a National Trade Policy (CNTP), 121, 130, 131, 135-36
Common External Tariff (see European Economic Community)
Common Market, European (see European Economic Community)
consensus-building, 20-21, 164-65; in Bay of Pigs crisis, 59-61; in SALT I, 89-91; in SALT II, 102-6;

210

in Taiwan Strait crisis, 44–47; in Trade Expansion Act of 1962, 131–34; in Trade Act of 1970, 144–46
conventional wisdom (see also the Appendix), identification of, 6–8, 23; cases and, 47–48, 55, 61–62, 65, 84, 86, 87, 98–99, 101–2, 111, 137; components, 8–23; inaccuracy of, 3, 159, 160, 162–64; normative vs. instrumental aspects (see evaluation)
Corwin, E. S., 15
Cowhey, Peter, 19
crises (see issue areas)
crisis management, 19, 54–55
Cronin, Thomas, 7, 13, 19, 176
cruise missiles (see SALT I and SALT II)
Cuba: Bay of Pigs (see Bay of Pigs crisis); Escambray Mountains (see Bay of Pigs crisis); Kennedy and, 50, 56, 62; military power in 1961, 54, 64; Soviet brigade and SALT II (see SALT II)
Cuban missile crisis, 52
Cutler, Lloyd (see SALT Task Force)

Davis, Kenneth, 147
decision-making process, 18
democratic accountability of President, 20–21; importance of, 163, 164; as a new criterion, 164, 165–66
Destler, I. M., 11
Dillon, Douglas, 54
"disciplined-configurative" mode of case study (see case study methodology)
Dobrynin, Anatoly (see "the Channel")
Donovan, Hedley, 5, 16
Dulles, Allen, 51, 53, 54, 57, 58
Dulles, John Foster, 33, 34, 39, 40, 41, 43, 45

Eden, Anthony, 34, 39, 40, 45
Edwards, George, 109
effectiveness, presidential, 164, 167–68
Eisenhower, Dwight D., 33–34, 35–48, 50; "brinkmanship," 35, 38, 43, 45; decision making, 40–44; quoted, 33, 35
Escambray Mountains (see Bay of Pigs crisis)
"escape clause," 125, 133
European Economic Community (EEC), 120–21, 127, 131, 132, 134–35, 137
"evaluation communities," 173–74
evaluation, presidential: agenda for future research on, 176–77; as a "calculus," 168; context of evaluation, 175–76; current, 2, 4, 23, 24; developing better standards, 3, 161–62, 164–69; evaluators (see evaluation communities); importance of circumstantial factors, 159–61; in opinion polls, 4–5; long-term vs. short-term outcomes, 164; principles for a general theory of, 171–72; process-outcomes relationship, 23, 24, 161; structure of a general theory of, 172–74

Flannigan, Peter, 139
Ford, Gerald R., 94, 96
Formosa Resolution, 35, 38, 43, 45, 46
fractionation (see SALT II: issues)
free trade, 123, 127, 135, 137, 141, 144, 148
Fulbright, William, 53, 57, 58, 81

George, Alexander, 6, 7, 12; on collegial model, 52, 164; on decision making, 17
Gilbert, Carl, 145, 147
Goodpaster, Andrew, 41

"grand design," 10-11
Greenstein, Fred, 175
Gromyko, Andrei, 95, 100
Gruenther, Alfred, 41, 42

Hargrove, Erwin, 166, 167
Harlow, Bryce (see Trade Act of 1970: administration lobbying)
Hatfield, Mark (see SALT II: Senate and)
"hedge your bets," 169
Helms, Richard, 79
Herter, Christian (see Reciprocal Trade Act of 1934)
Hilsman, Roger, 16-17, 19-20
Hodges, Luther, 124, 128, 134
Hoxie, R. Gordon, 14
Hughes, Emmet, 21
Hunter, Robert, 10, 17

Ichiang (see Taiwan Strait crisis)
Interim Agreement (see SALT I)
"intermestic" issues, 119
International Coffee Agreement, 139
Iranian hostage crisis (see SALT II)
issue areas, 25-26; crises, 25, 31-32; non-crisis security issues, 26, 72-73; non-crisis non-security issues, 26, 119-20

Jackson, Henry: Jackson amendment, 76-77, 81, 91; and SALT I, 76, 81; and SALT II, 100, 102, 109
Johnson, Lyndon B., 73
Joint Chiefs of Staff, 33, 35, 37, 40, 41, 43, 51, 53, 56-57, 64, 89
Jordan, Hamilton (see SALT II: administration lobbying)

Kennedy, John F., 49-65, 120-37; charisma, 60-62; and Cuban invasion, 49; decision making, 52-53, 57, 129-30; on foreign affairs, 2-3; as manager, 53, 55, 56, 58-59; perception of international crisis, 49-50; quoted, 2-3, 49, 125, 127; statements on Castro, 49; and Trade Expansion Act, 120-37; view of trade policy, 126
Kennedy, Robert F., 64
Kerr, Robert (see Trade Expansion Act of 1962: administration lobbying)
Kissinger, Henry A.: "the Channel" through Dobrynin, 74-75, 80, 83, 85; effect on SALT II, 109; on need for a "grand design," 10; as Nixon's "vicar," 82-83, 87; on policy "machinery," 18; policy making for SALT I, 74, 77-78; secret discussions on trade with Japanese, 139; and Trade Act of 1970, 139, 147
Koenig, Louis, 13-14
Kosygin, Alexei, 74
Kraft, Joseph, 5, 11

Laird, Melvin, 76
Laitin, David D. (see Cowhey, Peter)
Laski, Harold J., 7
leadership, 63
Lehman, John (see SALT I: administration lobbying)
Lewis, Flora, 5, 10, 11, 17
Light, Paul, 170
"linkage," 74, 99, 100
Long, Russell, 140, 141, 143
long-term versus short-term outcomes, 170
Lynn, Laurence E., 82

McGovern, George (see SALT II: Senate and)
management and oversight, 14-20; in Bay of Pigs crisis, 55-59; in SALT I, 84-89; in SALT II, 106-7; in Taiwan Strait crisis, 39-44; in Trade Expansion Act of 1962, 129-31; in Trade Act of 1970, 147

management of policy process, 16–17, 57–59, 62, 83–88, 129–31
"March 1977 proposals" (see Carter, Jimmy)
Matsu (see Taiwan Strait crisis)
methodology (see case study methodology)
Mills, Wilbur, 122, 123, 125, 131, 135, 138–39, 140, 143, 144
Minuteman III missiles (see SALT I)
MIRV (see SALT I)
Mondale, Walter (see SALT II: SALT Task Force)
Moore, Frank (see SALT II: administration lobbying)
most-favored-nation status, 125

National Association of Manufacturers, 136
National Command Authorities (see SALT I)
National Security Affairs, assistant to the president for, 72
National Security Council: in Bay of Pigs crisis, 52; Nixon-Kissinger "NSC System," 82–83, 146–47; in policy making, 72; Special Coordination Committee, 106–7; in Taiwan Strait crisis, 33, 37, 43, Verification Panel, 82; Working Group, 82
National Security Study Memoranda (NSSM), 83, 87
Nehmer, Stanley (see Trade Act of 1970: administration lobbying)
Neustadt, Richard, 6, 20, 176
Nitze, Paul, 55, 61
Nixon, Richard M.: attitude toward strategic arms policy, 73–74, 78; and Bay of Pigs, 50; and bureaucracy, 79, 80, 86–87; and linkage, 73–74, 77; quoted, 138, 139, 141–42; relationship with Henry Kissinger, 83; and SALT I, 73–94; "Southern strategy," 137, 141, 144, 148–49; and Taiwan Strait crisis, 33; and Trade Act of 1970, 137–49;
non-crisis non-security issues (see issue areas)
non-crisis security issues (see issue areas)
Nunn, Sam, 98, 99, 104–5

O'Brien, Lawrence, 122, 129, 130, 135
organization and staffing, 12–14; in Bay of Pigs crisis, 52–55; in SALT I, 82–84; in SALT II, 106–7; in Taiwan Strait crisis, 47; in Trade Expansion Act of 1962, 128–29; in Trade Act of 1970, 146–47
organization of policy process, 12
outcomes (see achievements/outcomes)
oversight of policy process, 19–20

Panama Canal treaties, 97, 110
"pay attention to the process," 169–70
Perle, Richard, 91
Pescadores Islands (see Taiwan Strait crisis)
Petersen, Howard, 122, 123, 126, 128, 129, 130, 135
Pious, Richard, 15, 21, 166
policy direction and design, 8–12; in Bay of Pigs crisis, 62; in SALT I, 77–82; in SALT II, 98–102; in Taiwan Strait crisis, 36–39; in Trade Expansion Act of 1962, 125–28; in Trade Act of 1970, 141–44
presidential accountability (see democratic accountability)
Presidential Review Memorandum 2 (PRM 2), 95
protectionism in Congress, 138, 144
Proxmire, William (see SALT II: Senate and)

214 / THE PRESIDENT AND FOREIGN AFFAIRS

Quemoy (see Taiwan Strait crisis)

Radford, Arthur, 39, 40
Rafshoon, Gerald (see SALT II: administration lobbying)
Rankin, Karl, 41
Reciprocal Trade Agreements Act of 1934, 120, 121, 122-23, 125, 127, 136
Reedy, George, 21
Reston, James, 5, 20
Ridgway, Matthew, 33
Robertson, Walter, 37, 40
Rogers, William, 79
Rossiter, Clinton, 13, 14, 18
Rusk, Dean, 54

SALT I, 73-94, 109; ABM defense and, 74-76, 90; administration lobbying efforts, 76, 90-91; B-1 bomber and, 91; cruise missiles and, 76, 90; defined, 144; Interim Agreement, 76; Jackson amendments (see Jackson, Henry); Minuteman III missiles and, 74-75, 76, 91; MIRV technology and, 75, 76, 91, 145; National Command Authorities and, 91; Trident submarine and, 74, 76, 91; two-track negotiations, 74-75
SALT II, 94-111; Administration lobbying efforts, 97-98, 102-6; defined, 147; Iranian hostage crisis and, 98, 110; issues for resolution, 96, 108; "March 1977 proposals" (see Carter, Jimmy); SALT Task Force, 97 (see also administration lobbying); Senate and, 101, 104, 109; Soviet brigade in Cuba and, 98, 105-6, 110; Soviet invasion of Afghanistan and, 98, 106, 110; Vladivostok agreement and, 94, 98
SALT Task Force (see SALT II)
Sato, Eisaku, 139

Schlesinger, Arthur M., Jr., 52, 58, 60
security (see issue areas)
Sidey, Hugh, 5, 20
Smith, Gerard, 74, 86
Smith, Walter Bedell, 33
Social Security Amendments Act of 1970 (see Long, Russell)
Sorensen, Theodore C., 122, 126; and Bay of Pigs, 50, 53; on policy process, 12, 51
"special case" of textiles (see Nixon, Richard: Southern strategy)
Special Coordination Committee (see National Security Council)
Special Group, 52
Special Trade Representative (STR): and Trade Act of 1970, 142, 146-47, 148; and Trade Expansion Act of 1962, 125, 133
staffing (see appointments)
Stans, Maurice, 139, 145, 146, 147
State, Department of, 57, 79, 80, 83, 124, 128, 133, 147
Stevenson, Adlai, 42, 45

Taft, Charles, 136
Taiwan Strait crisis, 25, 31, 32-48; Chiang Kai-shek and, 33, 36, 40, 42, 45; crisis erupts, 32; Eisenhower's response, 33-35; Ichiang, 34, 37, 42, 43; Pescadores Islands, 34; Quemoy and Matsu, 34, 40, 42; Tachen Islands, 34, 37, 40, 41, 42, 43; United Nations and, 33, 37, 42
Task Force on Trade Policy (see Ball, George)
Taylor, Maxwell, 55
Taylor Commission (Cuba Study Group), 53, 64
telemetry encryption (see SALT II: issues for resolution)
Textile Conference (1962), 132
textile industry, 124, 132, 137, 141, 145

Thompson, Kenneth, 176
timing of proposals, 170-71
Timmons, William, 141, 145
Trade Act of 1970, 137-49; administration lobbying effort, 144-45; provisions, 137-38
Trade Expansion Act of 1962, 120-37; administration lobbying effort, 129, 131-34; provisions, 123; and Trade Act of 1970, 133
Trident submarine (see SALT I)
Truman, Harry S, 33, 36

Vance, Cyrus, 95, 96, 107
Verification Panel (see National Security Council)
Vladivostok agreement (see SALT II)

Warnke, Paul, 95, 103-4, 107
Wexler, Anne (see SALT II: Administration lobbying)
White, Theodore, 5
Will, George, 5
Wilson, Charles, 33, 35
Working Group (see National Security Council)

ABOUT THE AUTHOR

RYAN J. BARILLEAUX is an assistant professor of political science at the University of Texas at El Paso. He attended Georgetown University and the University of Louisiana, graduating <u>summa cum laude</u> from the latter. In 1983, he received a doctorate in government from the University of Texas at Austin. A former aide to Senator J. Bennett Johnston, he is the author of numerous articles on U.S. government and public policy.

DATE DUE